THE FUTURE OF
GLOBAL
GOVERNANCE

MANAGING RISK AND CHANGE
IN THE INTERNATIONAL SYSTEM

MIHALY SIMAI

UNITED STATES INSTITUTE OF PEACE PRESS

Washington, D.C.

United States Institute of Peace
1550 M Street, N.W.
Washington, D.C. 20005

First published 1994

Printed in the United States of America

The paper used in this publication meets the minimum requirements of American National Standard for Information Sciences—Permanence of Paper for Printed Library Materials, ANSI Z39.48-1984.

Library of Congress Cataloging-in-Publication Data
Simai, Mihaly, 1930–
  The future of global governance : managing risk and change in the international system / Mihaly Simai.
    p.   cm.
  Includes bibliographical references and index.
  ISBN 1-878379-34-8 (alk. paper) — ISBN 1-878379-33-X (pbk. : alk. paper)
  1. International cooperation. 2. World politics. 3. Economic development. I. Title
JC362.S53   1994
327.1'7–dc20   94-13637
                                                                    CIP

Contents

Preface

For political decision makers, the prospect of change is much like the prospect of a blind date: although it may be desirable, it is unpredictable and the results may well run counter to one's preconceptions and plans. Unlike a blind date, however, change is inevitable. Political success has thus always depended on the abilities to understand and to master change. At this, the last stage of the turbulent 20th century, these abilities are being tested as never before.

In recent decades, changes have occurred at dizzying speed and brought dramatic consequences. We have seen a political landslide in Central and Eastern Europe and the former Soviet Union; the end of the Cold War; the evolution of a new international power structure; a technological transformation and information revolution; the emergence of competitive regional groups; the transnationalization of the international economic system; and a rising awareness of the dangers posed to the global ecosystem. The end of the ideological war between capitalism and communism has closed a major chapter in history, but it has also opened a new chapter, one of ideological conflicts waged on local and regional levels and in which nationalism, xenophobia, and ethnocentrism feature prominently. The victory of national self-determination and democracy in vast regions of the world has raised many expectations; however, if these expectations remain unfulfilled and the promises made by new, inherently unstable states are broken, then violent ethnic and social movements seem certain to arise and grow.

Change cannot be prevented, but its consequences must be managed. Unfortunately, the ability to promote change in the modern world is far ahead of the ability to calculate change's implications and to deal with its consequences. Although the Cold War has ended, the international community has yet to create a grand design for a new global order, and it may not develop one for a while. Some experts predict international institutional changes that will herald a new era in collective risk management and global governance. These expectations are fading amid devastating civil wars, social dilemmas, and economic difficulties. Thus far, change has produced more academic debates than concrete measures. In many countries, steps have been taken only toward reformulating national strategic interests and goals; there has been little focus on how to deal with change in an international sense.

A policy-oriented work with theoretical foundations, this book examines the tasks that confront the international community and assesses its capabilities to manage change. This book also suggests global measures that could improve multilateral risk assessment and management, and ties its conclusions to the new values and norms of international cooperation. It is not an addition to the globalist utopias, but contributes to the international dialogue of concerned people: academics, decision makers, and public opinion leaders. It is in favor of multilateral institutional cooperation but does not idealize the United Nations or other multilateral agencies. My approach is global, but I appreciate the inevitable strands of continuity with the past and take into account the new elements of bilateral cooperation and evolving regionalism.

In essence, then, the aim of this book is to seek answers to two overarching questions: One, what are the major political, economic, technological, environmental, and social changes confronting the world today, and what risks do they pose? And two, given what we know about these changes and risks, what new adjustments will have to be undertaken to make the world as peaceful and as stable as possible?

This book represents a new stage in my long-standing research on global political, economic, and social changes. My initial research was stimulated by the early global projections of the United Nations (in which I was participating) in the 1960s, at the end of the "golden age" of the post–World War II era. The results of the first stage of my research were published in 1976 in *Toward the Third Millennium*. My views at that time were strongly influenced by three assumptions: first, that, in spite of systemic differences, global gaps, and political conflicts, there was a strong international convergence of problems; second, that most problems required multilateral cooperation rather than bilateral or unilateral action; and third, that the world, with the help of the United Nations, could solve the existing and evolving demographic, technological, and economic problems in a global cooperative framework. This third assumption proved to be too optimistic. It did not take into account such important realities as the diverging interests of the major powers, the increasingly unequal and competitive character of the global economy, the implications of the oil price explosion, the collapse of the Bretton Woods system, the increasing systemic weakness of the Soviet Union, and the new wave of the arms race. However, the main conclusion of *Toward the Third Millennium*, that the post–World War II era was approaching its end, was correct.

Interdependence and Conflicts in the World Economy, published in the mid-1970s and based on my research and experience as an expert on the United Nations, analyzed the nature of evolving economic conflicts in an interdependent world and the interfaces between science, politics, states, and multilateral organizations. The main conclusion of *Interdependence and Conflicts in the World Economy* is that the growth in interdependence and interaction among states does not eliminate the sources of conflicts, and actually has become a source of new ones. This growth, however, has radically modified the character of conflicts and has introduced new incentives for their management and solution.

The third phase of my research was conducted within the framework of a multiyear program of the United Nations Development Programme (UNDP) dealing with the human dimensions of global development from a comparative perspective. Concentrating on the future of global employment problems and education issues, some parts of my research were published by the UNDP and the North-South Round Table in four volumes (*Human Development, Adjustment and Growth; Human Development: The Neglected Dimension; Human Development in the Changing World;*

and *Change: Threat or Opportunity for Human Progress*). These publications warn about the evolving "human crisis" dimension of change.

In the fourth phase of my research, I concentrated on the global agenda of the 1980s: increasing polarization, evolving new power structures, and changes in the functioning of the markets. My findings were summarized and published in 1990 in *Power, Technology and the World Economy*. A main conclusion of that work is that the global economy has entered a new phase characterized by deepening long-term problems, which have become major crises in areas such as the Soviet Union, Central and Eastern Europe, and many regions of the developing world. Another conclusion is that the new stage of economic and technological development has made the dominating patterns of international cooperation increasingly inefficient and irrelevant. I was not able to predict the political changes of the late 1980s and early 1990s, but my analysis of the global economy and the changing positions of the major countries resulted in projections about the socioeconomic sources, national and global determinants, and consequences of those changes.

This fifth—and, I trust, not final—stage of my research looks at the late 1980s, the 1990s, and beyond and argues in favor of a multilateral approach and multilateral institutions to deal with current and future global problems. This book is divided into five parts: a discussion of the historical development of global order concepts and the need for new formulations; an analysis of the new realities and formations in the international political system; a review of the search for collective security in an era of intense economic competition; a consideration of global multilateral cooperation; and a concluding assessment of challenges and opportunities.

"Mankind has always lived dangerously," observed the French philosopher Raymond Aron. This is the broad, yet unifying theme of my earlier and present work. Despite the demise of Soviet-style communism and the disappearance of the threat of imminent global nuclear catastrophe, myriad other dangers now confront the peace and stability of the world. Although some observers talk about the emergence of new opportunities that, if taken, will finally usher in an era of world peace, I believe that we must face up to the unresolved problems and dangers of the past while also dealing with threats that are only just beginning to appear. Above all, the world needs to acknowledge the existence of many nonmilitary problems that are emerging in various parts of the world, and it needs to address them much more intensively and efficiently through a multilateral and cooperative approach.

I should like to express my gratitude first of all to the United States Institute of Peace, which facilitated my research and provided excellent human and technical support and a creative, stimulating atmosphere. I am also grateful for the critical remarks and recommendations of my colleagues, especially W. W. and Elspeth Rostow, Samuel Lewis, Alexander George, Louis Sohn, Michael Lund, Otto Koester, Nigel Quinney (who also edited the manuscript), James Rosenau, Robert Cox, Modesto Vasquez, Robert Manley, Donald Puchala, William Diebold, Uner Kirdar, and the many others who helped me in the various phases of my research (including the participants of a workshop held at the United States Institute of Peace in 1992 on the future of multilateral cooperation). It was, however, my research assistant, Tim McInnis, who provided the critical support to a desperate Hungarian scholar, helping me to find my way to various institutions and parts of the United States and to navigate through the labyrinths of linguistics, references, footnotes, and computers.

March 1994

Introduction

The Global System in Transition

For the purpose of managing international peace and conflict, multilateral cooperation has important advantages over unilateralism. As the turbulent history of the 20th century has shown, unilateralism has often been accompanied by domination, fanaticism, and violence. By contrast, multilateralism is founded on international dialogue, mutual tolerance and respect, consensus building, accommodation of interests and values, and mutual understanding. Multilateralism has become increasingly more acceptable to nonstate actors, which have a growing influence on the international stage.

As history also reveals, however, neither a unilateral nor a multilateral approach has been very successful in preventing wars from breaking out. This is partly due to the character and magnitude of the threats to peace. But it is also the case that neither multilateralism nor unilateralism has ever been, nor probably ever will be, the absolute and independent source of international policy and action. Both approaches must thus be taken into account to understand present and future global problems, and the dichotomy between them must be understood when examining the potential sources of instability and conflict together with the future complexities of international cooperation, governance, and risk management.

The focus of this study is the global system and its political, economic, and ecological subsystems. This system serves as the context for analyzing the major global trends and changes shaping the new "human condition" of the world in the 1990s and in the early part of the 21st century. Today, there is a rare coincidence of historical discontinuities, with transformation occurring in many social, political, and economic processes and structures. In the global system, change takes many forms: regular and irregular, predictable and unpredictable, evolutionary and unsteady, linear and nonlinear, cyclical and noncyclical. On the global level, change is always multifaceted. The global system also contains elements of progress, decline, and retrogression that affect not only states but also groups of states, corporations, and international organizations. Some of these actors have been more astute than others in adapting themselves to a dynamic environment. But, when actors adapt their institutions as required by systemic change, does the old order simply vanish?

According to historical experience, the transition from one world order to another is never smooth. Transitional periods in the past have engendered uncertainty and tension; in those regions of the world most adversely affected by change, wars have erupted and nations have strategically realigned. Not surprisingly, patterns of transition differ according to the diversity of historical actors and forces.

The multidimensional complexity of the transitional phase of development is of critical interest to social science. This is the uncertain period between the old and new systems during which factors of each intermingle and compete, eventually producing change in the global order. Here, there is an interplay of a wide range of factors—geostrategic, environmental, anthropological, political, economic, social, technical, and organizational. Global actors also play a role. To understand the causes and implications of this interrelated and complex process requires special analysis.

On the threshold of the 21st century, the world is experiencing an especially profound and multifaceted historical change. A key element of this change has been the collapse of the Soviet Union, the last great empire of the modern age.

The decline of the great empires of the last half millennium has been protracted. It began with the collapse of the Spanish empire, which was followed by the successive disintegration of the Ottoman, Austro-Hungarian, and German empires. After World War II, all other great empires disappeared except for the Russian empire, the greatest continental empire of modern history. Although the Russian empire had transformed itself into the Union of Soviet Socialist Republics with the declared aim of creating an international community based on political and economic equity, the Soviet state simply revitalized the geo-strategic structure and goals of the Russian empire. Ultimately, this empire was liquidated by internal forces—by nationalism, anticommunism, and popular dissatisfaction with the state's inability to solve the basic needs and problems of the Soviet Union.

One result of imperial collapse has been an increase in the number of sovereign states, all of them patterned more or less along the lines of the European state structure. The current number of states is greater by far than at any other time in modern history, and it is still increasing. Between 1816 and 1946, 52 states were created and 23 destroyed. At the turn of the century, there were 50 states in the world, with only 26 of these being represented at the 1899 Hague Peace Conference. At the second Hague Peace Conference in 1907, 44 states were represented. Following World War I, 10 to 12 new states were either established or had their frontiers redefined. By the end of 1945, there were 63 states in the world. With the disintegration of the British, French, Belgian, Dutch, and Portuguese empires in the post–World War II period, 80 new states came into existence. The breakup of the Soviet Union further enlarged the ranks of independent states. By the end of the century, the number of states may exceed 200.

States are the primary units of the global political system, pursuing their perceived national interests wherever they may be. The experience of the past 20 to 30 years has shown that the global political system functions less well and less predictably if the potential sources of discord and conflict among a growing number of states are not managed, moderated, and resolved. The collapse of the Soviet-Russian empire represents a new era of interactive coexistence between smaller and larger states.

The disintegration of the Soviet Union has also ended an era of political and military bipolarity, closing the book on Cold War alliances, proxy wars, and the magnitude of the nuclear threat known in the period of mutually assured destruction. At the same time, that disintegration has brought about the partial collapse of Europe's political structure as established by the Allies at Yalta and Potsdam in 1945. The central element of this structural breakdown has been the unification of Germany. There have also been changes—most notably, the fragmentation of Yugoslavia and Czechoslovakia—in the peace regime established by the Versailles treaties after World War I. These changes and the multiplicity of ethnic and small-state conflicts they bring in their wake pose new challenges not only for European security but also for the global security system as established within the framework of the United Nations.

The global system is also being affected by the declining hegemony of the United States. This is certainly a long-term process: the United States is, and will remain for many years, the strongest power in the system. Still, the erosion of its hegemony involves the breakdown of those institutions, regimes, and arrangements that were based on it.

The late 20th century is a critical period for states: Will they, or will they not, be able to function effectively on behalf of their national interests in domestic and international arenas? The modern state system represents a concentration of power in the state, which in theory exercises full authority over the people and resources within its territory. The state is a secular power. It guarantees an individual's autonomy, although it also establishes a degree of social control through its institutions. Today, however, the traditional means of domestic social control are fast becoming incapable of dealing effectively with crime, drug abuse, and the many other social problems that are damaging to societal norms and cohesiveness. Internationally, these states may be facing an unfamiliar "post-Westphalian" world where secular and unitary states are no longer dominant.

Disintegration in the East is being paralleled by integration in the West. This latter process, reflecting the forces of globalization and transnationalization, is far from smooth. While the international commitments of states are everywhere increasing, as are the constraints on sovereignty, there is also resistance to transboundary regulatory institutions.

Certainly, the role of the state is changing. Domestically, relations between governments and their civil societies are going through important transformations, and the role of nongovernmental structures is growing. Internationally, the changes are even greater. The boundaries between international and domestic domains are being erased in many areas. Although great differences exist in the character and intensity of these changes vis-à-vis the state, one way or another even the strongest states are constrained, whether in real or in normative terms. In some areas—international capital and information flows, for example—states are either losing control altogether or imposing greater and often unsustainable burdens on their resources for retaining control.

Moreover, the state system is changing more rapidly than are international organizations (with the possible exception of the European Community), the result being that these organizations are incapable of dealing with the domestic policies of states having international consequences. The weakness of international organizations is a serious source of instability, particularly in the international economic system.

In economic terms, the last quarter of the 20th century symbolizes the end of the post–World War II era of global development, which was typified by large savings utilized for domestic investments and international capital flows, rapidly expanding world trade, major structural changes in output and consumption patterns, full employment, the expansion of social services, and surplus personal incomes—at least in the West. The East and the South never fully experienced global prosperity. Since the 1970s, a major shift has occurred in the economic policies of many governments, policies which had previously been based on the active involvement of the state in regulating economic processes for the benefit of the welfare state structures and full employment in the developed industrial world. This shift is no mere change in dominating ideologies, or a replacement of neo-Keynesians by monetarists. Rather, governments everywhere have become aware that their effectiveness in economic management has been substantially curtailed by both domestic constraints and the forces of the global economy.

Additionally, the last third of the 20th century has witnessed the end of a long technological era begun in the late 19th century. The transition to a new technological era based on a few main generic technologies has been under way since the late 1960s. The implications of technological change are reflected in the acceleration of what has been called the "creative destruction" of economic structures and fixed assets; at the same time, new production and consumption patterns have evolved, especially in the developed industrial countries. Information technology is making traditional transactions among firms, governments, and other microactors and macroactors increasingly obsolete. The unevenness of technological change is an important source of global polarization, resulting in shifts in comparative advantages and capabilities.

Geostrategic and technological changes have a major influence on the international order and on those forces shaping the processes leading to a new order. The present changes are of epoch-making importance. Indeed, the world is in a state of transition to a new historical order, the parameters and regulating forces of which remain to be determined, though it seems likely to be an order of dynamic, fluid, and rapidly fluctuating processes difficult to fully apprehend and control. Thus, it is necessary for the world to embrace collective multilateral governance to manage those factors of instability and risks already visible in the system with the aims of promoting more efficient conflict prevention, building multilateral cooperation regimes, and facilitating risk management. Rather than focusing on the institutional details of multilateral governance, decision makers and analysts would be better served by understanding the nature and structure of cooperation and the complex international processes where it must be applied.

The Nature of the Global System and Its Subsystems

A study that covers such a great variety of world problems cannot be equally comprehensive in all issue areas. Hence, the focus of this book is on those problems that require or influence collective actions. A "nonconventional" systems theory framework is employed because it seems the most relevant of competing theories for the analysis and synthesis of the interactions among the primary global actors and of important processes and their anticipated outcomes.

A *system* can be defined as the entirety of interactions and interdependencies among groups or items within a specified structure or framework. Naturally, different structures can be characterized as systems, and different theories seek to explain, describe, or quantify the intensity and nature of interactions, sources of change, and consequences of transformations within specific systems. Analysts of specific systems usually try to insulate a part of the empirical world against the randomness of the rest of that world. General system theory (or theories) deals with those problems that characterize all systems: equilibria and disequilibria, regularities and irregularities, sources and consequences of turbulence, and so forth.

This book looks at the *global system* (or *international system*). The global system encompasses the entirety of relationships among those actors that influence processes and changes beyond national frontiers. Operating in a structure characterized by the existence of states, these actors inevitably include the states themselves. Other important actors are intergovernmental organizations assigned the responsibility of managing destabilizing forces and risks, as well as certain nongovernmental institutions and organizations, like transnational corporations. A great number of relations have developed among these different actors in a wide variety of fields. Some of these relations are integrative; others can lead to disintegration and fragmentation.[1]

Further, the global system is, by its nature, embedded with social, ideological, and cultural structures. The role of social formations in systemic processes is especially important, because it influences virtually all of the system's components. In economic terms, social formations are defined as the structures of property, motivation, information, and institutions—all structures through which power is concentrated, diffused, and transferred.

For political, economic, and ideological reasons, nation-states have developed according to different societal formations. Freedom, democracy, particular moral principles, and pragmatic optimism, together with certain elements of social Darwinism, were key to forming the societal structure of the United States. The tsarist heritage of Russia, combined with a utopian communist ideology, had, in Russia's semideveloped economic environment, a major impact on the early social formation of the Soviet Union. China developed on the basis of cultural and social traditions developed over thousands of years, interwoven with major experiments in modernization, whether ideological, administrative, or economic. The process of social formation and transformation manifests great variety, flexibility, and adaptability, and represents a dynamic factor in the global system.

While the global system is constantly undergoing change, the amount and rate of change within its subsystems vary. A "subsystem" is an autonomous system having unique attributes that determine a certain logic to be followed by the actors and regulating forces within its parameters. However, all subsystems—political, economic, and ecological—have common characteristics. Their composition is, uniformly, of multiple interrelated actors whose interactions can be controverting of individual or common interests. Another common feature is that change, not equilibrium, determines their processes. The quantity and rate of change in subsystems may become a worldwide source of conflict, especially when reacted to differently by the world's various regions. Together, the international political system, the world economic system, and the ecosystem form the global system with its curious dynamics, synergies, and dissolutions.

The *international political system* is a multilevel structure. At its base it represents the totality of relations among states. These relations are characterized by power politics, interdependence, and diplomatic and military relations in peace and war.

Relations between states and the nonstate actors of the system are conditioned by several factors. Among these, domestic political motivations play a crucial role. Indeed, the international political system is broadly inclusive of domestic political structures, processes, and institutions, in addition to various relations between states and nonstate actors. After all, domestic factors define the quantity of national resources that can be devoted to international issues. They also define national objectives in international relations and discriminate among the different partners and forms of cooperation. National objectives include strengthening national security, increasing national wealth and welfare, advocating certain values and ideas, improving the national reputation, and pursuing national self-interest in other issue areas. States do not exist in vacuums, nor do domestic factors. Both are interactive components of the international system.

The leading part in international affairs is played by a handful of powers—the "price makers" of the system. Even these countries, however, must adjust their policies to accommodate one another's actions. Adjustment, of course, is the permanent requirement for the smaller states—the "price takers" in the system. It is as states adjust to each other, or to price makers, that political ideologies are generated by domestic actors. Although change is a constant characteristic of the international political system, major, epoch-making changes are produced by global crises that result from global wars, hegemonic decline, or large-scale and long-lasting economic contractions or depressions.

It has been suggested that the systemic model tends to minimize the importance of political ideologies, notwithstanding the ideological justifications given for the actions of states. One American scholar has argued:

> This de-emphasis on ideology, then, suggests that the analyst of world politics need pay little attention to what policy makers say about their policies. Clearly, they will say whatever will make their actions look good. They will talk about freedom, national self-determination, liberating people from Communist or capitalist slavery, and bringing about world peace, law, order and justice. But such concepts should not be confused with the concrete interests that are the real, underlying reasons for the state's behavior.[2]

In fact, political ideologies are more than window dressing for national policies. They express interests, values, attitudes, and culture in international relations, and they often reflect the influence of other factors. Ideology can play an extremely important and positive role in an era of major change. But creeds such as fundamentalism and orthodoxy can also rally nonstate actors, or even some states, to oppose and obstruct virtually all change, including the development of more cooperative relations with other groups or countries. The increasing influence of ideology today can be seen in the rising number of nonsecular Islamic states and in the revival of nationalism in Central and Eastern Europe. Plainly, ideological motives have also fueled international terrorism.

The international political system is the ensemble of national actions and interrelations. As a system, it expresses the political characteristics of the era, articulates mutually acceptable forms and instruments for seeking advantage in the system, defines the contests, determines the choices available to states, and places limits on their aspirations. It can also be a source of major and sudden shocks in the global system. A vital task of international governance is to reveal accumulating tensions within the international political system and to prevent the outbreak of conflicts and violence by means of collective institutions and instruments.

The *international economic system* (or world economy) is the totality of global production, consumption, and exchange activities undertaken by microactors working within national economies and/or the world market. They are conditioned and interconnected both within nations and internationally by the diverse and increasingly globalized markets (in goods, capital, labor, and technology), and are influenced by the economic policies, international agreements, and other actions of various national macroeconomic and international organizations that manage cooperation regimes.

The state-centered character of the international political system is in increasing conflict with the transnational nature of the world economy. This conflict is aggravated by the dual-track character of the international economic system, with growing technological and income gaps and inequalities between the richer and poorer countries. The international economic system of the late 20th century is a highly complex formation. It comprises about 200 political units in the framework of which an unspecified, but very large, number of microunits creates the global product. The number of consumers is approaching 6 billion. Behind this magnitude exist immense inequalities and quality-of-life differences. Ancient technologies, the dominant tools of production used by poorer regions of the world, today coexist with highly productive, modern technologies—sometimes within the same countries. Famine and poverty coexist with unprecedented levels of welfare.

The world economy comprises different sets of relations, like monetary, trade, and technology relations, which are themselves special systems regulated by the market and by cooperation regimes. These sets of relations have become vitally important to the existence of states. Economic relations are the media for interdependence and competition. Spillovers of economic shocks and crises are communicated or transferred by them.

Among the different actors in the system, there are economic and technological superpowers setting the norms, and there are dwarfs, whose yearly output is smaller than the annual cash flow of a medium-sized supermarket in any developed industrial country. The contrasts are not less dramatic on the microlevel: there are both global giants (transnational corporations) and barefooted entrepreneurs in the informal sectors of developing countries.

The global economy, and its way of functioning, is the main source of opportunity, income, and wealth; however, it is also a source of concern for many countries. Major changes take place in the global economic system as the result of radical technological innovations, the emergence or decline of major powers (competitors), and fundamental policy changes by the key countries of the system affecting income, output, trade, and investment. Changes are also interrelated with the global political system in terms of the role of economic power, the sources of instability, and the implications of political and economic conflicts and competition. The international economic system is also a key factor in the state of the global ecosystem.

Past theories of international relations have overlooked the *global ecosystem* as an integral component of the global system. The natural environment has mistakenly been presumed to be an inexhaustible source of natural resources; at best, it has been dealt with as a "global commons" that either should, or should not, be managed by cooperation regimes. Recently, however, deepening global ecological crises, as well as existing and potential international disputes over ecological problems, have changed the views of some scholars. The view of the ecosystem as an integral part of the global system, as a subsystem with special characteristics and postulates, is becoming widely shared, as seen in the development of international environmental policies, cooperation regimes, and law, and in attempts by grass roots organizations to safeguard the environment.

The global ecosystem (the atmosphere, hydrosphere, geosphere, and biosphere) is both the natural environment that sustains human society and the sum of interrelations between society and that environment. It has been characterized as a "self-organizing" or "self-regulating" system, in which the biosphere has become an increasingly active element. The global ecosystem is a highly complex mosaic of regional, subregional, and national microsystems where factors that have diverse environmental consequences interact. These microsystems affect the global system differently, but they are interconnected and mutually influencing. The macrosystem they form is a cumulative global network, which in turn influences how the microsystems function.

A major conflict exists between the functional requirements of the global ecosystem and those of the global political-economic system. The basic requirements for sustaining the ecosystem are relative stability and ecological harmony, or balance. The ecosystem changes when major imbalances emerge as the results of human actions or natural catastrophes. As a complex system, the ecosystem is stabilized by "feedback loops" (the corrective reactions of natural or human forces). In general, the dynamics of nonlinear systems are chaotic. Stability under such circumstances implies that trajectories of disturbance remain within a relatively well-defined framework. Environmental catastrophes are disturbances that cannot be contained and thus radically affect ecological balance. As a result of extensive human economic activity, the feedback linkages with the biosphere are changed radically. The needs of the political-economic system are dynamism, expansion, growth, and greater profit margins. This is often achieved at the expense of the ecosystem. Harmonizing the two sets of requirements is painfully difficult, requiring deliberate, well-coordinated international actions for achieving ecologically sound schemes for sustainable economic growth. It calls for responsible collective governance.

These, then, are the outlines of the global system and its subsystems. A word of caution is required before we proceed to employ the nomenclature of systems theory, however.

A widely recognized problem in social science analysis is defining terms and categories. In political science, researchers often work with analytically imprecise categories that are understood and applied differently by various schools of thought. For example, the concept of the increasingly fashionable category of "governance" has yet to achieve a universally accepted definition.[3]

An associated variable of some complexity in defining terms is the diversity and polyglotism of human cultures. Naturally, conceptual frames of reference and nuance vary by culture; a given intellectual construct in English may represent a different notion and be improperly interpreted and apprehended in French, Russian, or Swahili. For example, in certain languages "governance" simply means "the management of a household." Because of cultural differences, even seemingly opposite concepts as "chaos" and "order" are not necessarily understood dichotomously. In Chinese, the character for crisis simultaneously represents chaos and opportunity.

Similarly, concepts of "anarchy," "chaos," the "global system," and "world order" are neither easily transferable nor universally acceptable frameworks for students of international affairs. Indeed, even members of the same sociolinguistic group who accept the necessity of applying a systemic approach to the study of international relations are not always in agreement over the meanings of chaos and order.

Cultural differences go beyond mere linguistic differences. Human beings, who are in the final analysis *the* actors on the stage of international relations, are members of societies within which values, ideologies, customs, and history condition ways of thinking. It is not the task of this study to discuss the extremely complex role of culture in international relations. However, how the many political cultures influence the decision-making process and how political transactions are affected by biases and predispositions remain fundamental questions. Culture, together with other key factors (geographic and historical conditions, for example), is one of the most enduring variables conditioning changes and influencing the forms and content of governance.

The Structure of This Book

This book is divided into five parts. Part I begins with an overview of the historical development of concepts of global order and of attempts made in the past two centuries to institutionalize some of those concepts. It then asks whether, in light of past experience, we can arrive at a set of effectiveness criteria with which to evaluate and design a new global order. The conclusion is reached that, given the unprecedented nature of the risks confronting the post–Cold War world, qualitatively new approaches and policies seem necessary to strengthen global political, economic, and environmental security. But will new approaches arise automatically?

Part II begins the search for an answer to that question by examining the character of changes in, and issues facing, contemporary global and regional politics. As in all areas of international life, old and new problems coexist and intermingle. Some changes have as yet been only partial, while others, although more fully experienced, are still of uncertain duration and direction and their long-term implications remain unknown. However, changes in the perceived interests and policies of the main actors allow some conclusions to be reached. The evolving global structure will, it appears, be hierarchical, involving a number of important regional powers. Interrelations between domestic and international issues will become more complex and antagonistic. Although new opportunities have emerged for the collective management of the main sources of global political instability and risks, global politics have been left more confused and less predictable by the increasing diversity of interests among the main actors, by the simultaneous presence of integrative and disintegrative forces, by the appearance of new internal and external sources of tension and conflict, and by the political heritage of the Cold War. Consequently, major efforts are needed to strengthen the collective capabilities of humankind to address the problems confronting global security.

Global security must be understood in a comprehensive framework, one that includes economic factors. Recognizing that current and future interrelations between global politics and economic changes will differ in many ways from past experience, part III of this book analyzes the main trends in the world's economic system and the dangers they pose for global security. Globalization is a key process in this respect. Through such means as the information revolution and technological transformation, globalization has transcended a variety of national and regional divisions and bound societies together in an increasingly but unequally transnationalized economy. Globalization is also an expression of the growing interconnectedness of national economies. This interconnectedness is also unequal and the degree of interdependence is highly asymmetrical. The gap between the needs of globalization (liberal trading regimes, freedom of movement of capital and labor, and so on) and the responses of states is wide and growing wider. International intergovernmental organizations have proved to be incapable of dealing efficiently with the new requirements of international economic cooperation and global development.

Part IV asks a central question: What are the present weaknesses and potential strengths of the international system of multilateral cooperation in dealing with the new problems facing the global system? In this part of the book, the place and role of the mechanisms of global multilateral cooperation are examined in relation to bilateral and regional as well as worldwide cooperation in the post–Cold War era. Although the present crisis in the global multilateral system of cooperation may be only temporary, the major powers are clearly not yet prepared to increase the power of multilateral agencies across the board. The policies of countries toward the multilateral system are changing relatively slowly and not always in a positive direction. There is no grand design for the reform of institutions that acknowledges the evolving socioeconomic and political needs of collective security and risk management.

Part V, the last part of the book, is not just a conclusion, for it suggests what will be the main trends of the new era into the early 21st century. The argument of part V centers on the contention that the needs of international cooperation are, and will remain, highly diverse from the point of view of the countries involved in the various multilateral regimes and systems. The conditions for effective global governance may also develop in a highly unequal fashion. In light of the increasing problems facing humankind, faster progress toward more effective global governance requires the elaboration of a new vision, the implementation of major institutional reforms, the strengthening of the intellectual, political, and financial foundations of existing organizations, the exercise of bold and imaginative leadership, and the undertaking of new initiatives. If humankind is not once again to miss an historic opportunity to establish a more cooperative and secure world, these admittedly demanding requirements must be fulfilled.

Part I

The Conceptual and Historical Development of Global Orders

chapter 1

Order in the New Global Political Context

We stand today on the threshold of a new global order, confident that profound transformations are under way, but uncertain as to their eventual consequences. Future students of this era's history may be able to state with certainty the overall pattern and character of this unfolding order; we cannot. What we can do, though, is to assess our present situation in light of earlier historical patterns. Such an assessment can provide guidelines for understanding and interpreting the ongoing changes; it can also allow us to gauge, albeit tentatively, the extent to which the present transformation is historically distinctive.

A number of scholars have attempted just this task, comparing the previous transition period—from the imperial order of the 19th and 20th centuries to the era of U.S. economic hegemony and U.S.-Soviet bipolarism—with today's post–Cold War transition to hierarchical multipolarity, in which the United States tops a hierarchy that also features Western Europe, Japan, Russia, and China. Some experts have suggested similarities between the two transformations in the global political order. Ralph Buultjens, writing in 1992, raised the question of whether or not the following cyclical sequence of 20th-century development will continue to obtain:

First: Serious disputes among the major powers lead to a large and prolonged conflict, which destroys a large number of people.

Second: After an intense and costly struggle, the conflict is won by the power and powers that espouse values of freedom and liberty. This arouses high expectations that a new era of democracy has dawned. The victors establish or revive international peacekeeping institutions to prevent another catastrophe.

Third: Victory also results in the creation or redefinition of several medium and small states—entities that proclaim their commitment to sustain freedom and often embrace democracy.

Fourth: Despite initial efforts, these states are unable to maintain democracy and many soon lapse into types of authoritarianism. International peacekeeping structures prove ineffective.

Finally: The new states develop internal conflicts, engage in conflicts among themselves, or become adjuncts in big, fresh conflicts among major powers.[1]

This sequence expresses a widely shared pessimistic view about the present. Yet though anything is possible in the post–Cold War world, Buultjen's cyclical pattern seems unlikely to be repeated in the near future because it contains an assumption that does not hold true at present: today, there are no major powers challenging the status quo and preparing to engage in wars of succession.

At this stage, the transition process is marked by an absence, at least on the global scale, of the wars of succession experienced in earlier centuries between the established defenders of the status quo and their challengers among the newly powerful states. (Current civil wars in the former Soviet Union and Yugoslavia seem to be as much the causes of the ongoing transition as its consequences.) Two reasons for this lack of conflict spring immediately to mind. First, territorial conquest as an instrument of power politics has lost its global relevance. The importance of traditional, realpolitik means of exercising global influence—political domination over raw materials and human (labor) resources, strategic geopolitical positioning, and so forth—has been substantially devalued by the technological revolution, which has made the acquisition of knowledge and its technical and managerial application the keys to political and economic power. The most significant international markets today are those for knowledge-intensive goods and services in the developed industrialized countries, which absorb two-thirds of the world's supply of manufactured goods and about 90 percent of all high-tech products.

Second, wars of succession have lost their relevance in today's system because the major actors, both old and new, are interdependent and have strong common interests in ensuring peace, stability, and the smooth functioning of the international system. That system possesses more effective institutions for managing interdependent relations than did any previous historical international system.

There is also another explanation for the absence of wars of succession: given the start-up and maintenance costs involved, no power is able or willing to aspire to succeed the United States in the role of global hegemon. Ted Galen Carpenter has questioned whether even the United States, with its overwhelming economic, political, military, and diplomatic power, can retain hegemony. Carpenter concludes that although the international system is, indeed, presently unipolar, little in the history of international relations suggests such a phenomenon is sustainable for any length of time.[2]

Interestingly, issues of leadership and the functioning of the post-hegemonic order arose while the Cold War was still being fought. W. W. Rostow, in examining Japan as a world power, asked whether the emergence of Japanese world economic hegemony could be considered a realistic alternative to U.S. hegemony. His conclusion was that instead of a change of hegemon, world leadership would probably be diffused. Rostow emphasized that in the age of the fourth industrial revolution, there would be no single dominant state but rather a number of leading powers in the system, the distinguishing features of which would be peculiar kinds of cooperation and competition.[3]

Writing as the Cold War was drawing to its close, Robert Cox arrived at a not dissimilar conclusion in discussing the characteristics of the post-hegemonic world:

[Antonio Gramsci, wrote Cox] defines the condition of a world society and state system in which the dominant state and dominant social forces sustain their position through adherence to universalized principles which are accepted or acquiesced in by a sufficient proportion of subordinate states and social forces. This meaning of hegemony implies intellectual and moral leadership. The strong make certain concessions to obtain the consent of the weaker. The pax Americana of the post-World War II era had the characteristics of the Gramscian meaning of hegemony. . . . [4]

Cox concluded that a post-hegemonic era could see the coexistence of many different traditions of civilization within an atmosphere of mutual tolerance of a distinct set of values and a distinct path toward development. Cox recognized, however, that the achievement of such a world "is a difficult challenge to common ways of thinking."[5]

If, as seems unmistakably the case, the present transition period is significantly different from earlier transitions between global orders, is it also more likely to produce peace and stability than did those transitional periods marked by wars of succession? Sadly, current conditions suggest no. The world is experiencing destablilization that is eroding each of the subsytems of global security, as well as the interstices between them. We cannot know the outcome of this transitional period, but it will surely not prove a boon to humankind if the dismal conditions that exist today among the regulating forces persist.

This should compel us to act, to accept the challenge of striking some harmony among the regulating forces of the system and create a world order that has as its aim responsible world governance. By combining the conceptual and institutional lessons of history with sound, forward-looking policy analysis, we can discover how to amend the post–World War II order so that it becomes relevant and responsive to post–Cold War realities. The "world order" of which politicians and others speak must not become an intellectual fad, nor must it be allowed to become a mere "-ism" that disregards the consequences of its dogma. The world order must be understood and governed by a universal ideology based on the general values and interests of the world's population.

Should this challenge not be met, nations may well be forced to follow the apparent logic of events, precipitating an uncontrollable crisis. However, the determinants of crisis *can* be managed, and their effects mitigated, through responsible, preventive action taken collectively by both state and nonstate actors. This book seeks to identify these determinants and to explore how the institutions of world order can most effectively respond.

chapter 2

The Concept and Character of Global Order

Before proceeding further, a few definitions are in order. This brief clarification not only is essential for the purposes of this book but also reflects the necessity for specificity within the global system itself. Given the complex and multidimensional nature of the global system, the proper functioning of its subsystems requires that rules and norms be specifically elaborated.

The concept of *global* or *world order* is used here in both a broader and a narrower understanding. In the broader meaning, world order is the totality of globally valid norms, rules, and international codes of conduct designed for, and generally observed by, states and transnational actors in the international public policymaking process. More narrowly, world order is the entirety of legally binding norms and institutions that regulate interstate relations.[6] International norms and rules are usually based primarily on specific interests and values of the major powers, and, secondarily, on those of the whole international community.

These rules and norms cannot be isolated from, and in fact are parts of, the *regulating forces* that determine how the main components of subsystems function. These regulating forces are many, and include the "invisible hands" of global markets; social and technoeconomic factors, such as the socioeconomic conditions that determine how technology is used; government attitudes and policies toward technoeconomic problems; the international power structure dominated by the economic and political interests of major powers; the character and intensity of international cooperation; and the management and regulatory practices of international institutions and cooperation regimes.

Regulating forces help order international relations that would otherwise be entirely anarchical. According to some observers, anarchy does, in fact, reign. Robert Gilpin has defined the essence of international politics to be a recurring struggle among independent actors in a state of anarchy.[7] But anarchy has at least two definitions. The first is lack of government, the other is chaos, or disorder. Rules, norms, and regulating forces provide for some form of decentralized governance and order, and are thus valued by international actors. Violations of these norms, rules, and codes can result in sanctions applied by a legitimately established international authority, by a coalition of states taking enforcement actions, or by a single state willing and able to assume the role of international policeman.

Order and disorder, as well as predictable and unpredictable events, are not entirely exclusive elements of a complex global system. Individuals and groups have an immeasurable number of opportunities to react—rationally or irrationally—to domestic and international issues according to their intellectual capacities, cultures, and habits, being motivated by specific interests and goals. Behind their reactions, however, are the regulating forces that constrain the actions and influence the outcomes of the efforts of all actors.[8]

In an interconnected and dynamic global system, there are unpredictable processes that can neither be planned for, nor even anticipated. Therefore, regulating forces notwithstanding, any global order can only be relatively stable.[9] Indeed, although order is generally considered to be a static concept, no world order could ever be considered static. The survival and durability of world orders depend not least on their ability to promote and adjust to change.

The distinction between order and chaos, and anarchy and governance, is far from being of only theoretical importance. If the international system is determined by disorder and anarchy, then anything—including international violence, the threat and the use of force, terrorism, and international sanctions—would be a legitimate instrument of statecraft that could be deterred only by the punitive responses of other states. Order, however, implies institutionalized rules and a disciplined, accountable community of states. Order is a form of collective self-control, an ethic of sorts to which states subscribe via an international consensus on norms and, partly, on a codified legal framework.[10] At the same time, it should be noted that empirical experience does support the efforts of certain schools of political (and economic) philosophy to accommodate the simultaneous presence of order and chaos in the system.

chapter 3

Criteria for an Effective Global Order

Today, as the global system grows more complex and states and humankind find themselves with new needs, it is necessary to move beyond debating general concepts of world order and to begin discussing the institutional effectiveness of future global orders. If a set of effectiveness criteria can be developed, it could serve to guide consideration of the political and institutional changes necessary to improve the functioning of the international system.

Effectiveness is not and cannot be measured objectively. The reason for this is simply that the preferences of national populations (and of their political elites) can differ greatly; one need only think of the usual differences between the preferences of the ruling elites in totalitarian regimes and their counterparts in democratic regimes. However, if we presuppose a basically democratic future world, we can focus on a few human values and aspirations that will be widely shared and may offer general guidance as to how to gauge effective international governance.

From a democratic perspective, the efficiency of a country's political system is largely reflected in the capabilities of its government to accommodate, rather than suppress, differences in public opinion and to maintain domestic political stability by way of a social consensus achieved at relatively low cost and generative of significant social benefits. This requires the prudent and rational use of power, a democratic sharing of responsibilities and power, and a high intellectual level of professionalism in governance. It also requires substantial flexibility in institutional structures, enabling policies to be selected and adjustments to be made in a timely fashion.

These qualities are equally necessary in a system of effective international governance. The indicators of political effectiveness here would also include a state's capacity to understand and influence the nature of changes occurring in the international environment, thereby avoiding major crises. Very few countries can decisively influence the international environment. But, either individually or collectively, states can prepare themselves to confront sources of instability and external risks and to mitigate the effects of crisis.

Is it sound to formulate an unambiguous and immutable set of effectiveness criteria that could be applied to any global order? On the one hand, power has always been a critically important determinant in the establishment of global orders; therefore, aspects such as the source of power, its affirmative or cynical manipulation in instituting a global order, and the degree of acceptability of a particular power structure may offer some criteria for comparison and evaluation from an historical perspective. The costs of sustaining a given order and the benefits it yields may be equally important and interesting criteria for historical, political, and socioeconomic analysis.

On the other hand, however, global orders do not evolve in a vacuum. They are rooted in a given historical context. The diversity among political-historical actors and their unique world orders is probably greater than their commonality. The degree of efficiency of a global order, therefore, must be measured against the operational performance required by those who are its architects and members. Each set of efficiency criteria must be specifically related to the major problems of a given historical era and to the particular interests of that era's main actors.

Having said this, what would be the criteria for a *well-functioning* world order in the post–Cold War period? In delineating these criteria (or postulates), one must take into account the interests of not only individual nations but also humanity in general.

In political terms, the post–Cold War order must be effective in maintaining world peace, preventing the abuse of power in international relations, and, more particularly, forestalling violent regional or global conflicts on the basis of mutual obligations or contractual and institutional guarantees for the security of each country. The order must be one that holds countries accountable for their obligations to provide these security guarantees. A successful global order must be authorized by a collective mandate and have at its disposal effective mechanisms for the peaceful solution of international disputes and for peacekeeping and peacemaking operations. It should also be flexible enough to facilitate dynamic changes, especially those of a socioeconomic nature. In the absence of military blocs, it will be increasingly important for the leading powers to gain sufficient legitimacy and establish a consensus that will permit them to fulfill their managerial roles in certain international institutions.

From an economic point of view, an effective order must promote relatively widespread and sustainable development of the national economies comprising the system. (Sustainability is an increasingly important requirement in light of new social and ecological challenges.) It has to facilitate the international flow of labor, goods, services, technology, and capital, and assist in staving off international economic crises, trade wars, and similar disruptions.

With respect to the human dimension, the order must help establish international institutional guarantees against the massive violation of human rights (broadly defined), and should be patterned along principles of human solidarity that would facilitate collective action in global disasters and emergencies. A late 20th-century global order must protect the interests of future generations by directing collective responses to environmental problems.

These criteria imply that a new global order cannot merely be a functional improvement on the post–World War II order; significant changes are clearly required in almost all important areas of international cooperation. When the very character of its institutions and leaders are products of 20th-century history, the world cannot, of course, organize itself completely anew. However, the world must realistically address itself to the changes that will occur this decade, changes that will probably be gradual and incremental.

It follows from the above criteria that political efficiency in a global order must be evaluated against the extent to which the norms and institutions that shape the international organizational framework are able to constrain, or discipline, the behavior of states, thus making states predictable, reliable partners. In the absence of a strong norms-enforcing authority and an established code of conduct—both of which are likely to remain absent in a global arena of constant change—it will be crucially important in the future to enhance collective efforts to confront sources of international instability and manage risks that may otherwise result in global crises.

Any future global order must be organized in such a way that its legal and institutional structures have the capacity to manage political problems that are an admixture of past, present, and anticipated sources of instability. If this does not happen, the newly emergent opportunities for responding proactively to global demands will be jeopardized.

Although, as noted above, each global order has its own problems and character, today's policymakers would be wise to turn the pages of history books and discover what has been achieved and what has proved successful in the past. Perhaps history, a chronicle of human endeavors to order the world, can yield up insights of contemporary applicability; at the very least, history may tell us what *not* to do. In the next chapter we briefly review some of the *conceptualizations* of world order developed over more than two millennia; in the following chapter we give an overview of attempts made to *institutionalize* world order in the 19th and 20th centuries.

chapter 4

Past Ideas about Universality, Peace, and Order

Attempts to establish some order that respects certain normative values in a chaotic international relations system governed by national security interests and military power are by no means unknown in human history. "Every age has had its burden of misfortunes and dangers and has nurtured its hopes," wrote Aurelio Peccei, founder of that group of distinguished scholars known as the Club of Rome.[11]

Since the beginning of the turbulent 20th century, such efforts have been numerous. The many political ideologies and movements that have animated this century, the different "-isms" that have sought to claim this century as their unique era of influence, have almost all proffered concepts for a preferred world order. Liberals and communists, national and democratic socialists, nationalists and cosmopolitans, the variety of globalists, advocates of scientism, and believers in religious reform and fundamentalism: each group has elaborated concepts about a new order designed to improve the condition of humankind.

Some of the more benign of these concepts became sources of policy actions that resulted in the establishment of international organizations that have played a useful and sometimes

17

indispensable role in advancing the primary interests of humankind. However, many other concepts, values, and norms became the motive forces and justifications for different, more costly, policy actions. These costs were measured not solely in pounds, dollars, marks, or rubles, but also in human suffering and victimization, such as the millions of people killed or imprisoned in concentration camps and gulags.

It is beyond the scope of this book to undertake a systematic comparative analysis of the various interpretations of world order offered this century or before. However, a brief historical overview may indicate some of the possibilities and pitfalls awaiting present and future attempts to construct an effective global order. As this chapter shows, certain ideas that have been presented as original to the 20th century actually appeared long before. At the same time, however, one must bear in mind that each concept was "insular" insofar as it was developed and expressed within the confines of its own cultural and political milieu.

Conceptual Developments
before the 20th Century

Perhaps the earliest known world order concepts were developed in India around the 3rd century B.C. In the "Arthashastra," a collection of writings attributed to the Buddhist philosopher Kautilya, world order was called "mandal," or the circle of states. The relation of one state to another depended on geographical distance, internal strength, and cohesiveness. The neighboring state was considered as an enemy, and a neighbor's neighbor as a mediator. States were divided into six circles and the relations among them were based on friendship, animosity, or indifference. China's concept of world order was simpler, dividing the world into just two parts, the civilized and the barbaric.

Interestingly, world order concepts may have their genesis in religious doctrines. Virtually every great religion has claimed that world conditions would improve were its precepts to become universally adopted. For example, one world order concept with a religious base is "unity." Indeed, the dogma of unity as propounded by most world religions demands that those not already of the faith be persuaded to convert. In Islam, for example, this idea is expressed in the Qur'an (16:64 and 2:176). Similarly, the traditional position of Roman Catholicism has been *extra ecclesiam nulla salus*—no salvation exists outside the church.

The Roman Catholic church became the first real hierarchical transnational organization, controlling and coordinating its relatively autonomous units from Rome by establishing general norms, symbolic leadership roles, and a binding decision-making process. The church also created a global network for redistributing human and material resources between Rome and the semi-autonomous units.

Writing in the 5th century A.D., St. Augustine postulated the concepts of the City of God and the City of Man. The former was a sphere free of violence and corruption where all faithful Christians would reside. It was thought to be a sphere that could be realized in the social formations of that time. Medieval Christian empires held firmly to the belief that the world was to be hierarchically organized, unified by a common faith under the joint moral code of emperor and pope. In 1460, King George Podebrad of Bohemia, a medieval internationalist of sorts, called for a federation of Christian empires—a congress of kings and princes—with a permanent secretariat that would maintain an army, impose and collect taxes, and coin money.

In a similar, though secular, vein a French scholar, Emeric Cruce, proposed in 1623 a permanent congress of ambassadors rather than of kings and princes. Cruce was also the first, and, for centuries thereafter, the only European to widen the scope of the world order beyond Europe and advocate the inclusion of Ethiopia, Persia, the Indies, and China.[12]

With the appearance of the nation-state and the disappearance of unitary states, the realities of the world obliged new concepts to be formulated about how the world system functioned and could be ordered.

A variety of normative world order schemes usually appear in great numbers during turbulent periods of human history, when philosophers and statesmen alike venture to effect an ordered change in the hostile relations among countries. Utopian schemes reflect the ideological values of the day, whether religious or scientific. At times, they also reflect opposition to the rigid, hierarchical, and violent character of an era.

William Penn, in his "Essay Toward the Present and Future Peace of Europe" written in 1693, conceived of a new European order based on principles of cooperation. The main body of that order would be a congress of deputies dispatched by kings. The congress would hold annual meetings and all disputes among nations would be referred to it for resolution.[13] In the early 18th century, Castel de Saint-Pierre proposed a "perpetual Union" of the Christian rulers in Europe, where each major power would have one vote and the small states would be grouped and have a "collective ballot."[14] Toward the end of that century, Immanuel Kant, in his *Perpetual Peace* (1795), proposed a federation that nations could enter into and withdraw from at will.[15] At the Congress of Vienna in 1815, Tsar Alexander I of Russia sought to translate his interest in the question of how nations could become cooperatively associated by calling for a Holy Alliance of nations whose policies would be guided by Christian principles.

Throughout the 19th and the first half of the 20th centuries, an ever-increasing number of schemes, plans, and projects appeared, each offering a common solution to international problems under such slogans as cosmopolitanism, internationalism, and world federalism. In that era of great empires and nationalism, these proposals sought to offer a human alternative that was neither imperialist nor aggressively nationalist. Two main groups emerged: the liberal internationalists, whose ideas were based on reformed capitalism; and the socialist internationalists, who considered the establishment of socialism as the basic condition for the emergence of a new global order. Neither of these groups was homogeneous, and their heterogeneity was reflected in the influence they had on political actions.

Conceptual Developments since World War II

By the second half of the 20th century, world order concepts had matured, corresponding more closely to the processes and problems of the international system. Three—or perhaps four—major directions can be discerned in conceptual development since World War II. The first direction is the "Spaceship Earth" concept, which has been developed and advanced in many different ways by academics, religious groups, and other nongovernmental bodies. The reports issued by the Club of Rome represent probably the earliest and most comprehensive scientific justification of the concept. Formed in the early 1960s by a group of concerned scientists from different disciplines, the Club of Rome has sought to create a new global consciousness of hope amid the existing and potential global crises of population, environment, energy, and international governance by emphasizing the need for a new order of cooperation based on global scientific rationality. Although regarded with skepticism at first, Club of Rome reports have initiated great debates over the need for, and the practicability of, a more secure world— secure not only from war, but also from economic, social, and environmental threats.

Although they have not developed an explicit and detailed world order concept, members of the Club of Rome have been the first to proceed beyond the approach traditionally taken by political scientists to world order, an approach in which the political-military aspects of existing or normative world orders predominate. Club members have endeavored to shape a secure future world built on the foundations of common ground and intersected by the interests of all nations. Since the late 1960s, a variety of other groups have sprang up that have pursued similar goals. One influential product of this work has been the 1987 report of the World Commission on Environment and Development (the Bruntland Commission) entitled "Our Common Future," which emphasized the political, economic, social, and ecological conditions required for sustainable development. This report stimulated many global-level policy initiatives in the early 1990s, including the "Agenda 21," the final document of the United Nations Conference on Environment and Development that was held in Rio de Janeiro in June 1992.

The second conceptual direction taken since World War II could be called "global market integration." It centers on modeling the role of transnational structures, like transnational banks and corporations. Advocates of these models have suggested that technological progress, the development of transnational corporations, and increasing interdependence tend to make the traditional structure of the state obsolete; therefore, the state structure must be transformed to better allow for the global integration of markets. These transnationalists see the clash of interests between the political forces of the state and the techno-economic forces of transnationalization as the main global conflict of the future. Only a federative global government, argue some advocates of global market integration, would be able to resolve this conflict.[16]

Although the idea of a federative global government does not enjoy the support of all advocates of an integrated world economy, specialists throughout the United States and Europe have given serious consideration to the potential benefits of an international collective economic leadership achieved by the gradual integration of multifarious market sectors.

The third direction in conceptual development was taken in the 1970s by a number of developing countries, which attempted to establish a "New International Economic Order" (NIEO) that focused on economic and political issues. The advocates of the highly controversial NIEO accepted the present state-centric structure of the world and proposed solutions to problems—most notably, world impoverishment—that were consistent with this structure.

The principal assumption of the NIEO was that the traditional international economic order is exploitative and hierarchical, characterized by market processes that reinforce the economic dependence of the developing countries. As a result of these traditional market structures and forces, the developing world has remained subordinate to the developed world; political decolonization has not translated into economic decolonization. The objective of the NIEO was to redress this economic subordination and dependence through the political instruments of the United Nations and create economic parity in the market system. In 1974, the UN General Assembly adopted Resolutions 3201 and 3202, "The Declaration of the Establishment of a New International Economic Order and Programme of Action."

NIEO advocates sought to interpose principles of global solidarity into the systemic status quo that would safeguard the broader interests of the global economy and humankind, especially the politically and economically underprivileged. Satisfying basic human needs, according to the NIEO, should be the chief priority of a state's economic policy; and, either individually or collectively, states should be held accountable for the adverse consequences of their policies.

Proponents of the NIEO also proposed democratizing the norms of international cooperation and elaborating codes of conduct to govern transnational corporate activities, technology transfers, international lending operations, and the functioning of markets in raw materials (international commodity agreements, buffer funds, compensatory loans, and so forth), thereby taking into account the interests of both suppliers and users simultaneously. Issues like access to the markets of industrialized countries and the principles of nonreciprocal and nondiscriminatory treatment also received special attention. Politically, the NIEO called for noninterference, the peaceful settlements of disputes, and restraints on the use of violence to achieve political or economic ends.

In the long history of world order ideas, the NIEO is especially noteworthy as the first widely supported political initiative by the decolonized countries—wherein live most of the world's population—to change the existing order. However, although a substantial majority of the General Assembly voted to adopt the NIEO resolution, it was never implemented because of its failure to take into account the complex network of traditional market forces and the interests of the existing political and economic power structures.

The development of the NIEO had been largely influenced by the short-term success in the early 1970s of the oil-producing and -exporting nations, which had temporarily been able to increase their revenues by raising monopoly prices, thereby changing the pattern of global income distribution. The subsequent deterioration of the global economic situation (to some extent, a consequence of this power grab), together with the exercise of the consolidated political, economic, and technological power of the major industrial countries, effectively curtailed NIEO aspirations and restored the earlier relationships.

The NIEO had also overlooked a very important factor: the differences of opinion and conflicts of interest among the developing countries themselves concerning many of the new order ideas. The realities of a global political and economic system guided by the interests of powerful actors proved to be too strong, and the alliance around the NIEO too weak and temporary, for the NIEO to achieve its goals.

Since the late 1980s, the collapse of the communist regimes in Central and Eastern Europe, the dismembering of the Soviet Union, and the erosion of U.S. hegemony have stimulated new thinking about normative concepts of an evolving world order that would be based on the rule of law, universal democracy, and collective security. World order studies have become more widespread and are increasingly related to the new role of multi-lateral cooperation. This approach can probably be regarded as the fourth conceptual direction taken since World War II. The new problems and needs of states and other actors in international life will certainly serve to inspire further research on global governance as the underpinnings of a new era.

chapter 5

Past Attempts to Institutionalize World Orders

The Concert of Europe

Prior to the 19th century, attempts to order the global system were based on power, religion, political ideology, political and economic interests, and the range of compromises achieved among them. At best, these were only partial attempts at instituting a world order. A major effort to establish a more structured system of relations among the main actors of international life was made in the post-Napoleonic era. At that time, the industrial revolution had opened the way for greater mobility on the seas and oceans, and had provided the technological and military foundations for modern colonial empires. Additionally, weapons were becoming more destructive and efficient. With the defeat of Napoleon, a new status quo emerged in the global power structure that included both stable and uncertain, dynamic elements.

The establishment of the Holy Alliance and the Concert of Europe were practical steps taken by the great powers to create an international political order that was to formulate and advocate certain conservative norms in European public policy (like legitimism, traditionalism, and the suppression of "dangerous" radical movements). However, in international life, the Concert of Europe was merely an instrument for maintaining a stable balance of power within Europe and protecting the interests of the main European empires against new challengers, especially those from outside Europe. The concert was able to arbitrate a number of disputes peacefully, sustain a level of cooperation among the imperial powers, and accommodate changes to the political map of the continent.

The concert was widely criticized by contemporaries (and later by historians) for being too reactionary and too loosely organized to anticipate or manage the various threats and conflicts that endangered European security. Such criticisms, however, overlooked the fact that the Concert of Europe had been designed as an instrument of power politics in an imperial era to maintain a balance of power. Inevitably, the newly emerging, dynamic powers acted to undermine the imperial order that the concert was intended to sustain.[17]

The League of Nations

The first comprehensive attempt in human history to establish a world peace regime was the League of Nations, the concept of which was articulated in 1918 by U.S. President Woodrow Wilson in his "Fourteen Points." Wilson rejected the traditional European-dominated international order and its instruments of secret diplomacy, balance-of-power doctrines, and territorial conquest. Instead, he advocated national self-determination and national democratic rule, offering the vision of a democratic international political system and the model of an open, liberal world economy.

The creation of the league was also shaped by a framework of ideas, principles, and practical experiences learned from the Concert of Europe. The most important lesson was that the assignment of special responsibilities and positions to the great powers and their empires should be institutionalized. This was achieved in the Council of the League, which was composed of the representatives of the main allied powers. Also integrated into the design of the league were the new Wilsonian concepts of collective and universal security (although only in its narrower military understanding), the indivisibility of world peace, and the necessity for common action wherever peace was violated.[18]

Concurrent with the creation of the League of Nations, another vision of world order was being promulgated: the 21 Points of Lenin. Although this alternative vision had little or no impact on the functioning of the league, it did provide a contrast to Wilsonian ideas. Adopted at the second congress of the Comintern (the organization of the international communist movement established in 1919) in 1920, Lenin's scheme saw the Soviet Union as the model state for communist parties throughout the world, which were to be directed and organized transnationally from Moscow. Although this scheme was based on the principles of dictatorship and hierarchical relations, and thus counterpointed the Wilsonian democratic order, there were parallels between the two visions, most notably in their support for the notion of self-determination and their assault on European hegemony in global affairs.

In practice, the Soviet Union eventually discarded its concept of world revolution and concentrated instead on its domestic problems and increasing its economic and military power. The ideology of a hierarchical communist world order remained, however, and continued to influence the Soviet Union's international policies, especially the doctrine declaring interstate relations to be a form of international class struggle.

The short life of the League of Nations was marked by a series of failures and an inability to achieve declared goals. Ironically, the league, the main institutional form of world order, was held by many to be chiefly responsible for World War II. The organization was plagued with problems. First of all, it was based on a peace regime replete with potential conflicts that the league lacked the instruments to resolve. The League Covenant had made concessions to preexisting power politics, adopting such "regional understandings" as the Monroe Doctrine, which licensed certain powers to pursue their geostrategic priorities. Further, the league did not establish an efficient instrument for punishing those states that violated the peace.

Second, the league had little authority and few mechanisms to deal with the major political and socioeconomic issues of the era: the emergence of anticolonial forces; the Great Depression;

large-scale unemployment; poverty; and the rise of Nazism and other forms of violent nationalism.

Third, the United States, which was the strongest power after World War I, did not join the league. President Wilson, who had played the key role in formulating the main principles and erecting the main pillars of the new order, failed in 1920 to win the support of the U.S. Senate for membership of the new organization. Although more than two-thirds of the senators favored U.S. entry to the league, they attached conditions that Wilson rejected. As a result, those who opposed entry were able to garner sufficient votes to deny U.S. membership. The codification of the U.S. Neutrality Act of 1937 was another major blow to the League of Nations in that the act was taken to demonstrate a U.S. unwillingness to intervene in Europe.

U.S. participation could have guaranteed the league's functional success. As it turned out, not only did the United States not join, but also 17 of the league's 63 members withdrew before it eventually collapsed. Thus weakened, the league was unable to transform the international order or to defuse the sources of new conflict. It was even unable to maintain the existing balance of power.

Unrestrained by the league, the Axis powers pursued an aggressive, expansionist course that led directly to World War II. On one side of the conflict were the Nazis, whose "new order" established a system of oppression, racial supremacy, and hatred. On the other was the antifascist alliance, the aims of which were not only the defeat of the Axis powers, but also "to see established a peace which will afford to all nations the means of dwelling in safety within their own boundaries and which will afford assurance that all the men in all the lands may live out their lives in freedom from fear and want."[19]

The Post–World War II Order

The Allied victory in World War II ushered in a new world order, one that proved to be among the most successful of all such regimes. (We should perhaps say *"has* proved," for only now is it giving way to the post–Cold War order.) This order included the system of the United Nations (a term first applied to the democratic nations that fought against the Axis powers) and showed itself to be very durable, despite the historically unprecedented global changes and challenges that confronted it.

Over the past 50 years, the United Nations weathered, and sometimes actively confronted, a remarkable array of changes and challenges to global stability, including the Cold War and more than 130 hot wars; an economically devastating peace-time arms race (begun in the era of conventional weapons and carried through into the nuclear and space age); the political decolonization and birth of between 120 and 130 new states; a population explosion; a scientific and technological revolution with dramatic social and economic effects; the greatest expansion of the world economy and of global markets in history; profound changes in the patterns of output, consumption, and employment; the rise and fall of dictatorial regimes; and a deepening ecological crisis.

A major reason that the global order, along with its structure of international cooperation, was able to survive intact through this turbulent period is that the power structure was firmly supportive of it. Simply put, the post–World War II global order satisfied the power structure's interests and expectations.

The basic component of the power structure was the United States, which emerged from World War II as the only relatively undamaged, victorious power. Much stronger both economically and militarily than its allies, the United States assumed a hegemonic role in international affairs that facilitated the realization of the American vision of a new world order for much of the noncommunist world. This vision had changed since President Wilson formulated his Fourteen Points, but several building blocks nevertheless remained. The United States advocated a world system of legitimate, democratic, and secular states that honored the rights of individuals and facilitated their participation in society as democratic citizens. Economically, the United States favored a capitalist, open-market system based on private ownership. Internationally, it sought to advance national self-determination, peace, and global prosperity.

Many of these goals were shared by other leading members of the Allied coalition, and much of the U.S. ideology was embodied in the 1945 UN Charter, which expounded democratic norms and principles while simultaneously recognizing and accepting great global diversity. Indeed, the far-reaching normative aspects of the charter contributed to the longevity of the post–World War II order.

The Soviet Union assumed an antagonistic role toward Western assumptions and concepts of the post–World War II order until the late 1980s. According to the Soviet Union's official ideology, the basic determinants—or regulating forces—of the global system were socioeconomic pressures. The Bolshevik revolution had dissociated the Soviet Union from the global capitalist system and had enthroned the Soviet Union as the leading and central force in a new "socialist world system." Until 1928, the officially espoused view of the Comintern was that the socialist world system was to be developed through the extension of the Soviet Union, to which new countries would attach themselves as member republics. Later, this idea was abandoned. Faced with the realities of the post–World War II world, the socialist world system came to be seen as the structure of states within which the Soviet Union dominated.

The global system was therefore split into two contrasting systems, each ideologically exclusive in nature. The Soviet Union naturally became the chief international competitor to the United States, although after the 1970s the Soviet Union officially relinquished its ideologically motivated and self-proclaimed leading role in the socialist world.

Despite its ideological opposition to the Western order, the Soviet Union—along with countries in Central and Eastern Europe, China, and other communist nations—became an integral constituent of the global power structure and its intergovernmental organizations. In these forums, Soviet policies were somewhat ambivalent, reflecting on the one hand the geostrategic interests of a continental empire inherited from Russia's prerevolutionary past, and, on the other hand, the evangelistic nature of communist ideology. From a very early stage in its existence, despite being a relatively poor country with highly unequal performances among its various economic sectors, and despite consumption patterns very near those of the developing world, the Soviet Union made tremendous economic sacrifices to develop its defense sector and thus sustain a global military power position. Not until the mid-1980s did the Soviet Union modify its global aspirations and accept that it was economically unable to keep pace with the rising costs of remaining a military superpower.[20]

With Mikhail Gorbachev in charge, it became even more apparent that the Soviet Union had survived only as a one-dimensional power, one that had concentrated almost entirely on military might, leaving its economic power and influence to be marginal, static, and regional at best. The Soviet concept of two world systems—capitalist and socialist—also underwent a gradual change under the impact of Gorbachev's "new thinking." Long-standing ideas of an international class struggle were abandoned in the latter half of the 1980s, and "the general interests of humankind" was officially adopted as a guiding principle of Soviet foreign policy.

The United Nations will be examined in depth in part IV of this book. This brief historical overview has merely attempted to indicate the continuity over the last two centuries in the institutionalization of ideas of global order and to show that schemes for world order are not unique to the post–Gulf War era.

History has arrived at a new turning point. Cold War stability and the relatively predictable environment of the post–World War II era are giving way to uncertainty. New attempts to order the world must acknowledge and accommodate the perceived realities, dangers, and needs of the evolving era. Quite possibly, the quest for a new global order will prove elusive in the short run; already, the slogan of a "new world order" so popular in the early 1990s has been largely forgotten amid the political changes of the mid-1990s. Perhaps we must wait until the 21st century to discover the full ramifications—for good or ill—of those efforts begun as the Cold War ended.

The future is the outcome of the predictable and unpredictable. Those problems and tendencies that currently characterize the international political system (the subject of the next part of this book) may rapidly increase, or they may decline, or they may even disappear. New, unforeseen issues will certainly emerge. Some present trends may prove self-sustaining, others self-defeating. Even so, a careful analysis of today's chief political currents may well offer some sense of the present and future tasks for risk management in international politics.

Part II
Continuity and Change in the International Political System

chapter 6

States and Ideologies in the Post–Cold War Era

A remarkable coincidence of major global changes has set in train a transformation of the global political system. Powerful new forces are rivaling or replacing many of the political and socioeconomic processes that previously influenced the character and functioning of the system, refashioning it into a more complex and diverse structure. These forces bring with them hopes for a more peaceful and cooperative international political system, one fundamentally different from the confrontational character of the Cold War world.

We face many questions, each with profound implications for the future of global politics: What will be the chief characteristics of the post–Cold War political system? What will be its chief problems and major sources of tension and conflict? What will be the incentives and institutional guarantees for cooperation and conflict prevention? In our search for answers we must be forward-looking but eschew wishful thinking. For the moment at least, there are no guarantees that democracy in the former totalitarian regimes will be consolidated or that the transition to a new era of peaceful global progress will be smooth. Our task is far from easy. In this period of uncertainties, it is necessary but very difficult to predict the possibilities and pitfalls awaiting us.

History is at best only a rough guide to the future. Lessons of previous major changes indicate that transformation occurs when new trends and their regulating forces become strong enough to overcome resistance in the global system and are thus able to influence the course of events. This process is never clearly delineated, however; within the various international domains, both old and new elements intermingle for an indeterminable period. Beyond this very general observation, we can deduce little from past experience about future directions. Anyway, the policies of governments and the structures of international cooperation will have to deal with specifics and details, not with generalities, and they will have to search for solutions to concrete, not hypothetical, sources of tension and conflict.

Robert Jervis has suggested several reasons why it is difficult to predict the course of international politics: the limited stock of knowledge on which social scientists have to rely; the multiplicity of factors determining politics; the numerous policy options available to states; the tightly intertwined elements of international politics; the unknown ramifications of systemic changes; and the nongeneralizable nature of knowledge of past processes and events.[1] Jervis's argument is quite sound. International politics is, after all, composed of many different and interactive factors and forces that impact the system in any number of ways. The determinants of political change include the unique legal and institutional framework of a given international order, as well as the changing interests, values, and policy priorities of international actors and the dynamic interrelations among them. The task of prediction is further complicated by the uncertainties engendered by turbulence, which in any system often accompanies change.

Fortunately, while prediction is, to say the least, problematic, anticipation has a better record. For example, some analysts had for some time understood that the Soviet Union was heading toward an economic collapse with dramatic political consequences that would undercut the Soviet Union's capabilities to sustain its East European sphere of influence—not to mention its other global commitments. In 1982, in its well-known two-volume set, *The Soviet Economy in the 1980s*, the Joint Economic

Committee of the U.S. Congress anticipated all the economic problems of the Soviet Union, and several authors predicted that unless these problems were quickly solved the Soviet Union would collapse. Less then 10 years later the Soviet Union did indeed collapse, and it did so because of its economic problems. Yet, even in this instance, not one of the authors of the 50 articles in *The Soviet Economy in the 1980s* was able to predict the actual path of events that led to the dissolution of the Soviet Union, still less the timing of events or the role of different actors in the process.

Thus, we must be cautious in our efforts to discern the patterns and progress of change in the post–Cold War era. Caution, however, should not deter us from the attempt. If we are to realize the hopes for a more cooperative and peaceful global future, we must endeavor to understand the nature of the present clash between old forces and new realities and to anticipate both the opportunities and the obstacles that lie ahead on the path to a more efficient and equitable management of the global political system.

In the following chapters of this part of the book, attention is focused in turn on each of the world's major "traditional" regions and the changing interests, priorities, and roles of the main actors in the international system. First, however, some consideration is given to the overall global patterns in two key (and interrelated) areas that are certain to influence the main trends in the international political system: the impact of ideologies on politics; and the role of states and their relationship to changing political-economic processes.

Ideology and Politics in the New Era

The Cold War vividly illustrated the extent to which ideologies can influence politics. During the 40-plus years of their post–World War II confrontation, communism and Western ideologies helped to mold the perceptions and goals of politicians, political parties, and publics within countries. Less apparently, but no less importantly, they also shaped the international political system and its institutions by creating, sustaining, or disrupting international coalitions formed to pursue common goals.

Among the leading ideologies in today's world, some may encourage attempts to create and sustain a peaceful and democratic global political system, while others may obstruct such efforts, but none will have a decisive influence over the shape of the system.

Communism failed to fulfill its promises to create a world free from need and war. Socialism in general has lost its ability to mobilize the masses both within and outside the industrial world with its internationalist perspective. Meanwhile, although certain values of liberal internationalism—like the honoring of human rights and democracy—are enjoying increasing acceptance in many parts of the world, contemporary forms of liberal internationalism may be ineffective in addressing the concerns of the developing world, concerns like poverty, polarization, and mass unemployment. Pope John Paul II has squarely identified the problem:

> The Marxist solution has failed, but the realities of marginalization and exploitation remain in the world, especially in the Third World, as does the reality of human alienation, especially in the more advanced countries. . . . Indeed, there is a risk that a radical capitalistic ideology could spread which refuses even to consider these problems, in the *a priori* belief that any attempt to solve them is doomed to failure, and which blindly entrusts their solution to the free development of market forces.[2]

Capitalism as such is not, of course, a closed or homogeneous ideological system. Its radical versions have been unresponsive indeed to fundamental global problems, but its reformed versions recognized those problems at an early stage.

The international political system has accommodated some fanatical ideologies such as violent nationalism and fascism, which lamentably are gaining ground again in various parts of the world. Fueled by growing socioeconomic problems and political impasses, these creeds preach such divisive doctrines as racism, ethnic hatred, and religious bigotry. Such ideologies cannot be expected to encourage global solutions to the problems of poverty, environmental degradation, and crime.

A number of other influential ideologies, such as environmentalism and neofeminism, focus on single issues. These ideologies exert some influence on international cooperation through nongovernmental movements, but overall their ability to shape global changes is limited.

The main churches and the political movements inspired by them (some of which are very active internationally) are in a difficult position. They contain progressive elements, which are searching for a coherent ideological response to many present and future issues, and extremely conservative constituencies, which are resistant to change. Interestingly, many Western political analysts expect future global ideological confrontations to center on religious movements; more precisely, they expect a major clash between Islamic and Western ideas and values.

However, it is not the religion of Islam that confronts the Western world, but rather the political movement of militant Islamism, which interprets Islamic texts and traditions as supportive of authoritarianism and exploits the failure of the West to meet popular expectations in many parts of the world for equitable economic and social development. Militant Islamism has come to occupy the ideological vacuum created by popular disillusionment with the socialist and liberal models. With its violent methods, with strong political, ideological, and financial support from several states, and with the rapid spread of the Muslim faith in different parts of the world, militant Islamism has generated considerable concern. That concern has been further fueled by the dissolution of the Soviet Union and the birth of several independent Central Asian republics with Muslim majorities. These republics, some analysts speculate, will become part of a belt of fundamentalist, anti-Western Islamic states stretching from North Africa to Central Asia. Such speculation seems misplaced, however. The new states have large non-Muslim ethnic groups, and the majority of the Muslim populations seem more interested in establishing secular regimes than in creating theocracies. Furthermore, Islam is not a homogeneous force in international relations. It is extremely diverse and decentralized, and does not yet offer any specific global ideological or systemic alternative. For the foreseeable future, Islamic states will have to accommodate themselves to a global community of nations and accept the rules of the game in global politics. It is also in their interest to work as partners with other states in global and regional organizations.

In the complex and challenging era of the late 20th century and beyond, open systems of thought that do not claim a monopoly on truth will best suit a highly diverse, multicultural world. An optimal international system should resonate with the best elements of each ideology. Sadly, human history offers no examples of a system achieving this. In the distant future, a "convergence of values" as a guideline for rational global actions may emerge from a growing realization of the common interests and problems of humankind. For the next few decades, however, a more realistic and more pressing task is to look for common denominators among diverging interests and ideas that will permit a harmonization of actions.

States and Political-economic Processes

Notwithstanding the increasing role in international relations played by nonstate actors such as transnational corporations and nongovernmental organizations, and despite the fact that the processes of globalization represent new challenges to the state system, states will remain decisive players in the global political system. Consequently, the shape of that system in the post–Cold War era will be heavily influenced by the ways in which states interact and the extent to which the freedom of action of individual states is constrained by other actors working independently or collectively.

Among the almost 200 states now in existence, profound inequalities exist in almost all areas: territorial size, size of population, military strength, economic power, and so forth. Some long-established, mature states possess stable institutions and considerable political experience; others are fragile constructs, with artificially established borders, weak institutions, and questionable political legitimacy. Such differences constitute only one of the divisions and sources of potential conflict among states. With the Cold War over, the main actors of the global political and economic systems are developing new interests, linkages, and relationships. The end of the military confrontation between the two Cold War blocs has also altered the respective roles of economic power[3] and political-military power in determining the global position of states.

In general terms, political-military strength cannot, of course, be treated independently of economic factors. A nation's military strength depends, for example, on such essential variables as the amount and structure of its natural resources; its level of scientific and technological development; the size, composition, and diversity of its research and development (R&D) base; the size and composition (by age and qualifications) of its population; the volume, performance capacity, and adjustment potential of its economy; the level of consumer goods and other supplies available to its population; and its mode of needs-satisfaction (equal distribution, incentives, and so forth).

The consequences of this interrelationship between political-military and economic power are illustrated by the example of the Soviet Union. Although the Soviet Union was able to develop a military potential of devastating strength comparable to that of its rival, the United States, it was unable to establish a well-functioning economy, having invested a large part of its resources on military R&D and on the constant development and upgrading of weapons systems. The Cold War and the arms race exhausted the Soviet economy (and the economies of its Warsaw Pact allies) and caused considerable domestic economic imbalances and bottlenecks. Although it was able to sustain a large and relatively modern army with massive nuclear capabilities and other strategic weapons systems, the Soviet Union became increasingly vulnerable and weak in all other areas that are the true foundations of power. (Even on the basis of the Leninist concept of peaceful competition between two systems, which posits the rate of increase and comparative level of social productivity to be the factors that decide winners and losers, the outcome of the Cold War contest was predetermined.) The West was well ahead of the East in scientific and technological progress, and could calibrate its flexible economies and societies more successfully to the constantly changing stipulations of the Cold War than could the rigid communist regimes.

The ability to create and strengthen an economic power base and to employ economic power greatly depends on the effectiveness of political institutions. Societal cohesion, political stability, transaction costs (of applying political power), institutional flexibility, bureaucratic competency, and effectiveness of government: all are very important to the efficient functioning of a national economy and to international competitiveness.

The base of economic power is more decentralized and diversified than that of political power, making the exercise of economic power a highly complex matter. Decisive factors in determining economic power are productivity, international market competitiveness, the level of innovation, and the effectiveness of supporting political institutions. Other factors include export performance, the capacity to effect capital investments abroad, and the strength of a nation's currency and its role in international money markets. The role of firms—their market presence and their capabilities to functionally promote their own interests in the economic power arena—is another cardinal component of the national economic power base.[4]

Changes in the world economy—the transition to a new technological era and the evolution of new economic power relations—preceded, and in many ways stimulated and then reinforced, the political changes of the late 1980s and early 1990s. As the ideological, political, and military confrontation between the North Atlantic Treaty Organization (NATO) and Warsaw Pact countries dissolved, and as the problems between North and South became increasingly socioeconomic, the role of economic power and its capacity to influence the relative power positions of countries in the world became crucial. For some time before the end of the Cold War, economic power, in relation to political-military power, had been increasingly exercised. The balance of deterrence maintained by the United States and the Soviet Union effectively neutralized the global role of military might as a discretionary policy option for the majority of states, greatly facilitating the emergence of economic superpowers.

In both theory and practice, the coupling of politics and economics within and among nations has always been a hotly debated issue, encompassing questions concerning the primacy of one sector over the other and the short-term versus long-term implications of this interrelationship. Economically irrational decisions taken in the political arena (heavy taxes, high and nonproductive expenditures, the proliferation of regulations that disadvantage small and medium-sized business, and national policies that neglect the education and health sectors) are counterproductive to the development of the national economic system and detrimental to international competitiveness.

Economic factors have played a key role in the evolving new power structure. Those analysts who, after the Gulf War, suggested that the post–Cold War order would be unipolar and centered around the United States did not take into account the factor of economic power. It is true that the United States is today the only major power and maintains the strongest multidimensional power base in the world. Today's world, however, does not follow the same political, economic, and military patterns that characterized the post–World War II era.

The other main actors of the system are now in a much stronger economic power position, both in relative and absolute terms, than they were in the late 1940s. Indeed, the international system will be increasingly multipolar—though with a hierarchical power structure—and will have to adapt to disparate, diffuse power elements of varying capacities. Multipolarity implies that there will be new concentrations of power and interests. Changes in the relations among global and regional powers will inspire the creation of new structures, which may cooperate or conflict.

The new interrelations between political and economic processes also influence the growing interdependence among countries. Economic interdependence has a major impact on political interests, systemic cohesion, and the scope of potential conflicts. It remains to be seen if political and economic interdependence will lead to the development of new international institutional guarantees for the peaceful management of change. If it does, then perhaps we shall no longer see the use of force by second-echelon states to increase their power and influence. Such guarantees would require binding norms and better mechanisms for harmonizing interests and managing conflicts and risks.

In these early stages of the post–Cold War system, the major global powers have an unprecedented opportunity to strengthen global cooperation and enhance common security. Compared with the rest of this century, today there is less international discord and tension in the system, brighter prospects for major accomplishments in disarmament, and the real possibility to improve international relations. Major advances have also been made in the recognition of human rights in the former Soviet Union, in Central and Eastern Europe, and in other parts of the world, including South Africa. The global summit for children organized by the United Nations Children's Fund (UNICEF) in September 1990 reflected a new interest in global social issues. The 1992 global summit on the environment and development organized by the United Nations produced no breakthroughs in terms of organizing collective actions, but it did elicit important commitments from all countries to implement programs for the protection of the global ecosystem.

Systemic cooperation faces formidable obstacles, most notably the diversity of interests, values, and attitudes within and among nations and regions. This diversity is bound to increase in the future, engendering yet more difficulties. Thus, a much greater commitment to cooperation is needed from all countries—especially those that carry the most weight in the international political system and possess the largest concentrations of human and material resources. Progress toward that commitment depends not only on the declarations or intentions of countries but also on their domestic policies, as well as on a wide range of other independent political variables, both domestic and international.

Critical Questions

In this increasingly complex and diverse world, a number of questions can serve as guidelines for future policy analysis and evaluation:

1. What are the optimal national policies and behaviors that will result in greater security? Which policies and behaviors threaten to result in confrontation, hostility, and heightened tension in the post–Cold War period?

2. How can responsibility and accountability be increased in a future international system that includes many more actors and thus many more diverging and converging interests?

3. Can the present system of international organizations be reformed to undertake the effective governance of the changing world, or are radical changes required to combine and coordinate global and regional cooperation structures?

4. What are the priority areas around which an action-oriented global consensus could be formed?

5. How should the evolving global institutional system function to cope with systemic realities and become more relevant to complex international problems?

The following chapters search for at least partial answers to these questions. The realities of the political system of the 1990s are the backdrop against which these answers will be formulated.

Before proceeding, however, a few organizing principles for the following analysis must be established. First, as much as possible, the focus will be on long-term processes rather than short-term trends and events of evanescent significance. Second, the various dominant actors (nation-states *and* regions) are analyzed not only as potential sources of conflicts and risk but also as actual or potential contributors to the future of global cooperation to produce a more secure environment. Third, both the present and the evolving interactions among the main actors will be taken into account. Fourth, attention will be centered not on the post–Cold War rhetoric and the declared intentions of governments but on their changing interests, positions, and possibilities within the international political system. Fifth, the role of domestic political and economic factors will be examined.

chapter 7

The United States in an Evolving Multipolar World

The United States and International Political Stability

After many decades of the Cold War, strategic thinkers in the United States are having to reconsider their worldviews. No longer need they respond to the threats posed by a fellow super-power with an immense nuclear arsenal. Instead, they face the prospect of low-intensity conflicts that may involve the use of modern, highly destructive conventional weapons; given the spread of nuclear weapons to smaller powers, these conflicts may even escalate to nuclear confrontations. These types of wars threaten not the United States directly but rather countries friendly with it or the security of a distant region. As such, the U.S. public may become less interested in foreign affairs in the future. The turbulent world may, of course, produce new concerns.

The United States will also find itself in a new, more unpredictable global political environment replete with diverse and difficult economic and social problems. The United States will be expected to play a leading role in maintaining stability in this environment. However, the criteria and instruments of leadership are also changing. The requirements of post–Cold War leadership will be new, creative ideas, bold political and socio-economic initiatives, and flexible, multilevel global policies.

The rest of the world is no less anxious about the future role of the United States than is the United States itself. Although a few states remain suspicious of U.S. intentions toward their domestic regimes and the international system as a whole in the absence of another countervailing global power, the great majority of countries recognize that the United States played a crucial role in bringing about the collapse of the Soviet system. They do not question the need for a strong and stabilizing U.S. presence in the new political environment. They are concerned, however, that a U.S. commitment to stability might not advance some of their chief interests. It remains to be seen the extent to which the United States will redefine its national interests and reformulate its policies in harmony with the changing interests of other countries, especially its main future partners.

National interests change slowly, as do the perceptions of those who make policy according to those interests. The national interests of a global power are extremely complex, centering on its national security interests but also involving—as is the case for all countries—political, military, and socioeconomic components. Setting national goals is not the same as achieving them, even for a global power. The United States has always been keen, for example, to counter any shift in international political environments that might increase its strategic vulnerability or create instability in its regions of influence. Nevertheless, despite its intentions, the United States has often been unable to curtail the growing power of its potential rivals and competitors.

Continuity and novelty can both be discerned in the various factors shaping contemporary U.S. interests. Along the lines of the traditional realist approach, Robert Art has proposed the following primary areas of interest for the United States: defense of the homeland; preservation of prosperity based on international economic openness; assured access to Persian Gulf oil; prevention of certain wars; and, when feasible, the promotion of democratic institutions and certain humanitarian values abroad.[5] Samuel Huntington has formulated three areas of U.S. strategic interest: maintaining itself as the premier world power; preventing the emergence of a political-military hegemonic power in Eurasia; and protecting its concrete interests in the Third World.[6]

As for U.S. policymakers, their thinking may be indicated by the following draft of a Pentagon document that was leaked to *The New York Times* in March 1992:

> Our first objective is to prevent the reemergence of a new rival, either on the territory of the former Soviet Union or elsewhere, that poses a threat on the order of that posed formerly by the Soviet Union . . . whose resources would under consolidated control be sufficient to generate global power. . . . There are three additional aspects of this objective: First, the U.S. must show the leadership necessary to establish and protect the new order that holds the promise of convincing potential competitors that they need not aspire to a greater role or pursue a more aggressive posture. . . . Second, in the non-defense areas, we must account sufficiently for the interests of the advanced industrial nations to discourage them from challenging our leadership or seeking to overturn the established political and economic order. Finally, we must maintain the mechanisms for deterring potential competitors from even aspiring to a larger regional and global role.[7]

These ideas are not original. They express the political consensus that has characterized and shaped U.S. policies over several decades; they also correspond to the formulations of Art and Huntington.

It is evident, however, that the implementation of those general principles of U.S. strategic interests in an increasingly multipolar world will have to be different than in the past. No pragmatic reformulation of U.S. security interests and strategies could disregard the following realities:

1. As the only remaining global power, the United States cannot avoid assuming greater responsibility in global affairs; and yet, the United States cannot afford to assume the entire moral, political, and financial obligations of being either a global social worker or an international policeman.

2. Global competition in a multipolar environment will differ from that in a basically bipolar world. As the role of economic power in global affairs increases, the United States will have to pay more attention to its domestic sources of strength than it did in the past.

3. Because the United States will be collaborating with different partners and competitors on various issues, in many cases

multilateral cooperation with its predictable norms and reciprocal obligations will be more advantageous to the United States,
especially over the long term, than any bilateral or unilateral
approach to problem-solving.

4. During the Cold War, U.S. foreign policy evaluated global
change—including European integration, the strengthening of
Japan and the newly industrializing countries, and civil wars in
Angola and Mozambique—mainly from the viewpoint of its strategic implications for U.S.-Soviet relations. In the future, U.S.
policy calculations will be more complex and difficult, especially
as regards the development of autonomous goals, interests, and
actions by a united Europe and the increase in the global economic and political power of Germany and Japan. The United
States will have to be both a partner and a rival with these
powers, protecting its global position and interests. All international relations will reflect this new duality, but it will be most
apparent in relations between the United States and its traditional partners. Foreign policy will have to be flexible, especially
in economic affairs.[8]

5. Defining new U.S. policies toward the successor states of
the Soviet Union will be a long-term, difficult process. U.S.
strategists must look beyond the transition from communism to
capitalism and the question of how to help consolidate and
strengthen Russia. They must consider not only Russia's nuclear
capabilities but also the historical role of Russia in Eurasia and
how best to balance power in this region.

At each of the important turning points in post–World War II
global politics, a new "presidential doctrine" has been constructed
to guide U.S. foreign policy. The complexities and mutability of
the post–Cold War world may well make the formulation of a
new doctrine a lengthy process. However, it seems very likely
that the idea of selective engagement will eventually become the
strategic principle and pragmatic approach of U.S. foreign policy, acceptable to both Democrats and Republicans. It may be
noted that selective engagement is hardly a new idea. Before
the Cold War, and with the exception of the two world wars,
selective engagement was the hallmark of U.S. foreign policy.

In the past, U.S. strategists and decision makers have sought to
divide the world into zones according to the level of engagement

undertaken by the United States. Of all zones, Europe has been considered the region of primary U.S. strategic interest, although there have been other regional priorities as well. In the post–Cold War system, however, these priorities are subject to change.

In a 1991 article dealing with future U.S. strategies, Ted Galen Carpenter expressed a relatively widely shared view:

> Instability per se in distant regions does not threaten American security. There is no longer any challenge from a would-be hegemonic power such as Nazi Germany or the Soviet Union. . . . In the post–Cold War world there are likely to be numerous quarrels that ought to be irrelevant to the United States. Interfering in such imbroglios in an effort to maintain stability poses far greater dangers than the remote possibility that a limited conflict might spiral out of control and ultimately threaten America's well-being.[9]

Clearly, no single country is able by itself to carry the burden of maintaining global order and stability in a complex international system. U.S. self-interest demands, however, that the United States be disproportionally involved in trying to maintain global order and stability. The dangers that threaten the United States are many—the spread of weapons of mass destruction, fierce economic and technological competition, environmental problems, and monetary troubles, to name but a few—and its interests in a stable world almost innumerable—ranging, for instance, from the safety of Americans traveling abroad to the security of the foreign investments of major U.S. companies.

There are also Europe-specific expectations of the United States. Without the United States, no European country would be able to sustain the political balance in Western Europe, where a united Germany will become increasingly powerful and nationalistic trends will become stronger. A U.S. commitment to help restrain the forces of violent nationalism is also important to many countries in the Commonwealth of Independent States (CIS) and in Central and Eastern Europe. In instances of potential or actual civil war (as in the former Yugoslavia), the United States is widely expected to go beyond rhetorical declarations and participate actively in peace initiatives organized through the United Nations or regional structures.

Furthermore, citizenries in Central and Eastern Europe, the CIS, the Middle East, and other parts of the world would like to have—in conjunction with multilateral guarantees—as many unilateral U.S. commitments as possible to support stability, democracy, and human rights while their countries undertake the delicate task of constructing democratic institutions.

The United States in the New Strategic Environment

The increasingly complex multipolar system that is emerging from the ruins of the bipolar Cold War structure will be hierarchical. At the top of that hierarchy will be the United States, which will remain the strongest and only multidimensional power in the world. The U.S. market is larger, in terms of goods and services produced, than the markets of Japan, Germany, Great Britain, and France combined. Furthermore, through its superior military potential, the United States has the capacity to project its power throughout the world. The United States is the least vulnerable major power in terms of its supplies of raw materials, and it has the world's largest and most diversified scientific and technological potential.

However, the gap in economic, scientific, and technological capabilities between the United States and other major international actors has been substantially narrowed over the past 40 years. Indeed, in many areas it has altogether disappeared as other powers have become increasingly competitive. The globally ascendant position of the United States in the technological and economic areas that are extremely important to future global competition has not suffered an absolute decline, and yet the relative position and role of the United States has been declining for some time. For example, in global finances the United States has become the greatest single debtor country in the world (although the U.S. net position is still good).

Despite this relative decline, the United States represents a concentration of power that is unprecedented in modern history. According to W. W. Rostow, the United States maintains the "critical margin" of power in world affairs.[10] Yet, as Rostow also observed: "If the United States seeks to do something which runs against the grain of majority thought and feeling in the world, it can be easily frustrated, or indeed vetoed."[11] Although it may be noted that the United States equally retains *its* veto power, Rostow is correct. Furthermore, although the United States will continue to shoulder the largest burden in maintaining international stability, it may not do so indefinitely, especially if its agenda is frustrated by other powers.

The United States is needed as a major international guarantor of an evolving global order based on the joint responsibility of states to maintain freedom and justice. At the same time, the world needs an economically strong and politically stable America that can keep its household in order and is willing, able, and ready to credibly reaffirm its commitment of 1945 to build a world free from fear and want. No one can realistically expect the United States to sacrifice its national interests on the altar of a fragmented world.

Writing about the future world order and the role of the United States, Henry Kissinger made the following observation:

> Ironically, America's victory in the Cold War has produced a world quite contrary to the recent American experience. During the Cold War, the industrial democracies relied on American protection and for nearly two decades, on American capital. The ideological conflict lent plausibility to the American penchant for crusades. But the dependence of our allies on American protection has declined; hence, they will prove less and less willing to subordinate their judgment automatically to Washington's. Europe and Japan will develop increasingly autonomous defense capabilities. Similarly, the days of America as the principal source of worldwide investment capital are clearly over. . . .
>
> What we need to do is something we have never done before: define distinctions between the essential and the desirable; between what is possible and what is beyond our capacities. The redefinition of national security which this implies should lead to a concept of national interests different from the two-powered world of the Cold War—more discriminating in its purpose, less cataclysmic in its strategy and above all, more regional in its design.[12]

Isolationism has a long tradition in the United States, and there is concern both within and outside the United States that "neoisolationism" may emerge as a powerful force shaping public attitudes, especially as external threats to U.S. national security fade. A return to the pronounced isolationism of the 1920s, when the U.S. Congress voted not to join the League of Nations, is not anticipated. Today, the United States is part of an interdependent global structure and domestic political and economic issues inevitably spill over into the international system. Support among the U.S. public, legislature, and administration for institutionalized forms of cooperation is much higher now than 70 years ago. The United States is involved in most contemporary multilateral cooperation structures, especially the United Nations system.

Still, some similarities do exist between the attitudes of certain segments of today's American political establishment and public and the isolationist tenor of the 1920s. Then, a costly war had recently ended. Today, the costly Cold War has ended. In the 1920s, a strong domestic force sought to avoid involvement in the tangled, potentially costly affairs of the League of Nations. Today, there exists a strong desire to minimize U.S. participation in international affairs and to focus on improving U.S. domestic socioeconomic conditions. This aspiration is entirely understandable in light of the hundreds of billions of dollars spent annually on defense over the past few decades.

The neoisolationist trend in U.S. national politics is a major risk factor, not only for the world as a whole, but also for the United States itself. Given its enormous stake in today's global political and economic systems, the United States would lose much if its introspection were to obstruct or jeopardize the changes necessary to ensure the functioning of the future international system.

It would, however, be equally dangerous for the world if the United States encountered long-term domestic economic and social instability. The 1929 crash in the U.S. stock market was the catalyst for the greatest economic depression ever known, and was to a large extent indirectly responsible for the triumph of Nazism in Germany and for events leading toward World War II. Domestic imbalances in the United States during the 1980s created major problems for the world by increasing interest rates and contributing to the debt crisis, thus aggravating the problems of the developing world. The stock market crash of 1987 was a severe shock to global capital markets and caused great concern within the rest of the world, which was becoming increasingly apprehensive about the inherent dangers of the unrestrained growth in U.S. borrowing in an environment of low domestic savings.

The United States' transition to the new global environment probably will occupy the better part of the 1990s, and will entail political, military, economic, technological, and institutional transformations. Domestically, the transition will have profound political and psychological effects (which must remain beyond the scope of this analysis). At the outset of this decade, President Bush made a commitment to strengthen the global system of cooperation:

> Out of these troubled times, our fifth objective—a new world order—can emerge; a new era—freer from the threat of terror, stronger in the pursuit of justice and more secure in the quest for peace, an era in which the nations of the world, East and West, North and South, can prosper and live in harmony.
>
> A hundred generations have searched for this elusive path of peace, while a thousand wars raged across the span of human endeavor. Today, that new world is struggling to be born, a world quite different from the one we have known, a world where the rule of law supplants the rule of the jungle, a world in which nations recognize the shared responsibility for freedom and justice, a world where the strong respects the rights of the weak.[13]

In the 1992 presidential campaign, this commitment was reaffirmed by Democratic candidate Bill Clinton.

Global events and the domestic debate during the first years of the Clinton administration have underlined the complexity of the role that the United States is expected to play in the post–Cold War era. First of all, expectations have grown concerning U.S. involvement in multilateral structures. Second, even though long-term threats to the global system that also endanger U.S. security interests are not yet readily discernible, the role, size, and deployment of U.S. military forces will have to be planned on the basis of certain assumptions concerning potential adversaries. Many defense analysts emphasize the importance of high-tech, rapid response forces, which require expensive logistical support. For the United States, sharing the responsibilities and costs of global conflict prevention and management with its allies has become a very sensitive issue as Cold War alliances erode and its main security partners become ever-stronger economic and political competitors. Awareness of the increasingly competitive economic system has accentuated the importance of such longer-term domestic goals as upgrading the quality of the U.S. labor force, improving infrastructure, accelerating technological progress, and restoring the equilibrium of the federal budget. All of these goals represent attempts to improve the competitive position of the United States in the evolving global system.

chapter 8

The Political Consequences of European Unification and Fragmentation

The second millennium has been a Europe-centered epoch. It began with the period of European recovery in the year of 955, when Emperor Otto defeated the Magyars in a fierce battle near Augsburg. Over the next 10 centuries, Europe established a new culture and an efficient combination of political, military, economic, technological, and scientific power. European power reached its zenith early in the 20th century, when 10 empires were centered on the continent, 9 of which had colonial territories in other parts of the world. European politics, however, have produced some remarkably belligerent regimes and devastating wars, especially in this century. These conflicts, together with an imperial reach that exceeded Europe's military grasp, led to the decline of European power in the mid-20th century.

Although the Cold War was a global confrontation, it was in Europe that the iron curtain was drawn and parted. Long before the Berlin Wall fell and the Soviet Union dissolved, most observers perceived that the Warsaw Pact nations were losing the Cold War. The Soviet Union and its allies could not bear the enormous strain that the arms race imposed on their weak and inefficient economies. Inexorably, the more economically efficient, socially flexible, and technologically progressive West drew further ahead of the East. Moreover, the people of Central and Eastern Europe and the Soviet Union had in various ways revolted against their dictatorial regimes. Ideas of freedom, democracy, human rights, and national self-determination had loosened the one-party system, weakening its political structure and raising popular expectations.

No contemporary analyst dared divine, however, the sequence of events or the timing of the collapse. Because of the balance of mutual deterrence and an emerging rationalism in international behavior based on the "new thinking" that emphasized general human interests, some expected a major historical compromise to be struck between the two main powers. Other, more pessimistic analysts continued to anticipate a major conflict between the superpowers. The armies of both sides operated on the basis of the latter assumption.

The end of the Cold War came with the disintegration of the Soviet empire and the collapse of the Central and East European communist political structures. The differences among the various regimes and the progressively diverging interests within these communist countries undermined the intraregional cohesiveness created by Soviet dominance and the common interests of ruling elites. The dissolution of the Warsaw Pact and Council for Mutual Economic Assistance and the withdrawal of Soviet troops from Eastern Europe have not, however, turned out to be straightforward and unalloyed strategic gains for the West. In Europe, where the features of the new geopolitical era are particularly pronounced, the recent changes have created great political uncertainty.

Dangers to Future European Security

The uncertain political future of Europe raises important new security issues. Europe was a classic example of the consequences of bipolarity during the Cold War. The continent had been divided into two military blocs that, because they presented such a high level of mutual risk, effectively neutralized each other in war-waging options and capacities. The two blocs imposed a high level of discipline on their members and were able to control conflicts between them. Indeed, the Cold War represents the longest peaceful period in the history of Europe. Only two, relatively minor conflicts were fought on European soil during this period: the quashing of the Hungarian revolution by Soviet forces in 1956 and the Cyprus conflict between two NATO allies, Turkey and Greece.

With the end of the Cold War, this relatively simple and balanced military and political structure has disappeared. The character of threat has also changed. Countries in Western Europe have no obvious strategic enemy, and none seems likely to emerge on the horizon of global politics for some time. Where, then, are the new security dangers? They may lie in the reemergence of chaotic patterns of interstate relations—or, as John Mearsheimer has characterized the matter, Europe may be moving "back to the future."[14] These patterns of instability may result in increasing antagonism and violence. Notably, the spread of nationalism may, as in earlier periods of European history, undermine the establishment of a new, cooperative global order.[15]

For the moment, however, it may be unhelpful to think in terms of traditional power politics and apply the balance-of-power concept to an era of European integration and global politics. In Western Europe, neither the liberal nationalism of the 19th century, which was championed by the bourgeoisie and associated with the pursuit of individual liberties and national independence, nor the more exclusionary nationalism of the first half of the 20th century, which was typified by the racism, bellicosity, and totalitarianism of Nazism, enjoy much support. Neo-Nazis do exist in Germany and elsewhere, and the dangers of nationalist revivals directed against immigrant laborers are real, but for the most part violent nationalism is not on the political agenda of Western Europe in the 1990s.

A more immediate, concrete threat to European security is rooted in the political and strategic environment that has emerged since the dissolution of the Soviet Union and the collapse of communism in Central and Eastern Europe. Unsolved and reemerging ethnic and national issues and territorial disputes have already resulted in violence in the former Yugoslavia and parts of the former Soviet Union.

For the West, these conflicts pose severe problems, and not just in terms of humanitarian and refugee issues. There are many nuclear weapons in the East—not only in Russia, but also in other republics of the former Soviet Union. There are also many nuclear power stations, the accidental or deliberate explosion of which would imperil the whole of the continent. Other problems include the danger of ethnically motivated international terrorism and the political and strategic fallout that the direct or indirect involvement of a major Western power in Eastern conflicts would produce.

The future domestic and foreign policies of Germany will have a profound impact on both European and global politics. Similarly, the future of post-Soviet Russia is bound to affect the future of all of Europe. Will the Russian empire be restored in a recognizable form, or will it assume a different form within the CIS? If the empire disappears altogether, how soon will Russia be able to consolidate its economic, political, and military power and become a major factor shaping continental politics, thus ensuring its leading role in European and global affairs?

Another source of uncertainty for Europe is the potential impact of the changes under way in the South and East Mediterranean, an area which extends from Turkey to the Maghreb. Demographically, 1990 was a historical turning point, at which the population of the South and East Mediterranean became more numerous than that of the countries north of the Mediterranean. Furthermore, the South and East Mediterranean region is stockpiling modern weapons and experiencing an upsurge in Islamic fundamentalism and an increase in political unrest and social problems. All these developments threaten to ignite new conflicts, which may disrupt Europe's vital fuel and raw material supplies and unleash a flood of refugees to Western Europe.

Perhaps the greatest nonmilitary threat to European security is posed by economic and environmental problems.[16] Economic difficulties are especially severe in Central and East European countries, where the difficult transition from a socialistic system to a capitalistic one will last throughout the 1990s. Dismantling the centrally planned past and constructing a promising future amounts to a social process of creative destruction, which, its long-term benefits notwithstanding, causes enormous disruptions. The risk factors of economic and environmental security are not confined to the eastern region of the continent, however. Their efficient management will require more intensive regional cooperation and the active participation of all European multilateral cooperation structures.

Post–Cold War Challenges to European Political Unification

The future of European security will depend primarily on the nature, speed, and consequences of economic and political unification in Western Europe, and on the extent to which that process encompasses the East.

In spite of a variety of setbacks, the prospects for European political stability and economic prosperity remain good, although new challenges call for the development and projection of a new vision of Europe's future by its leaders. European states are being compelled by the domestic and international environment to formulate and articulate more clearly their perceived national interests; and while the benefits of a collective approach to common problems are still widely recognized, the limits of that approach have become clearer. Europe's primary objective of maintaining its competitiveness in the global marketplace requires, of course, the continuity of policies enacted against its chief competitors and deepening cooperation across a wide spectrum of subjects ranging from regional security to science and technology. In the new era, however, the interests of European states are changing and views are diverging on a number of pressing issues. Some of these differences have been brought to the surface by the conflicts in the former Yugoslavia and the unification of Germany.

German unification has spurred efforts by some European Community (EC) members to seek closer political integration through a federation of European states. These members call for new structures that would form a strong framework able to accommodate a strengthening, united Germany. Cynical observers have asked if the united country will be the Germany of Europe or if the united continent will be the Europe of Germany? Might there also be a third alternative, namely, a future alliance between Germany and Russia, with countries in the Western part of the continent having to look for the continuous security presence and assistance of the United States?

The final answer to these questions can only be given by the unpredictable forces of history. At this stage, one can only say that the content of the answer will be greatly determined by the outcome of those efforts initiated in the early 1990s in Maastricht. The Maastricht Treaty, which aims at the monetary and political union of the member states of the EC, may, if implemented, represent a turning point in European history.

Of course, a retreat from the Maastricht commitments or other setbacks to the integration process are possible. The potential dangers are many: a marked rise in neonationalism and right-wing populism; a major economic or political catastrophe, which would render joint solutions unworkable or impose intolerable political or economic burdens on one or more member states; the failure to satisfy the aspirations of future political elites, especially in Germany; and the inequitable distribution among the small and medium-sized powers of the gains and losses of integration.

The debate on political integration has ignited deep disagreements among EC members over the process of becoming a "United States of Europe." In the early and mid-1990s, the debate among member countries has not been about movement toward, or away from, integration but rather about two models of European integration, each of which has its own group of supporters. One group wants to strengthen central institutions and accelerate progress toward a unitary state of Europe as a final goal. The other group advocates increasing European cooperation in a wide range of areas while maintaining decentralized structures, thereby creating a system that is sufficiently flexible to accommodate differences in the relative economic strengths of member countries and in their diverse domestic interests and practices.

EC members have clashed over such questions as the character of European political institutions, the relationship between national and regional political structures, and the nature of a common army. Events in Central and Eastern Europe, interestingly enough, have provided ammunition for opponents of unification. As one columnist has written: "The architects of Europe should learn from the collapse of the Soviet Union and Yugoslavia, two federations masquerading as countries. Their recent history has shown that while nationalism can be suppressed for a time, it cannot be destroyed. Any attempt to impose a rigid central government system will be resented and cause a revolt."[17]

Among the many difficulties facing the EC in the 1990s, five seem particularly challenging. One is connected with the process of transferring power from states to supranational structures by way of treaties, rules, and directives. This process is far from easy. Indeed, the defenders of the nation-state have included two safeguard provisions in the Maastricht Treaty: the first is that states will retain principal control over such sensitive areas as foreign and defense policy, internal security, and immigration; the second is enshrined in the principle of subsidiarity, which stresses that collective action can be taken "only if and in so far as the objectives of the proposed action cannot be sufficiently achieved by the member states and can therefore, by reason of the scale or effects of the proposed action, be better achieved by the Community."[18]

A second, related problem is that several conditions of the single market program remain to be fulfilled on the national level. For instance, agreements on the creation of a single currency and a central bank, even after ratification by national legislatures, will be difficult to implement. Social policy is another sensitive and disputatious area where agreements have yet to be reached.

A third difficulty lies in deciding if, when, and to which countries EC membership should be extended. Austria, Finland, Norway, and Sweden will probably be the next candidates to join the present 12 members; the Czech and Slovak republics, Hungary, and Poland, are waiting in the wings; and the Baltic states and other CIS countries, as well as a number of Central and East European countries, are also interested in joining.

The debate about who should be admitted, and when, reflects long-standing disagreements and differences in national interests. Germany, for instance, has been more supportive of the participation of Central and East European countries than have other member states. Generally, EC members fear economic dilution and the political difficulties that a more diverse membership might bring. Expansion may, indeed, overextend the EC in terms of its operational efficiency and disrupt the delicate balance of interests and opportunities among its present members. For their part, the nations of Central and Eastern Europe consider

"Europeanization" a panacea for many of their political and economic diseases. These countries would like to become integral parts of a European system that has enjoyed unprecedented success in terms not only of stimulating economic progress but also of resolving many complex political issues and bringing together such traditional enemies as France and Germany.

Europe's relationship with the developing world, and especially with its traditional client regions, presents a fourth difficulty. These developing countries expect greater economic and technological support from Europe. Within Europe, there is widespread concern that millions of workers from the developing world will migrate to Europe, imposing massive, perhaps intolerable strains on its labor markets.

The fifth difficulty concerns Europe's relations with the United States and Japan. Although all European countries are interested in developing political and economic cooperation with these two global powers, EC member states differ on the degree of cooperation that should be sought. Differences also arise regarding the multilateral dimension of relations with North America, Japan, and other major powers. Thus, for instance, negotiations on the General Agreement on Tariffs and Trade in the early 1990s were a source of discord within the EC.

Russia and the Commonwealth of Independent States

The strategic importance and military power of the former Soviet Union make its transformation one of the central problems of global, and especially of European, politics. Changes in the former Soviet Union are still at a relatively early stage, and the vicissitudes and shocks of the transformation process will probably continue throughout the 1990s.

The Soviet Union disappeared, and the CIS cannot be considered as its successor. The CIS is a loose cooperation regime and not a cohesive and structured union of states. Its frontiers are flexible and its members' participation in the network of bilateral and multilateral arrangements and agreements does not require firm and long-term commitments, except in the area of defense cooperation. Even on the topic of defense, the agenda of the CIS is not the same for all its members. For some, the key issue is the redistribution of power and resources; for others, it is how to dismantle the old center and still maintain all the potential advantages of earlier ties. Some member republics emphasize the importance of security cooperation as a means of handling frictions among the Soviet Union's successor states. Relations with Russia are of central importance. In fact, it is Russia and not the CIS that will shape the future of the region. Eighty percent of the territory, about two-thirds of the economy and natural resources, and about 90 percent of the research potential and military strength of the former Soviet Union lie within the frontiers of Russia.

With its present structure and power, the CIS cannot become an instrument for sustaining a new Russian empire. But could it instead become an instrument of new democratic confederalism, enabling the new nations to convert symbols and slogans of freedom, market relations, and popular representation into practical and tangible results? This will depend on the success of the ongoing process of political and economic transformation, especially in Russia; on the readiness of CIS member states to work together as reliable partners; and on the alternatives offered by the global market. What is certain is that it will take a long time—even under optimal domestic and external conditions—to overcome the serious economic, political, ideological, moral, and economic crises beleaguering the members of the CIS. Internal political struggles and ethnic or religious conflicts seem sure to hamper constructive changes. And as both imperial Russia and the Soviet Union discovered, transitions are always hard to accomplish in a country of such size and in the face of a deeply rooted bureaucratic inertia.

The future of Russian foreign policy will depend on the interaction between domestic developments—notably, the progress of the process of consolidation, the strength exhibited by Russian nationalism, and the effects of the interplay among forces of regionalism, separatism, and democracy—and external factors—particularly the responses of the main powers to the new geostrategic position and great power status of Russia.

Despite the present uncertainty and instability that runs throughout the CIS, certain aspects of Russia's future attitude toward global politics seem discernible. The geostrategic position of Russia has changed radically. A belt of independent states, now large enough to be more than a typical buffer zone, has been interposed between Western Europe and Russia and has pushed Russia far away, geographically, from Central Europe. Russia's relations with Western countries will be influenced by specific bilateral interests in cooperation, and thus will be more diverse than they were in the days of the Soviet Union and bloc politics. Russia will try to maintain the best possible relations with the United States and Germany. At the same time, Russia will be interested in establishing close ties with its economically dynamic Asian neighbors in the east.

Russia will be committed to protecting the interests and maintaining the influence of large Russian minorities (totalling 25 to 30 million people) residing in other commonwealth states. Russia will seek to sustain "special relations" with these states; indeed, it may increase its efforts to hold all the commonwealth republics together for strategic purposes.

As reflected in the new constitution approved by Russian voters in late 1993, Russia's primary security concerns will be focused within its own frontiers, where it will try to block secessionist trends. Russia may also engage in territorial disputes with former Soviet republics and potentially expansionist Islamic powers in the region. There will be powerful domestic political pressures to maintain a relatively strong army for internal purposes, prestige, and regional security. The military doctrine adopted by Russia in 1993 indicates that the territory of the former Soviet Union will be regarded, at least for the moment, as the zone of Russia's preponderant security interests.

Having abandoned its crusade for world communism, Russia's relations with its former allies will be guided increasingly by specific economic interests. Pro-Western in its outlook, Russia will look for structural cooperation with Western powers and will be less interested and involved in the developing world, except in respect of its immediate neighbors. Russia will try to win the friendship and influence the policies of neighboring countries through the development of regional cooperation zones and similar arrangements.

Finally, Russia will be more interested than the Soviet Union was in global and regional multilateral institutions generally, but especially in Europe and in Asia. Given its domestic problems and limited resources, Russia will be interested in overall global stability and will strive not to disrupt the status quo.

While one can predict these characteristics of Russia's future policy with some certainty, what remains an open question is the extent to which the establishment of independent nation-states in place of the Soviet Union will increase or decrease global and regional stability over the longer term. This question cannot be answered in abstract terms by idealizing and advocating the process of change or by regarding events in the former Soviet Union as heroic chapters in the struggle for national self-determination against autocracy. The issue of self-determination is always complicated, especially in a region of mixed ethnic or religious populations. Russia contains more than 100 ethnic minorities. In Ukraine, religious and ethnic differences sharply divide its western and eastern parts. Ethnic diversity in the Asian republics is similarly intertwined with religious differences. Russian minorities can be found everywhere in the former Soviet Union, and in some places they comprise almost 50 percent of the citizenry. Given the variety of separatist movements and the strength of ethnic frictions and political rivalries, even the establishment of independent states upon the ruins of the Soviet empire represents only the first act in long era of political instability.

The policies of the major global powers toward the new states within or outside of the CIS will continue to focus on Russia. Concerned about the future of the former Soviet army, control of the enormous Soviet nuclear arsenal, and oversight of the Soviet military-industrial-science complex, the United States is keen to avoid chaos in the region and to stabilize a loose political structure able to provide sufficient security for the new states. Among the European powers, Germany has the strongest political and economic interests in developing a new partnership with Russia. The EC as a whole will have to redefine its relations with the individual states of the former Soviet Union. The CIS region does not pose a direct security threat to Europe. However, the potential for mass emigration from an economically stricken area may encourage Europe to accommodate the economic interests of the CIS, including developing a cooperative structure with a number of the new states. Such an approach also has an economic rationale, for CIS countries could become important markets for European goods and capital and sources of raw materials and scientific capabilities.

The relations of the former Soviet Union with erstwhile allies in Central and Eastern Europe are complicated because of their geographic proximity and historical role as a security belt or buffer zone between Russia and the West. These countries are still dependent, though to a diminishing extent, on supplies of oil, natural gas, and electricity from the east, and on a former Soviet market that purchased most of their exports. Most of the Central and East European countries have unresolved differences with some of the newly independent states. Ukraine, for instance, incorporates the former eastern part of Poland and controls a region that historically was Hungarian.

In short, while the disintegration of the Soviet Union has produced many opportunities for closer economic and political cooperation, the international community, and especially the European states, also face many new challenges, such as converting the former Soviet Union's defense industries to peaceful production, establishing structural safeguards for the management of ethnic strife, containing migration pressures, and sustaining the process of democratization.

Central and Eastern Europe

Like the CIS, the Central and East European region is a source both of uncertainties for the international system, especially for Western Europe, and of new opportunities to accelerate the region's modernization and become more closely integrated into the European mainstream and the global economic and political systems.

Although this region is often considered homogeneous by external observers, it is in fact one of the most heterogeneous areas in Europe in terms of comparative levels of economic development, religions, languages, cultural traditions, and ethnic groups. The countries of the region—Albania, Bosnia-Herzegovina, Bulgaria, Croatia and Slovenia, the Czech and Slovak Republics, Hungary, Poland, Romania, and Yugoslavia—have a combined population of about 130 million people and are burdened with 14 divisive minority issues, 6 of which range from volatile to actively violent, as in the case of the former Yugoslavia. Each country has its own specific internal and external problems. The extent of popular support for the governing regimes and the character of new political institutions varies widely among them. Of the various international and domestic factors, forces, and problems that are shaping the region's future, the deep economic crisis is probably the most influential, since it brings together inherited structural deficiencies, institutional weaknesses, and external constraints. It also reflects the new sources of tensions caused by the transformation process. Neither a rapid improvement in the region's economic performance nor a spectacular reverse in declining standards of living can be expected. The countries of Central and Eastern Europe will have to undergo a long and painful internal process of social and political restructuring. This reality contrasts markedly with the expectations of the population, thereby heightening popular discontent, deepening sociopolitical instability, and further aggravating ethnic problems.

The political and ethnic frontiers established in this region after World War I, and which were basically restored by the Paris peace treaties after World War II, created sources of latent tension in the system that the dictatorial regimes of the past 40-plus years were unable and ill prepared to defuse. While the communist regimes vainly tried to ignore the underlying antagonisms by emphasizing loyalty to social classes over loyalty to nations, their actions only contributed to the divisions within and among their nations. The regimes limited the movement of their peoples, provided few guarantees for honoring the rights of national minorities, and in some cases (like Romania) undertook the forcible assimilation of minorities. The Soviet Union, by promoting the establishment of autocratic economic regimes that were connected bilaterally with the Soviet economy and had very little interest in real multilateral cooperation, strengthened the new economic foundations of nationalism.

With the demise of regional Soviet hegemony, not only did old ethnic problems rise to the surface, but also a new element—separatism—appeared on the political canvas of multinational states, which resulted in the dismembering of Yugoslavia and Czechoslovakia.

The revival, or strengthening, of nationalism is not of course confined to Central and East European countries. According to one expert, there are more than 5,000 ethnic groups in the world that desire national independence.[19] Nationalistic and ethnic violence blights areas as diverse as Western Europe, the Middle East, Africa, India, and China. Nationalism in Central and Eastern Europe, however, is particularly strident and presents great dangers to both regional and international security. Historically, the region has been a buffer zone between the great powers, and its conflicts (often exploited by the great powers) have played catalytic roles in precipitating both world wars. The mass murders—especially of Jews and Gypsies—of the Holocaust have become part of the world's historical memory of this region.

During the Cold War, the struggle for national identity and self-determination was considered by the West to be a legitimate goal and political instrument in the fight against Soviet domination. Today, Western encouragement of such goals is no longer to be heard, but nationalism remains, unconstrained by either dictatorial regimes or an established tradition of democratic tolerance. The process of transition to a Western-type market system is still in its early phase. Stabilizing democracy, consolidating the economy, and achieving integration within the global market system will take a long time.

The transformation process in Central and Eastern Europe has demonstrated the truth of an old tenet of systemic change, namely, that political institutions are the easiest and fastest elements to change. It is much more difficult to change values, popular perceptions, and attitudes. The elementary political goals of those who fostered the transformation process in Central and Eastern Europe are democratization, pluralization, and reintegration into Europe. New democratic constitutions have been adopted in most countries and constitutional reform has been introduced in others. New political institutions have been established that correspond to the notions of civil society and Western democracy. In 1990, the first democratic elections since the late 1940s took place in all of the Central and East European countries. These elections yielded new governments that were in most cases formed by fragile coalitions or received only slim majorities of the popular vote.

How strong and safe is democracy in the region? Four factors give cause for concern. First, the region has no strong democratic traditions. Second, the middle class, which is arguably the most important social group to the efficient functioning of Western parliamentary democracies, is small. Third, apathy and dissatisfaction among the masses are growing. Fourth, the socio-economic difficulties—rising inflation and unemployment—spawned by the transition to the market system may increase popular discontent and pave the way for extremism and auto-cratic forces.

More encouragingly, the social composition of today's Central and East European countries differs greatly from that of the early Cold War period. No longer traditional peasant societies where authoritarian rule can easily be enforced, these societies have large professional groups, a broad industrial working class, and a small but growing entrepreneurial middle class. Most of these groups were suppressed by dictatorial regimes during the Cold War. Any open or disguised political effort to introduce new dictatorial regimes would thus encounter strong internal opposition, not to mention adverse international reaction that would prove highly damaging to countries so heavily dependent on external economic relations.

Some political groups in Central and Eastern Europe would prefer to reinstate some variant of the system that operated there before World War II—as the Polish historian Jerzy Jelicki put it, these groups consider "what existed in between" (namely, the defeat of Nazi Germany and the Cold War) as "enclosed in historical parentheses." This ambition is impossible to realize. The world, and Europe especially, has been fundamentally changed. Germany today is a strong democratic state in a democratic European system. European institutions are formidable safeguards of democracy. The return of Central and East European nations to Europe, and the development of their relations with the EC, must be based on democratic values and institutions.

A democratic political culture is, among other things, the result of a long learning process. The Cold War period of dic-tatorial rule was not fertile ground for cultivating such a culture. If the countries of the region are to begin to learn democracy, they must become organic parts of a community of nations in which basic democratic values determine the functioning of inter-state relations. In addition, they must receive external help to ameliorate the economic ill-effects of their first experiments in democracy; inflation, unemployment, increasing inequalities, and a declining standard of living will generate only fear, alienation, and distrust among the majority of people. For 40 years, the etatist regimes of Central and Eastern Europe, under the slogan of communism, sought to convince their citizens of the necessity of sacrificing their present welfare for the promise of a better future. Many people see a parallel between this and the present vague promises of democracy, an association that could be destructive of these countries' aspirations, governments, and institutions.

Under such circumstances, the success of democratic changes in Central and Eastern Europe requires not merely wise new leadership, good governance, and popular support for the new system, but favorable external conditions. Several decades must elapse before we can know whether this region will eventually become Europeanized, with open frontiers that freely allow the flow of goods, capital, expertise, technology, and labor, or whether it will instead face the drawing of a "golden curtain" by the West.

The Unified Germany in the European and Global Systems

Few observers of European politics would question that the united Germany will play a key role in shaping Europe's political and economic future. German unification has itself already come to be regarded as a major watershed in the international political system.

The division of Germany was never expected to be the final verdict on that nation. The question was not if, but when and how unification would take place, at what price, and paid for by whom. Would the issue of unification lead to World War III, or to a regional conflict sparked perhaps by a civil war? What, if anything, would remain of Germany after such a war? A few East German experts optimistically anticipated a gradual, peaceful confederation of a social-democratic Federal Republic of Germany and a democratized socialist German Democratic Republic. The way unification actually took place was unexpected, in that it contributed to the improvement of the international strategic environment. It was a peaceful change, occurring by consent of the great powers.

The costs of German unification have been very high. In economic terms, estimates (including the costs of modernization in the former East Germany) vary between $600 billion and $1,000 billion, but all analysts agree that the process will be longer and much more expensive than originally anticipated. The human costs have also been substantial; unemployment, for instance, affected 20 percent of the former East German labor force by the end of 1993.

Nevertheless, despite the price that has been paid, the unified Germany is an economically strong, politically stable democratic state. Already the most important power in Europe and a leading player in world trade and finances, Germany is set to acquire all the attributes of a major international power, indeed of a superpower. Its population is around 80 million; the German labor force is highly qualified and well motivated; its share in global output is close to 10 percent, the third largest in the world; and Germany is the largest trading nation, with 30 percent of global trade in manufacturing. Germany is also a leading power in new technology. And, in keeping with its historical tradition, Germany has a large, well-trained, and disciplined army.

In European and global political arenas the unification of Germany has raised new hopes and awakened old fears. The hopes center on Germany's potential to assist the promotion of progress and stability in European and global politics and economics. The fears are rooted in German history. Although it is widely recognized that the political configurations of the new Germany, Europe, and the global community are quite unlike those of the periods preceding both world wars, the sheer fact of Germany's historical responsibility for those wars has become a cause of concern and uncertainty. One of the main questions has been whether, after the collapse of the Soviet empire and the diffusion of power in global politics, any power will balance the increasing role of Germany in Europe. If not, what will be the consequence for European and global politics? These issues have become especially salient for the two other major powers in Western Europe, France and the United Kingdom. France, seeking to increase stability and reduce the risks that recent changes have brought, has found it especially difficult to forge a new international identity that would define its strategic interests and relations amid the new configuration of forces.[20] Some French politicians and strategic thinkers advocate developing firm Franco-German cooperation in all possible areas as the key to balancing Germany. Others seek a balance in the interaction among France, Germany, Great Britain, and NATO.[21]

The most reliable guarantee of a peacefully inclined Germany would seem to be the development of an economically integrated and federated structure in Europe. As a member of joint political institutions governed by binding rules, Germany would find it very difficult to pursue dangerously divisive political goals. The achievement of such a structure would very much depend, of course, on the politics of the unified Germany.

Will the present, positive German attitude toward Europe and the process of European integration change? The high economic costs and the political problems of reunification, together with the growth in unemployment and domestic discontent, has resulted in some segments of the German public, especially at local political levels, displaying "Eurofatigue," strident nationalism, and xeno-phobia. Although these sentiments have not prompted any change in Germany's long-term political goals or any weakening of its commitment to European unity, the possibility remains that shifts in German domestic politics may diminish Germany's readiness to push ahead with European integration.

European Security Regimes: Competition or Complementarity?

The new and highly complex political structure in Europe has made the role and the efficiency of the security regimes on the continent a crucial issue. Although European nations will continue to have armed forces, European security organizations will stress that military forces and doctrines are to be used not to threaten or conquer but rather to provide reassurance and enhance stability. Effective arms control agreements and strong institutional guar-antees for crisis management and conflict resolution can do much to translate this ambition into reality. Agreements to remove troops from foreign soil (as in the case of a number of former Soviet, though non-Commonwealth, republics where Russian troops are still present); downsizing and restructuring armed forces and defense industries; and redefining the role of nuclear weapons on European soil, reducing their numbers to the lowest possible level, and working toward the nonproliferation of weap-ons and military technology are all vital security requirements.

In the post–Cold War world, the military dimension of security has lost much of its earlier prominence. Among the nonmilitary aspects of European security, fostering economic cooperation and respect for human rights are two crucial areas for the work of international institutions. Economic security problems will not be restricted to Central and Eastern Europe, and will spread to many parts of the continent. Indeed, the success of Central and Eastern Europe's transition to the market economy will largely be determined by the ability of all European countries to achieve noninflationary and environmentally sustainable economic growth, reduce unemployment, and dismantle protectionist obstacles to the movement of people, goods, and capital on the continent.

All of Europe will be concerned with the rights of ethnic minorities, the protection of which depends heavily on the development and maintenance of democratic political structures. In the eastern part of the continent, the fragility of democratic institutions in an era of major domestic economic difficulties may create temptations to use nondemocratic instruments or extreme political measures to achieve economic objectives. European institutions must therefore be given the authority to help protect and strengthen fledgling democracies.

Compared to all other continents in the post–Cold War period, Europe possesses the widest variety of institutions concerned with regional security: NATO, the EC, the Western European Union (WEU), and the Conference on Security and Cooperation in Europe (CSCE). A number of other institutions deal with problems of economic security and cooperation. The oldest of these, the UN Economic Commission for Europe, covers all of Europe; others involve countries on a subregional basis, like the EC, or a global basis, like the Organization for Economic Co-operation and Development (OECD), which includes all developed industrial countries. The majority of these organizations were established in the political environment of the Cold War, which played a crucial role in defining their respective mandates.

The North Atlantic Treaty Organization

Established in 1949 as a military alliance, NATO was the primary bulwark for the defense of Western Europe, committing and directing a major proportion of European armies in pursuit of common goals. With the unification of Germany, the disintegration of the Soviet Union, the dissolution of the Warsaw Pact, and the changes in the character of the political system in Central and Eastern Europe, the original assumptions on which NATO was based have radically changed. In the absence of the Soviet threat, two alternatives became apparent to decision makers: either to dissolve NATO or to provide it with a new role within the newly evolving security system of Europe. The latter option was chosen. On May 28, 1991, the NATO defense ministers approved the broadest strategic and conceptual change in the organization's 42-year history. Moves already made have included reducing the number of NATO troops, restructuring the remaining NATO forces, and reformulating military doctrines to emphasize the defensive character of the alliance.[22] This is only a first step. NATO will have to continue to extend itself geographically to correspond to Europe's new security needs, and it must do so in harmony with the changing collective security structures of the United Nations. It should be noted, however, that the belief that NATO must be open and responsive to the security needs of Central and Eastern Europe and to neutral European states is not shared by all NATO members.

Apprehensive of potential threats from the former Soviet Union, three countries—Hungary, Poland, and Czechoslovakia—sought membership in NATO in 1992. A document adopted by the foreign ministers of these countries stated: "In Europe there is no place for different levels and types of security. Security must be identical for all. There is a need to create conditions for the direct inclusion of Poland, Czechoslovakia, and Hungary in the activities of the NATO alliance."[23] Other countries from the region, including Russia, have also sought to establish more structured relations with NATO. Although NATO has been reluctant to extend its security guarantees to Central and Eastern Europe, it has become increasingly evident that a new concept of European security will have to be elaborated. Such measures as the establishment of the North Atlantic Cooperation Council in 1992 to permit a security dialogue and political and military cooperation with the former members of the Warsaw Pact are inadequate.[24] Similarly, the creation of information-exchange and training-exchange programs involving NATO and Poland, the Czech and Slovak republics, and Hungary represent technical rather than political-strategic steps toward a new security regime.

NATO members have disagreed on the question of coordination between NATO and the other institutions in Europe with security mandates, namely, the CSCE and the WEU. Serious differences of opinion have arisen between the United States and some of its NATO allies concerning the future security structure of Europe, especially after the Maastricht Treaty. The outcome of the ongoing debate about NATO's future role in European security will depend on how "Atlanticism"—that is, a U.S. role in European political and security matters—is perceived over the next decade.

A security partnership between Europe and the United States seems clearly to be in the long-term interests of both and could serve as an important safeguard against the potentially adverse consequences of economic competition and any future dangers that German or Russian political developments may present. In the past, the Atlantic alliance has served European security well. Not only has it amassed great military power for deterring war but also, and more significantly, it has brought together former foes. NATO has acted as a confidence-building instrument, integrating the armies and the strategic policymaking processes of erstwhile enemies. It has also created close cooperative arrangements in defense-related economic activities. NATO's enduring role in European security will provide for the continued presence of the United States in Europe.

Europe neither needs nor can afford two parallel defense forces. NATO has the military background, the infrastructure, and the credibility to serve as the military arm of a united and broadly based European security structure. As is generally recognized, NATO has a strong comparative advantage in security matters over other European institutions. The future of NATO in European security matters will depend on its ability to sustain that advantage, to protect against potential military threats and nuclear proliferation, and to become the pivotal instrument of collective defense for all countries within the CSCE structure. This implies a NATO role in regional peace enforcement and conflict prevention. NATO, however, must assume a stronger European identity in its membership, mandate, command structure, and, according to some experts, even in its name. For example, it has been suggested that NATO be renamed the European-American Treaty Organization (EATO) and have a substantially new European content.[25]

NATO's political structure could, over time, become amalgamated with other European security bodies. In the interim, under any new institutional umbrella for NATO, the mandates of the various security regimes would inevitably overlap or run parallel with one another. To establish an optimal complementarity, the different political, military, and economic interests of the existing institutions would have to be reconciled and harmonized through a series of compromises. This would help to avoid the paralysis and inaction that has characterized the response to the Yugoslavian tragedy.

The Conference on Security and Cooperation in Europe

Whereas political changes in Europe or the United States may result in NATO becoming an organization with formidable military forces and weaponry but no serious role in Europe, the CSCE may increase its role but lack the instruments necessary to accomplish that role. The CSCE was established as an all-European security organization in the mid-1970s, during a period of détente. In the new security environment of the 1990s, it has a few advantages over NATO, among which is its broader territorial framework. The scope of the CSCE was defined in such a way as to ensure that all of Europe participated in the security process, as well as the non-European territories of the Soviet Union, the United States, and Canada. This broad geographic scope has facilitated the participation of all the successor states of the Soviet Union. The participation of the United States and Canada was, from the very beginning of the CSCE, considered a fundamental guarantee of the future security of Europe.

The Final Act of the Conference on Security and Cooperation in Europe (better known as the Helsinki Final Act), which was signed on August 1, 1975, and served as the original political platform of the CSCE, was an historic compromise among neutrals and countries belonging to two opposing military alliances. Despite their differences on many issues, the partners reached a common understanding in certain areas of European security and cooperation by simultaneously pursuing subjective political goals in important security-related matters. For the United States and most of its Western partners, the CSCE was an important instrument in the struggle against totalitarian communist regimes. The West sought to secure the freer movement of peoples and ideas across the iron curtain and promote the spread of human rights by making it a key issue in inter-European affairs. (Although generally unrecognized, the CSCE did indeed help to promote political changes in Europe by advocating political rights, stimulating the liberalization process, and recognizing the work of opposition groups in Central and Eastern Europe.)

The primary aim of the Soviet Union as regards the CSCE was to achieve acceptance of the European status quo and the frontiers established after World War II. Poland and Germany also shared this ambition. Some of the smaller East and West European countries saw involvement in the CSCE as a way of forging closer economic contacts with other countries and increasing their freedom of action within the alliance systems. All the countries of Europe were interested in creating a more secure continent, less susceptible to the dangers of a nuclear holocaust.

In the future, the role of the CSCE in European security will be based more on the converging interests and goals of its member countries. A flexible organization, the CSCE has already moved to accommodate the recent political changes and define the new security agenda for Europe. A process of restructuring is under way, changing the CSCE from a consultative body without permanent institutions into one with permanent secretariats and new bodies that focus on building democratic institutions, safeguarding human rights, and preventing conflicts through arbitration, monitoring, and the gathering and dissemination of information. The CSCE has all the requisites of a truly peaceful cooperation regime in issue areas ranging from economics and human rights to military security. It could become the largest coordinating body for European cooperation, bringing all subregional and functional cooperation regimes under its umbrella. With its Eurasian-Atlantic structure, the CSCE could serve as a bridge connecting three continents.

The CSCE structure has several weaknesses, however. The rapid expansion of its membership to include 50 states has complicated the decision-making process, as all decisions (except those related to fact-finding missions and mediation) must be reached unanimously. Its decisions carry political and moral, rather than legal, weight, and do not even have the strength of international agreements, the breach of which can result in the imposition of sanctions. Also, the CSCE lacks the instruments and the commitments from its member countries necessary for it to deal with the problems of minorities and ethnic conflicts.

The European Community and the Western European Union

The EC has played a multifaceted role in promoting European security. In addition to strengthening European economic security, the EC has played a key role (similar to that of NATO) in bringing together traditional enemies and establishing democratic structures based on the equality of member states. It has also performed a limited but direct role in political and military security, with its members participating in NATO and the WEU.

The WEU was created in 1955 to defend Western Europe, control the rearmament of Germany, and cooperate with NATO. The WEU has since functioned successfully as a forum for discussing and articulating European military security policies. Although its objective to control the rearmament of Germany has lost its relevance, the WEU has grown in importance, reflecting the growing sentiment, especially pronounced within France, that Europe should develop its own defense capabilities, which would be independent of NATO.[26]

There has been much disagreement, especially between the United States and France, about the WEU becoming a parallel military force in Europe. France, which in 1966 withdrew its forces from NATO's integrated military command, wants the WEU to be reactivated because it is convinced that the United States will remove U.S. forces from Europe in the 1990s.[27] French advocacy of an independent European defense capability is also motivated by apprehension at the increasing strength of Germany and by the belief that the EC, when it becomes a political union, should have a security arm. The Maastricht Treaty envisions such a defense establishment.[28]

A Future European Security Regime?

The 1992 Helsinki summit of the CSCE reflected a de facto, though perhaps only temporary, institutional compromise in European security matters. According to agreements reached at that summit, the CSCE would be the political center of a system of interlocking organizations—NATO, WEU, and others—that would function in their own way and cooperate only occasionally. The division of labor among institutions on the basis of comparative advantages and the extent of mutually reinforcing activities remain to be worked out and will no doubt be influenced by how willing countries are to finance parallel structures.

This institutional compromise lacks any grand strategic design. For the moment, with changes occurring at remarkable speed, an overall approach may be unwise or unworkable. Understandably, attention today is focused on preventing existing and emerging conflicts from escalating into widespread violence. Eventually, however, a grand strategy will have to be devised, one that takes account of changes in the global system affecting the demographic, strategic, and economic conditions of Europe, and one that mirrors the radical redefinition of European identity that will shortly result from the economic and political integration of the EC.

A comprehensive security regime in Europe that extends east and west and that possesses efficient institutions for economic cooperation and peacekeeping would have a positive effect on global stability, especially in the Middle East and Africa. As part of a global network of regional partnerships shaped by changing political and economic conditions and centered on the collective security system of the United Nations, the European regime could greatly assist global risk management and strengthen the global economy.

Failure of Europe to produce a credible security regime that corresponds to Europe's new needs would present the danger of long-term instability on the European continent and perhaps signal the return to some form of realpolitik, with its divisive unilateralism and contending spheres of influence. In an era of weapons of mass destruction, sharpening economic competition, and increasing polarization, an unstable Europe of feuding countries vying for unilateral advantages would inevitably destabilize a large part of the world.

chapter 9

The Politics of Change in Asia

Key Security Issues for the Asian Continent

Over the course of the past decade, Asia, and especially Pacific-Asia,[29] has been widely proclaimed as the future growth center of the world. This prediction may well prove accurate, for the emergent economic powers in the region have a higher growth potential than do states anywhere else in the world. However, the potential for instability is equally great. Most of the major global risk factors will be present in this remarkably hetero-geneous area: proliferation of nuclear weapons; ethnic conflicts; dramatic population growth and the consequent pressures for mass migration; ecological problems; and water shortages.

The end of the Cold War has produced different consequences in Europe than in Asia, where the socialist-communist regimes of China, Vietnam, and North Korea have remained in power. Even the disintegration of the Soviet Union has brought much less immediate change in Asia than in Europe. With its immense Far Eastern reaches, Russia remains a major Asian power, and most of the Asian republics of the former Soviet Union have become members of the CIS and have stronger ties to Russia than, say, Ukraine.

The Cold War system in Asia was always distinct from that in Europe. The majority of Central Asia was part of the Soviet

Union and thus interconnected with the domestic problems of that country. Elsewhere in the region, tensions ran high as conflicts erupted or threatened to erupt between such neighbors as India and Pakistan, North and South Korea, the Soviet Union and China, the Soviet Union and Japan, Taiwan and China, and Vietnam and China. Western involvement in these and other regional conflicts further heightened the dangerous atmosphere. Yoshikazu Sakamoto, a Japanese scholar, characterized Asia as a "secondary" Cold War arena, and yet the arena where the "hot wars" of the global Cold War regime were fought.[30]

While the bipolar Soviet-American confrontation was a fundamental factor in shaping the political processes in Asia, there was always greater multipolarity in military and political affairs there than in Europe. The geostrategic network in the region included the United States and its relationships with the Soviet Union, China, the two Koreas, and Japan. Sino-Japanese and Sino-Soviet relations were also key components of the strategic network. Unlike Europe, the region was unable to develop an organized security system like the CSCE that encompassed both sides of the Cold War divide.

The collapse of the Cold War system has permitted some progress in resolving long-standing conflicts—as in Cambodia, where a peaceful settlement was finally negotiated—and ameliorating old antagonisms—for example, the two Koreas have shown some readiness to engage in dialogue. However, other disputes persist, such as China's claim on Taiwan and Japan's claim on the Kuril Islands occupied since 1945 by the Soviet Union (and now by Russia). Moreover, new, diverse sources of instability and violence now also threaten the region, notably the disintegration of the Soviet empire and ethnic conflicts within India and other Asian states.

The prospects for regional cooperation are unclear. The Asia-Pacific Economic Cooperation group, which includes the United States, Canada, Australia, New Zealand, China, Japan, and nine other countries, remains a loose negotiating forum and seems highly unlikely to become a cohesive regional organization. However, Japan, China, and India will probably play key roles in the future formation of geoeconomic or geostrategic subregions having a scope beyond the Association of Southeast Asian Nations, which is the only regional organization that has functioned effectively in economic, and to a lesser extent, political areas. Linkages in trade and capital flows among countries of the region are increasing. The Asian Development Bank is playing an important part in the provision of development financing. Another, much looser regional structure is the UN Economic Commission for Asia and the South Pacific, which is a forum for conducting socioeconomic analysis and negotiations and organizing functional cooperation instruments.

Japan in Asia and Beyond

Japan will play a singularly important role in shaping the future security of the Pacific-Asia region. Japan's role is also globally important, and has implications for global peace and stability.

With the Soviet Union having ceased to exist and Russia unable for the present to assume a position of global power, Japan has suddenly found itself the second most important economic power in the world. This is an unprecedented occurrence for Japan. In the past, strategic thinking in Japan has concentrated on the dynamic and strategic U.S.-Japanese partnership and on Japan's interests and policies in its relationships with the Soviet Union, China, and others within a bipolar global system where Japan could comfortably exist as the third most important economic power in the world.

Japan is a formidable force in a global system where economic power defines the relative power capacities of countries. Japan can be typified as a superpower of the new technological era, in which power is determined not by great armies, vast territories, or abundant natural resources but rather by knowledge and access to information and the ability to use these resources to increase economic capacity and competitiveness. Although Japan does possess, and could easily further develop, a high-tech military capacity, the future sources of Japan's power are its scientific, technological, and economic capabilities. The foundations for these sectors are the Japanese educational system, high levels of savings and investments, cultural cohesion, a keen sense of social responsibility, and a well-structured relationship between industry and government that enables fairly rapid and coordinated adjustments to be made to the economy and a rational approach to be taken to the efficient use of resources.

Japan is very forward-looking in choosing its economic partners and in seeking to reduce its high level of dependence on imported raw materials by making structural changes in its economy. Japan has managed to diversify its raw material and fuel purchases since the early 1970s; in the early part of the 1990s, Japan has systematically striven to decrease its dependence on the U.S. market, focusing more on Asia and on its new foreign direct investments.

After World War II, Japan underwent a political transformation to become a democratic state, at the same time making profound adjustments to its economic system. Although the character and functioning of the Japanese political structure have often been targets of domestic and foreign criticism that centers on collusion between Japan's government bureaucracy and business establishment, that structure has supported and facilitated more or less constant economic growth, a steady increase in the standard of living, and a spectacular performance in foreign markets as exporter and investor.

This post–World War II transformation owed much to Japan's strategic partnership with the United States. The early Cold War years provided Japan with a secure international identity as an increasingly important power in Asia and a valuable ally of the United States. The nature of the partnership has since changed. Japan has outgrown its once subordinate position and become an equal partner with the United States, with which it increasingly shares responsibility in international security matters. Japan is now also the United States' chief economic competitor.

Unlike the U.S.-European relationship, which rested fairly securely on common cultural foundations, relations between the United States and Japan have remained vulnerable in the absence of basic common values. With the end of the Cold War and the disintegration of the Soviet Union, the main purpose of the U.S.-Japanese military alliance—Soviet containment—has disappeared,[31] and both countries are presently reformulating their goals in international politics. Future U.S.-Japanese political and security relationships will surely recognize Japan's graduation to great power status and its autonomy in pursuing its own interests within Asia and elsewhere. Japan's neighbors, mindful of the aggressive and expansionist record of Japan before 1945, hope that Japan will remain tied to the United States in security matters. As one diplomat in Singapore observed in 1991: "The U.S.-Japanese security treaty of 1960 is an important pillar of peace and stability in Asia and the Pacific. If Japan stopped relying on the U.S. nuclear umbrella and became an independent military power, it would destabilize the region."[32]

The future of Japanese-Chinese relations will also be crucially important in shaping Asian politics. Historically, the two nations have regarded each other ambivalently: they are geographically close yet psychologically distant; they share mutual respect and suspicion; they have a record of both conflict and cooperation.[33] China's future interests Japan for two reasons. One is economic. For Japan, cheap and disciplined Chinese labor and China's abundant natural resources are highly attractive. The other interest is political. An economically strong and modernized China might well enhance its military capabilities. Should China become politically unstable, the potential dangers of external military adventures would menace the entire region. Should China instead retain its political stability, Japan would still feel threatened by the regional influence that a well-armed China would wield.[34]

In its relations with Russia, Japan will continue, as throughout the Cold War, to press for the return of the "Northern Territories," those islands to the north of Japan that were occupied by the Soviet Union at the end of World War II. Over the long term, however, the character of Russian-Japanese relations seem likely to become warmer. With its expertise and financial resources, Japan could help in the economic development of Siberia and the Russian Far East. For its part, Russia, which seems likely to become a marginal security concern for Japan, may become Japan's main trading partner.

The post–Cold War period offers great opportunities for Japan to act as a stabilizing force, not only in the global economy, but also in the global political system. Japan has become the largest donor nation to the developing countries, and has committed considerable sums to the protection of the global environment. Japan has, however, provided only very limited assistance to Central and Eastern Europe and the countries of the former Soviet Union. Were Japan to increase its imports from, and its direct investments in, those regions, it could greatly assist them as they make the transition to democracy and the free market. Japanese expertise in technological development and quality management also could be invaluable to other nations; indeed, many Japanese feel that Japan's economic development should serve as an economic model for other countries.

In economic and political terms, Japan could increase its role in regional security affairs by assisting in the peaceful unification of Korea, strengthening the fragile peace in Cambodia, and spearheading the creation of a comprehensive Asian security structure. Japan could also become a main pillar of a future system of global multilateral cooperation. In recognition of its present economic status and potential political role, Japan should be made a member of the UN Security Council.

But is Japan prepared to take these opportunities? Is its political system sufficiently open to the world? Would closer involvement in cooperative regimes be in the long-term interests of Japan? More importantly, would cooperation be perceived by the political elite of Japan as something that is in *its* long-term interests? These questions have sparked much debate both within and outside Japan.

Japan has become an economic giant not least by avoiding massive participation in the very costly arms race of the Cold War. This freed Japan to concentrate most of its energies on increasing its technoeconomic potential and international competitiveness. The strengthening of its international competitiveness has been very much in line with Japan's traditional values, chief among which is the subordination of individual and group interests to the pursuit of national strength. The argument has been made that Japan "has no goals and ideas of its own to offer the world and thus lacks the ability to lead effectively," and that "the values that shape the Japanese paradigm are not, by definition, designed to benefit the rest of the world."[35]

Although this argument is one-sided and suspect, it does help to explain why the potential dangers, and not the potential benefits, of a stronger Japan have become the focus of international debates regarding Japan's future development and role in the global system. Japanese competition in the world market is presently considered by the vast majority of industrial nations to be one of the greatest risk factors of the future. Even before the collapse of the Soviet empire, public opinion polls conducted in the United States revealed that Japanese economic power was increasingly perceived as a greater threat to U.S. interests than was the military power of the Soviet Union.[36]

Japan's global economic role could indeed become a major source of conflict, sparking trade wars among industrial nations. Economic conflicts in the post–Cold War world will inevitably have greater political implications than before, in part because of the disappearance of common interests that characterized Cold War bipolarity and moderated disputes within both blocs, and partly because of the gradual erosion of the cohering force of day-to-day strategic and tactical coordination among powers that influenced the thinking of the political leadership. Nonetheless, depending as it does on the markets, raw materials, and, albeit to a declining degree, technology of other nations and regions, Japan has vested interests in the maintenance of a relatively liberal global economic system. In the long run, Japan would pay a much higher price for the system's collapse than would most of its partners in the industrial world.

The nature of Japanese participation in the Gulf War may have signalled Japan's future course. On one hand, concerned to pursue its autonomous interests, Japan was reluctant to commit itself too strongly to a course of military action that endangered its oil supplies and export markets. On the other hand, Japan's commitment to the U.S.-led coalition reflected Japan's acceptance of the need to punish aggression in international life and its desire to avoid confrontation with the United States, particularly on strategically important issues.

Japan's increasing military potential has generated concern both domestically and within China and many other Asian countries. For some time, the Chinese have differentiated between an "appropriate" and an "undesirable" buildup of Japanese military forces. When, in 1987, the Japanese defense budget rose above 1 percent of gross domestic product (GDP) for the first time since 1945, the Chinese press warned about the expansionist ambitions of Japan.[37] Even Japan's involvement in UN peacekeeping operations has provoked strong protests from Singapore, Korea, and other Asian countries.

The strength of the Japanese armed forces has not yet been judged a source of serious risk and instability by Japan's strategic non-Asian partners. During the Cold War, Japan's partners encouraged it to increase its military capabilities to accomplish three tasks: to build up a modern and efficient air-defense system; to be able to blockade the three straits around Japan, and thus contain the Soviet Pacific fleet; and to share with the United States the task of securing communications in the Pacific.

In the mid-1990s, with the Soviet threat gone, a number of Asian countries that were occupied by Japan during World War II fear that other, domestically rooted motives might inspire a further increase in Japanese military capabilities. Such fear seems unwarranted, however. Few, if any, groups in Japan would support a policy of militarization. Furthermore, although Japan has already developed an impressive high-tech defense industry, which has its own interests and dynamics, including the need for constant modernization, there seems little chance that defense could become an important new sector for Japanese economic growth. Japan's long-term interests dictate that it pursue peaceful cooperation with its main partners in the region and beyond. Only the rise of an expansionist power within Asia or the eruption of regional military conflicts would be likely to trigger Japanese militarization in the remaining years of the 20th century. In fact, the defense white paper approved by the Japanese government in December 1992 substantially reduced the growth in military expenditures.

China: The Evolving Superpower

The new era is a perplexing political environment for the People's Republic of China. During the Cold War, as a part of the nonaligned world, China had assumed an independent role in Asian and global affairs while maintaining flexibility in "equally distant," pendulum-like relations with the two superpowers, both of which generally sought to maintain good relations with China. In simplified terms, when faced with U.S. criticism of its human rights record, China would intensify cooperation with the Soviet Union; when relations with the Soviet Union were tense, China would play the American card.

Despite the historical rivalry between China and first tsarist Russia and then the Soviet Union, the disintegration of the Soviet Union has presented China with new risks. Although during the Cold War the two powers clashed violently at times, the People's Republic found security in the existence of an ideologically similar regime on its northern border. Today, not only is that sense of security gone, but also the political example of the changes in the Soviet Union may well encourage opposition forces in China. Furthermore, the transformation of the former Soviet republics, especially those in Central Asia, into independent states may stimulate nationalist and secessionist movements among ethnic groups in a number of regions of China.

Seeking to repair some of the damage done to its security by the demise of the Soviet Union, since 1991 China has taken significant steps to establish close economic and security cooperation with Russia. Interestingly, the two countries share many common strategic concerns, including political uncertainty in Central Asia, the potential role of Japan within the region, and the future of Korea.

Changes in China's domestic political environment have always exerted an unusually powerful influence on the formation of its foreign policy and on its capacity to act in international affairs. China has tremendous economic potential; even with its domestic problems, China could become a new superpower in the world economy within the next 20 to 25 years. China has demonstrated its flexibility and growth capabilities by its rapid increase in agricultural output, an achievement that has solved China's food problems since the late 1970s. Since the early 1980s, China has made major changes to its political and economic systems in pursuit of greater openness, economic efficiency, and the expansion of its manufacturing industry and trade.

During the past few decades, China has also suffered serious economic and political setbacks caused by internal power struggles and the pursuit of unwise, ideologically motivated policies. The "great leap" at the end of the 1950s; the Cultural Revolution of the 1960s and the activities of the "Gang of Four" in the early 1970s; and the Tiananmen incident of 1989: all have inflicted great damage on China's economy and societal cohesion.

By the mid-1990s, the economic changes begun in the early 1980s have set in train a process of decentralization that has strengthened the role of social groups with interests and values different from those of the political center. Further steps toward decentralization and democratization might help to create a new framework that will gradually transform the character of China's political structure. Alternatively, a new tension may develop between the political system and the values represented and spread by the process of marketization. Such issues as the continuation and nature of reform, the economic and political power of the provinces, the degree of democratization, and the future role of the party may influence also the struggle for political succession. As in the past, in the future domestic political problems may have a negative effect on China's international role, creating tensions with its neighbors and endangering the security of the entire region.

Under stable circumstances, China's regional and global economic and political role will increase substantially. On North-South issues, China will be a strong voice for the South, especially with regard to the inevitable socioeconomic problems of the coming decades. At the same time, China will probably also increase its role as the foremost arms supplier to the developing world.

Some U.S. experts envisage the emergence of a new belt in Asia, centered on mainland China and encompassing not only predominantly Chinese areas such as Taiwan, Hong Kong, Macao, and Singapore but also countries such as Malaysia, Thailand, and the Philippines where Chinese minorities make substantial contributions to the national economies.[38]

A United Korea—But When and How?

The hostile character of relations between the two states of the divided Korean Peninsula—a legacy of the Cold War—presents a substantial danger to the peace and stability of Asia. Although recent global changes have diminished the probability of an armed conflict between North and South Korea and allowed the two countries to establish a more direct relationship, the sources of that conflict have not disappeared. At the same time, especially since the unification of Germany, the possibility of Korean unification has been discussed in the context of the future Asian security agenda.

The debate over unification has raised some interesting problems. The systemic differences between the two Koreas, their very different economic performances, the character and interests of their ruling elites, the high concentration of military hardware on the Korean Peninsula and the nuclear potential of the North, and the sheer economic cost of the process are major obstacles to unification. There are, however, interesting similarities between the two countries. For instance, about 25 percent of the population in both Koreas work in agriculture and fishing. Long working hours and a high participation rate in the labor force are common to both countries.

Within the region, the prospect of a united Korea arouses apprehension that such a state could become a second Japan—a regional power with a significant global role. North Korea has an army of about 1 million personnel and possesses nuclear capabilities; South Korea's military force is close to 750,000 strong. Together, they would comprise the third or fourth largest army in the world. These military capabilities, together with a combined population of 70 million, a large, well-trained labor force with an austere way of life that facilitates a high level of savings and investments, experienced entrepreneurs, and an excellent international marketing structure and trade position—South Korea is already ranked 10th or 11th in its volume of world trade—would make a united Korea a formidable force in regional politics.

What kind of state might emerge from the union of the two Koreas? Would a united Korea necessarily be a democratic Korea? To the north, in the Democratic People's Republic of Korea, a dictatorial regime has maintained a rigid control over society; to the south, in the Republic of Korea, a military regime has only recently been replaced by a democratically elected civilian government. With their Confucian traditions and ethical foundations, East Asian societies tend to view individual rights, freedom, and public duties differently than do the mature democratic societies of Europe and North America. Yet, the evolution of new domestic sociopolitical forces and the changing external environment are clearly fueling pressures for the adoption of democratic values and institutions.

As of the mid-1990s, the prospects for unification appear to be fading once again. No major power in Asia expects progress toward unification to occur in the next few years. Consequently, the present task for those powers with influence in the region, as well as for the two Koreas themselves, is to manage relations between the North and South peacefully.

South and Central Asia

The regions of South and Central Asia are closely interrelated and contain within them a great number of sociopolitical and territorial sources of tensions and conflicts.

The two main powers of South Asia, India and Pakistan, have been locked in conflict since the partition of British India in 1947. During the Cold War, the United States tended to support Pakistan, while nonaligned India established close ties with the Soviet Union. Since the end of the Cold War, however, the strategic importance of Pakistan to the United States has substantially declined while a number of the political differences that previously separated India and the United States have disappeared or diminished in importance.

The end of global bipolarity has done nothing, however, to defuse India's internal conflicts; such conflicts are, indeed, perhaps inevitable in a diverse multiethnic state exposed to destabilizing external forces. Ethnic problems in Kashmir, Punjab, and Tamil-Nadu remain bitter and unresolved; similar conflicts seem likely to erupt in other parts of India. Despite these often bloody domestic difficulties, India has played, and will continue to play, a prominent role on the international stage, concentrating not only on the general problems of the developing world but also on a pragmatic and positive approach to global security issues. In this context, India's relations with the United States and the countries of the former Soviet Union have assumed great importance.

The explosive potential of the strategic triangle of China, India, and Pakistan poses a long-term threat to the stability of the region and requires new multilateral efforts to maintain peace. Although relations between India and China have improved significantly in recent years, India remains concerned over Sino-Pakistani ties and the potential for China to help build up Pakistan's military and nuclear capacities. The collapse of the Soviet Union and the uncertainty of India's relations with the successor states has forced India to reconsider some of its traditional strategic assumptions concerning Soviet strategic guarantees. Defense cooperation with Russia will remain an important option for India, but in the evolving strategic environment of South Asia, and in the absence of international security regimes or security guarantees, both India and Pakistan may seek to bolster their security by increasing their defense capabilities.

The political landscape of Central Asia, extending from Turkey in the west to Kazakhstan, Kyrgyzstan, and Tajikistan in the east, has been reshaped by the disintegration of the Soviet Union, the civil war in Afghanistan, and the consequences of the Iranian revolution. The ethnic tensions and artificially established frontiers that divide the region ensure that instability will continue for the foreseeable future. Multiethnic Afghanistan may be in a process of disintegration; new separatist movements may arise among the Hazaris in Iran and the Pashtuns in Pakistan; and ethnic struggles may have far-reaching consequences in the former Soviet republics in Central Asia. Because this region borders on Europe, Russia, China, India, and the Arab world, its instability has serious geopolitical implications.

The Southeast Asian Security Zone

The present and potential sources of instability in Southeast Asia are many and varied: antagonistic relations between neighbors; adverse economic and political consequences of the Indochina wars of the past four decades; explosive ethnic and social problems; competing claims by several countries to a number of small islands and oil fields on the seabed; separatist movements in such states as Indonesia, Myanmar (Burma), and Thailand; and a host of domestic problems.

Although the peace settlement reached in Cambodia has radically changed the regional strategic environment, opening the way toward a new, more peaceful era, the multiplicity of problems presents constant dangers to regional security and underscores the need for security and cooperative regimes. The Association of Southeast Asian Nations (ASEAN) is not chiefly a security organization, although it does have a mandate to settle disputes and has developed a code of conduct for regional relations. In January 1992, Vietnam and Laos requested to accede to the Treaty of Amity and Cooperation, which ASEAN's members signed in 1967. ASEAN member states warmly welcomed Vietnam and Laos's request. In 1992, the heads of government of ASEAN member states declared their intention to promote common security and their commitment to make the region a nuclear-free zone of peace and freedom.

As the influence of the Asian region on the global political and economic systems grows, the size, technological level, and deployment of Asia's national armies and the mechanisms and regional management of Asian security affairs will become increasingly important for the rest of the world. The new political and economic interactions of the main Asian powers, together with their specific roles within the different Asian subregions, are rapidly restructuring the Asian geostrategic environment. The strategic alliances and nuclear umbrellas offered in the past by the United States and Russia to Asian nations are, in many instances, being discarded or devalued as those nations develop new relationships among themselves, frequently without regional institutional guarantees for dispute settlement or peacekeeping operations. Even so, the United States and Russia will remain important participants in Asian politics. Indeed, the position of the United States as the main economic partner of the most important countries in Asia, U.S. military strength and special interests in the Pacific region, and the interests of a number of Asian countries in seeing the United States act as a strategic balance to various evolving regional powers will demand a strong U.S. involvement in Asian economic and security affairs.

chapter 10

Old Problems and New Opportunities in the Middle East

The post–Cold War era began in the Middle East with the Gulf War, the most important achievement of which has been to set in motion a peacebuilding process between Israel and the Arab world.

Nowhere else in the world are the sources of international instability more numerous, the risks to the evolving global order greater, and the linkages between domestic and external problems stronger than in the Middle East. Violence is a constant variable in the Middle East. Between the end of World War II and the end of the Cold War, the region witnessed 15 interstate wars and more than 500 major uprisings, revolutions, insurrections, and coups. The region's geographical location, ethnic, socioeconomic, and political characteristics, and strategic importance to external powers has produced a unique network of international risk factors. In the coming decades, the Middle East may well become the testing ground for the viability of any new global order.

The Middle East is closely connected with many other regions. It is part of an Islamic cultural belt that extends across Asia and Africa. Its ideological, political, and economic problems directly influence northern Africa. Like Central Asia, the Middle East has been profoundly affected by the disintegration of the Soviet Union. The Middle East is tied to Europe not only by oil but also through the Mediterranean countries. NATO, in fact, has been extended to this region through Turkey.

Throughout most of its history, the Middle East has been a target for foreign conquest. In the 19th century, the external powers competing for control of the region were Russia, Great Britain, France, and later Germany, all of which sought to capitalize on the decline of the Ottoman Empire. These powers drew national frontiers irrespective of local ethnic identities. They extended the concept of nation-states to an area where it did not, and in many ways still does not, apply.[39] As a result, almost all Middle Eastern countries have territorial claims against at least one of their neighbors.

During the Cold War, the Middle East was perhaps the most complex and conflict-ridden area of the world. Both superpowers adjudged the region vital to their strategic interests. Its oil resources and geostrategic position attracted the United States. The northern part of the Middle East, which bordered the Soviet Union's southern tier, was regarded by the Soviet Union as a key sector of its strategic defense system. Furthermore, the sole channel for the Soviet navy and commercial fleet to enter the Mediterranean from the Black Sea was through the Bosphorus strait of Turkey, a member of NATO. Both the Soviet Union and the United States found their efforts to secure strategic allies in the area facilitated by the traditional conflicts between Middle Eastern states, which were looking for external allies as sources of arms, economic assistance, and military guarantees against attack by their neighbors. From the early 1950s onwards, the superpower conflict led to the establishment of regional client states.[40]

West European countries, and to a lesser extent Japan, have also been involved in Middle Eastern political processes. Their primary interests have been the security of oil supplies and the sale of arms. While they have more often than not supported the common policies of the West, all have nonetheless maintained special bilateral relations with individual countries based on traditional ties and particular interests. China has also become an important participant in the power games of the region, mostly through its arms shipments.

With the end of the Cold War, external actors are less inclined than before to look for Middle Eastern allies and more circumspect in supporting states with records of dubious respect for human rights or democracy. Today, stability in the region is the chief goal of external powers—hence the breadth of international support for the coalition that ousted Iraqi forces from Kuwait. Over the long term, however, great uncertainty surrounds the aims and roles of all external powers except the United States. Since the Camp David accords of 1978, and especially since the Gulf War of 1991, the importance of the United States as a mediator of Middle Eastern conflicts has grown.

Post–Cold War changes have allowed traditional sources of conflict to reemerge. Although politics has been perceived as the chief progenitor of Middle Eastern conflict, in fact economics has served as the background for most regional conflicts, especially because of the highly unequal distribution of wealth throughout the area. Economic inequality in the Middle East is perhaps a more salient source of instability than it is in other regions of the developing world, where disparities in incomes among neighboring states tend to be less pronounced. Per capita income gaps between Middle Eastern countries are enormous: in 1989, per capita income in the United Arab Emirates was $23,798; in Saudi Arabia, $10,330; in Syria, $980; and in Egypt, $640.[41] Despite the absence of reliable statistics for income distribution across the entire region, it is generally accepted that around 1 percent of the Middle Eastern population enjoys a standard of living comparable to that of the wealthiest individuals in the developed world, while 60 to 70 percent of the population lives in poverty. Illiteracy, malnutrition, unemployment, high rates of infant mortality, and low life expectancy are widespread.

The countries of the region can be divided into three groups: those with high oil revenues and relatively small populations; those with high oil revenues and large populations; and those poor and populous countries that must rely largely on foreign assistance. In economic terms, the oil-producing and -exporting countries, even those that have pursued radical political policies, are closely interconnected with the West as major suppliers of oil, major investors in international money markets, and major importers of manufactured goods, commodities, and services that their oil-dominated economies cannot provide. This economic interconnectedness brings with it certain common strategic and security interests with the industrial world. The other countries of the region have significantly less well-developed economic relations with, and thus are less dependent on, the industrial world.

Many of the roots of the region's domestic economic problems lie in negligence and government mismanagement. Most countries are ruled by either dynastic elites, military dictators, or a blend of the two. The nature and conduct of these regimes do not encourage cordial and cooperative intraregional relations.

The Middle East is one of the most militarized regions of the world. In the 1980s, defense expenditures accounted for between 8 and 10 percent of GDP, almost double the global average. In the same period, the region purchased 36.5 percent of global arms exports, and about half of all arms shipments to the developing world went to the Middle East.[42] Some Middle Eastern arsenals include chemical, biological, and nuclear weapons and intermediate-range missile-delivery systems.

The Arab-Israeli Conflict

The establishment of the state of Israel in 1948 occurred at a time when the Arab countries were themselves searching for their own national identity in a postcolonial Middle East. To a large extent, they found that identity in their opposition to Israel, which was seen as an alien body in an Arab world. Israel became a scapegoat for many Arab problems and a symbol of Western interference in Arab affairs. Over the next 40 years, Arab-Israeli relations became intertwined in a complex web of antagonisms that included Arab hostility to Western influence and culture, the clash between Arab dictatorships and Western democracies, inter-Arab rivalries, regional ethnic and religious disputes, and the Cold War. The fundamental question was not one of territorial claims or access to water, but rather the acceptance by the Arabs of the legitimacy of the Israeli state.

In the 1990s, however, the international environment within which Arab-Israeli relations are shaped has changed. With the dissolution of the Soviet Union, several Arab states have lost a previously important source of political support and military hardware and have become far more dependent on the West.

China, the largest non-Western arms supplier in the world, has restored diplomatic and trade relations with Israel. The political and military credibility of the United States and its position as external arbiter of regional disputes have increased substantially as the result of the Gulf War.

The position of Israel has also changed, in part because of political developments in the Soviet Union, which, from the late 1980s, permitted large numbers of its Jewish citizens to emigrate to Israel. The subsequent collapse of the Soviet Union changed the strategic balance in the Middle East and diminished the strategic importance of Israel to the United States. At the same time, Israel's vulnerability became clearer as the Arab states obtained medium-range missiles and other high-tech weapons—this vulnerability was underscored by Iraq's use of SCUD missiles against Israel during the Gulf War. However, Israel became stronger diplomatically. Between 1988 and 1992, 35 countries established or reestablished diplomatic relations with Israel.

The prospects for some accommodation between Israel and its Arab neighbors have improved in the aftermath of the Gulf War. For instance, Syria, which together with countries such as Iraq and Libya had been one of the chief supporters of anti-Israeli actions, transformed its international orientation by supporting the U.S.-led coalition against Iraq. Since then, Syria has also facilitated the restoration of Lebanon's political integrity.

With its diplomatic and military position enhanced by the outcome of the Gulf War, the United States restarted the Arab-Israeli peace process with a conference in Madrid in December 1991. A negotiated settlement between Israel and its Arab enemies is not without precedent. The Camp David accords, signed in 1978 by Israeli prime minister Menachem Begin and Egyptian president Anwar Sadat, may serve as a model for future Arab-Israeli compromises. Seemingly fragile and based on mutual diplomatic recognition, exchange programs, and tourism, the accords between Israel and Egypt have weathered many challenges since 1978. The United States acted not only as a broker of the Camp David negotiations but also as a guarantor of the settlements reached.[43] Such U.S. support will be even more important to any future plan for Middle Eastern peace.

The most important result of the Madrid initiative—indeed, probably the most significant step toward peace between the

Arab world and Israel since Israel was established—has been the accord reached in 1993 between Israel and the Palestine Liberation Organization on limited Palestinian self-rule in Jericho and the Gaza strip. With the question of the future of Palestine and the Palestinians lying at the heart of the Arab-Israeli conflict, the accord, if implemented, will change the political environment and improve the prospects for resolving other regional issues. One must not forget, however, the extremely complex nature of the Palestinian problem for the domestic politics and future security of Israel, and for Jordan, a majority of whose post–Gulf War population is Palestinian.

The process of achieving and implementing a lasting settlement between Israelis and Palestinians is certain to suffer setbacks. Many problems remain to be settled, including the return of Palestinian refugees, antagonisms among the various Palestinian political organizations, the complexion of the future Palestinian political system, and Israel's demands to ensure the security of its borders. The Israelis and the Palestinians have a long road to travel from formal recognition to mutual acceptance.

The Difficult Politics of Regional Relations

The lasting success of any Middle Eastern peace regime will depend largely on the character and future of inter-Arab relations, which are in turn profoundly affected by the new international realities of the post–Cold War era and the economic and political instability of the Arab world.

Explosive population growth, rapid urbanization, the uneven distribution of oil resources, economic mismanagement, giant defense budgets, and faulty development practices (including the inefficient use of oil revenues) serve as the domestic background to inter-Arab relations. Major ideological rifts, some a reflection of the two main trends in Islam, divide many Arab states. The delicate balance between the influence of traditional Islamic institutions and the processes of Western-style modernization is another source of problems. Supporters of Islamic fundamentalism and proponents of democracy compete to maintain or achieve political power. In those few countries where democratic institutions exist, their functioning is complicated by this ideological and cultural clash. With the influence of Marxism waning, future domestic, political, and ideological struggles will center on the separation of secular and religious authorities and the tensions between modern and traditional religious values. These struggles may lead to the establishment in some countries of anti-Western theocracies and dictatorships.

Ideology has always played a prominent role in the struggle for hegemony in this region, not least by extolling not the concept of the nation-state but rather the vision of a regionwide community of Arabs. Nation-states are alien to Middle Eastern history. The Ottoman Empire was based on self-governing religious and ethnic communities, each subservient to the broader, multiethnic empire. Pan-Arab movements, which were instrumental in breaking up that empire, advocated the idea of an "Arab nation" composed of a community of believers united by their loyalty to God rather than to individual states. During much of the Cold War, various Arab leaders competed for the loyalty of the masses throughout the region by stressing their pan-Arabist credentials and promising to unite the Arab world. Although pan-Arabism proved unable to accomplish its aims, its influence meant that the contest among Arab states for regional hegemony was not based solely on their respective economic and military capabilities.

Those contending for regional leadership actively sought external support and exploited Soviet-American enmity to this end. Egypt, which with its political and military power, intellectual influence, and international role had been accepted as the traditional leading power in the region, relied heavily on Soviet support after the Suez War in 1956. After the 1973 war with Israel, however, Egypt realized the limits of Soviet assistance and began to consider a peaceful accommodation with its longtime enemy. In the 1980s, with Egypt having lost its leading role in Arab politics by signing the Camp David accords with Israel, Iraq and Iran vied for regional supremacy. Even Libya entered the ring, laying claim to a leadership role in ideology and politics.

The nature of the struggle for regional hegemony has changed in the post–Cold War period. With the dissolution of the Soviet Union, Arab states no longer enjoy superpower support for aggressive, anti-Israeli policies, and the Palestinian issue has lost its Cold War component. Furthermore, the Gulf War not only inflicted a severe blow on Iraq's ambitions but also demonstrated the limits of any Arab nation's ability to use military force to achieve its foreign policy goals.

Today, an additional new challenge confronts the rivals for Middle Eastern hegemony, namely, competition for political and economic influence in the Muslim republics of the former Soviet Union. In this struggle, fundamentalist Iran and secularist Turkey have become the main contenders, each courting different groups in that region. Iran has appealed to the Shiite fundamentalists in Azerbaijan and Turkmenistan and to the Farsi-speaking majority of Tajikistan. Turkey has appealed to those who seek to establish secular democracies and to the large number of Turkish-speaking Sunni Muslims in the six Central Asian republics. This competition to fill the power vacuum created by the weakening influence of Moscow is part of the broader contest between Iran and Turkey to strengthen their influence throughout the Middle East. Despite their ethnic differences with the rest of the region (neither country is an Arab state), both Turkey and Iran could enlarge their roles as other, smaller countries look for economically powerful regional allies. All present and potential contenders for regional hegemony have learned from the Gulf War the neeed to pursue political settlements rather than military solutions to regional problems.

Among those problems, ethnic and minority issues figure prominently. The most numerous of the ethnic groups without a state of their own are the Kurds, who are spread throughout Turkey, Iran, Iraq, and the former Soviet Union.[44] Their struggle for independence began in the 1880s in major uprisings against the Ottoman and Persian empires. In the 1920s, the prospects for the establishment of an independent Kurdish state in the eastern part of present-day Turkey brightened briefly, but then were dashed. Since then, the Kurds have fought against the status quo by political and paramilitary means. Like the Palestinians, the Kurds have become pawns in regional conflicts; for instance, they were encouraged by Iraq to fight against Iran, and they were supported by Iran in their struggle against the Iraqi regime.

The creation of an independent Kurdish state would radically change the balance of power in today's Middle East. Not surprisingly, those countries with sizable Kurdish minorities strongly resist the idea of Kurdish statehood, and regional autonomy seems the most that the Kurds could realistically expect to achieve in today's political climate. Demands for Kurdish state-hood will surely persist, however.

Other ethnic and religious minority groups in the region include the Copts of Egypt, a Christian sect who have become targets of Islamic fundamentalist attacks in the last 15 years; the Christian Maronites in Lebanon, who have established a fragile modus vivendi with the Muslim majority; and the Shiites in south-ern Iraq, who are being encouraged by Iran to fight against the Sunni regime.

All attempts made since World War II to quell ethnic violence have ultimately failed. The political model of "Lebanonization"—the official recognition of quotas and the granting of narrow political rights to Lebanon's different religious and ethnic com-munities—has collapsed in the region. In this antagonistic envi-ronment, with ethnic tensions being exploited by external forces seeking to destabilize the regimes of their adversaries, managing interstate relations has been very difficult and ad hoc arrange-ments have proved all too fragile.

Through political, economic, and military means, foreign inter-ventions could impose a temporary calm on the region, but permanent settlements of Middle Eastern problems will require the creation of a regional collective security system that guar-antees the peaceful coexistence of all nations. The opportunity to establish such a system may be presented if peace talks between Israel and its Arab neighbors yield positive results. Success in those talks may start a self-sustaining process of peace, which could result in greater stability, democratization, the seculariza-tion of politics, and even demilitarization.

chapter 11

The Politics of Latin America, Africa, and the Developing Countries of the South

Some of the region-specific changes related to the role of the South in the evolving global political system have been discussed above in connection with Asia and the Middle East, regions that have been playing a more central role in global politics than they did in the past, and which will be profoundly influenced by the end of superpower rivalry. In this chapter, besides the specific problems of Latin America and Africa, some of the general issues of North-South politics are raised.

Latin America:
A Subcontinent without Interstate Conflicts?

The process of decolonization, which resulted in many wars in Africa and Asia after World War II, took place in Latin America in the 19th century. Consequently, the countries of Latin America were integrated into the global political and economic systems much earlier than were those states that gained independence after 1945. Still, the countries of Latin America share many of the socioeconomic problems that affect the newer nation-states of Asia, Africa, and the Middle East. Those problems, present to varying degrees throughout the continent, are threatening Latin America's fragile democratic structures.

Some of the continent's problems are rooted in its Spanish colonial heritage: historical traditions of authoritarianism and militarism; slow economic development; and highly inequitable social justice. Other problems are of a more recent vintage and are the results of the collapse of raw material markets, civil wars, drug trafficking, high levels of debt, and policy errors committed by recent and incompetent dictatorial regimes.

During the Cold War, Latin American social discontent, coups, and civil wars became global issues and several Latin American nations became battlegrounds for global political and ideological struggles. Both the United States and the Soviet Union involved themselves—albeit in different ways—in local conflicts in such countries as Nicaragua, Honduras, and Grenada. With the Cold War now over, Latin American problems will probably have less impact on global politics; the end of the Cold War will not, however, eliminate the problems that have inspired conflicts in the region.

Latin America has never been homogeneous. Three chief divisions are evident today: Mexico, which will increasingly become part of the North American complex; Central America, with its small, underdeveloped countries and intense sociopolitical conflicts; and the South, which encompasses countries of varying size and levels of development. Even within these divisions, each country is different in terms of its degree of political pluralism, social heterogeneity, and domestic stability. If poverty is not reduced and inequalities grow, the next decade may witness explosive sociopolitical crises that may endanger the progress achieved in political democratization.[45]

These crises are likely, however, to be confined within national borders. Since World War II, there have been few interstate conflicts. Most of the region's earlier conflicts concerned frontier disputes; these have now largely been settled. Many other conflicts were ideologically motivated and were often initiated and sustained by external powers; today, only Cuba poses the danger of an ideologically driven conflict.

The risks of large-scale military interstate conflict in Latin America during the 1990s are minimal. Although there are disputes between countries, no major structural (including ethnic) sources of regional conflict exist. All of the countries are weak economically and cannot afford costly military operations beyond their frontiers. The region also possesses institutional mechanisms for conflict resolution. Since their establishment, Latin American countries have sought to formulate common principles and guidelines for dispute settlement. In 1890, the Pan American Union was founded with the aim of achieving an order of peace and justice among the American nations and defending their sovereignty, territorial integrity, and independence. After World War II, the inter-American system was revitalized with the creation in 1948 of the Organization of American States (OAS) as the successor to the Pan American Union.

The record of the OAS is mixed. Some of its members—notably, the United States—have preferred to take unilateral action rather than collective measures. Even since the end of the Cold War, the organization has proved unable to respond effectively to domestic coups in Haiti and Peru. Nevertheless, the OAS is undoubtedly the most important and representative institution on the continent for conflict management and resolution and offers a comprehensive organizational framework for cooperation. The OAS could usefully broaden its focus to include nonmilitary threats to regional security, such as those posed by environmental degradation, and could play a greater role in protecting fragile democracies in the subcontinent.

Latin American countries can be expected to remain important actors in formulating the agenda of the South as a whole, especially on such issues as debt, regional cooperation, and structural adjustment. Within their own hemisphere, a key issue for the countries of Latin America will be relations with the United States. In their search for a more harmonious relationship with their powerful neighbor to the north, Latin American countries will find that the North American Free Trade Agreement presents a new challenge to the process of bargaining over such issues as trade, foreign direct investments, migration, and environmental protection.

Africa: From Turmoil to Stability?

The single most important post–Cold War change in Africa—the historic compromise between the majority of the black and a part of the white communities in South Africa and the beginnings of the end for the apartheid regime—has been only loosely related to the end of the Cold War. Developments within South Africa and increasing pressures on it from the international community have been chiefly and directly responsible for South Africa's sea change, which has opened a new chapter in African politics.

Since its division among the European imperial powers in the late 19th century, Africa has been tied to European politics. This link has been weakened by decolonization, although many African nations still maintain strong ties to the former metropolitan countries—especially to France and Great Britain as members of the Franc Zone and the British Commonwealth. Africa became enmeshed in Cold War politics through the process of decolonization, with some newly independent African countries seeking Soviet support, and both superpowers exploiting African ethnic divisions to enlarge their spheres of influence. As in Latin America, while the end of the Cold War has significantly reduced the level of external intervention in African conflicts, it has not changed the continent's fundamental internal, political, and socioeconomic realities. With the end of Soviet assistance to many African regimes, the United States has also become less engaged in the affairs of the continent, and with the larger external powers displaying little interest in filling the resultant political vacuum, Africa is facing increasing isolation and marginalization in international politics. As a consequence, in the post–Cold War era Africa's role in the international political system will be more strongly influenced by domestic factors than by external ones.

Africa is politically, economically, and ideologically divided along many lines. Yet, despite their divisions and disparities, African countries suffer from many of the same ills: rapidly growing populations, inefficient governments, corruption, mismanagement, declining per capita income, dwindling food supplies, famine, and the rapid spread of AIDS. The boundaries of most African nations were drawn by their former colonial masters in an arbitrary fashion that took no account of the distribution of the indigenous ethnic groups. The consequence has been a plethora of ethnic conflicts, which have led to a state of almost constant political instability, an increase in the number of refugees from 500,000 in 1970 to over 15 million in 1990, and a very high level of military spending throughout Africa.

The majority of African countries have been governed by dictatorial regimes. The parliamentary systems established immediately after independence proved unable to sustain the broad-based political coalitions created during the struggle for independence. Confronted with ethnic tensions and unrealistically high popular expectations for rapid socioeconomic development, the parliamentary systems were transformed into single-party instruments for serving either privileged political elites or specific ethnic groups. Military coups, civil wars, guerrilla movements, and, in South Africa, constant violence instigated by the apartheid regime and its opponents have characterized the continent's postcolonial political history.

Governments staffed by bureaucrats, the military, or the urban middle class have been responsive to the problems of the urban population but almost completely neglectful of the rural areas where most people live. In Zaire, for example, even the roads in rural areas have been reclaimed by the jungle. At the time of its independence in 1960, Zaire possessed more than 100,000 kilometers of usable roads; in the early 1990s, only about 20,000 kilometers are usable, and only 2,000 kilometers have been paved. Economic development has been hampered by inefficient industries and state enterprises, limited markets, and wasted investments. The process of democratization, in progress since the 1980s, has increased the political participation of groups previously excluded from power, but it has also led in many cases to extravagant demands by those groups for the immediate redistribution of national resources. Such demands have served only to paralyze governments and fragment societies.

With its many internally divided countries, Africa cannot overcome the trap of underdevelopment. The small, declining or stagnating economies that depend on the export of commodities are struggling under the impact of socioeconomic crises, food shortages, unemployment, and political unrest. Subregional cooperation and integration would be a fruitful response to the problems of African countries; however, this is increasingly difficult to initiate in an environment of poverty.

Integration efforts in the past have generally inspired more suspicion than cooperation. A few subregional cooperation regimes have been established, including the Arab Maghreb Union, which aims to promote peace and development; the Southern Africa Development Cooperation Conference (SADCC), which aims to reduce its members' dependence on South Africa; and the Economic Conference of West African States (ECOWAS), an economic cooperation structure formed by several West African countries, which intervened in Liberia in 1990 to prevent a widespread massacre in that country. The only regionwide entity is the Organization of African Unity (OAU). Founded in 1960, the OAU has the declared goals of promoting unity and solidarity among its members, defending their sovereignty, territorial integrity, and independence, and eliminating all forms of colonialism in Africa. With its members facing grave economic and social problems and unwilling or unable to make strong commitments to the cause of regional cooperation, the OAU is virtually powerless to address the civil wars and other conflicts that plague the continent.

Africa will increasingly depend on different forms of international assistance and cooperation with the United States and countries in Europe and Asia. Unfortunately, the developed world is showing decreasing concern for Africa and for the developing world generally.

The New Politics of North-South Relations

The Cold War era presented different opportunities and possessed different characteristics and problems in the South than it did in the North. Most of the conflicts in the South had socioeconomic roots and were not directly related to the Cold War confrontation, although they were often exploited by the competing blocs, which sought allies and even proxies among the nations of the South. The sources of North-South confrontation during the Cold War were also more socioeconomic than political-military in nature, and their management required institutions for multilateral and bilateral bargaining.

In the bipolar world of the Cold War, the former colonies came to occupy an intermediate position between the two superpower blocs. The "third world" (a coinage of French socialists and a concept that was not readily accepted by Marxists and a number of Western neoclassical conservatives, who denied the possibility of a third alternative to world socialism and world capitalism) became an arena in which the two blocs competed for political influence. Political influence not only permitted the establishment of military bases but also facilitated access to the South's raw materials and expanding markets, especially in arms. The struggle for political influence brought the South into the global Cold War arena.

The process of political decolonization with the arbitrary mapping of frontiers accentuated traditional problems and created new sources of conflict. Most of the 130 small wars waged after World War II occurred in the South, many of them becoming war of proxies despite being rooted in local issues. More than 20 million people died in these conflicts. Between 1960 and 1987, the military spending of the developing countries increased three times faster than that of the developed industrial countries, rising from $27 billion to $173 billion. Between 1979 and 1989, the cost of the military hardware acquired by the South equaled twice its combined GDP in 1985.[46]

Global political changes in the second half of the 1980s had a moderating influence on some of the crises in the South and encouraged the settlement of political disputes by nonviolent means. Namibia achieved independence. The war between Iraq and Iran ended in compromise. A political settlement was reached in Nicaragua. Soviet troops left Afghanistan. A political compromise was achieved in Angola and Cambodia. The international coalition formed during the Gulf War brought together former Cold War adversaries in a common venture. The South, however, is still far from tranquil. Old and new sources of instability and risks constantly undermine the stability of governments and impede the progress of democratization. Furthermore, the end of the Cold War has "introduced an extra element of uncertainty into the strategic considerations of the developing countries in that they can no longer rely on the automatic protection of one of the two major military powers in a regional confrontation with their adversaries."[47]

The proliferation of weapons of mass destruction is a growing danger to the developing world. In the early 1990s, at least 10 developing countries were working on the development of nuclear weapons, 22 on chemical and biological weapons, and 25 on ballistic missiles.[48] Encouragingly, the prospects for arms control have improved with the end of the Cold War, which has effectively terminated supplies of free or inexpensive highly sophisticated arms to developing countries that cannot otherwise afford to purchase such weaponry. In a move that might enhance post–Cold War stability, the Japanese government has decided that those countries which are heavy importers of armaments or which increase their defense expenditures will not receive Japanese assistance.

Although opportunities for the peaceful resolution of conflict in the developing world are greater than in the past, if they are to be realized much more intensive and better organized international cooperation is necessary, especially at the regional level. The dangers of regional conflicts in the South escalating into global crises have receded in the post–Cold War world, but those conflicts are increasingly internationalized through arms sales and various forms of external intervention (including peacemaking and humanitarian assistance operations), as well as through their creation of large numbers of refugees.

The termination of the era of political decolonization and the ongoing domestic economic transformation in the developing countries have brought major changes in the international economic position and political role of the countries of the South. At the same time, the developing world is facing problems that are largely unprecedented in the history of the North. The great number of interconnected political, economic, demographic, and social problems; inefficient and unrepresentative governments in many countries; the strong demonstration effect of Northern luxury goods, which is stimulating rapidly rising expectations; a North that is not ready and able to help: all are fueling political instability and ethnic, tribal, and communal conflicts. Yet, the South has made some progress toward democratization. For instance, in some African countries a "second liberation" is said to be under way, bringing with it the beginnings of the establishment of democratic institutions and a new political culture. Latin America is another area where democratization has made significant strides forward.

The collapse of the communist regimes in Europe and the end of bipolarity is bringing other changes. Some are conceptual in nature. For instance, "third world" is gradually disappearing from the vocabulary of international relations now that the "first" and "second worlds" have lost their meaning. Other changes involve the group of nonaligned countries. During the Cold War, the chief political instrument of collective third world politics was the Non-Aligned Movement, which was born at the 1955 Bandung Conference of Asian-African Nations. Although the movement has been accused by its opponents of being more an instrument of international political and economic demagoguery and extortion than one of constructive action,[49] it did introduce new forces and initiatives (like the New International Economic Order) into global politics. Within the United Nations system, the Non-Aligned Movement pressed for greater respect for human rights, the liquidation of colonial regimes, and the right of self-determination.

Nonalignment has lost its raison d'être in a world without opposing blocs. Whether the movement can survive as a collective body of Southern states, or whether it will be transformed into something else, is an open question. In the post–Cold War era, the countries of the developing world better understand their situation and vulnerabilities, and many of their political leaders have articulated their common interests in a more peaceful and demilitarized world. At the same time, those leaders recognize the importance of developing greater solidarity in the new era among the nations of the South and using their collective strength for bargaining with the North. There is also greater awareness of the fact that the principle of sovereign equality enshrined in the UN one-country, one-vote decision-making system still gives the South, which includes a numerical majority of the nations of the world, significant voting power.

The interests, especially the economic interests, of the countries of the South have become more diverse, however. South-South cooperation will become more difficult as Southern countries compete for markets and external economic resources (capital, technology, and so forth), make special arrangements with groups of Northern states, and pursue different policies on such matters as commodity pricing.

The disparity between the developed and developing worlds seems set to increase during the 1990s as global competition intensifies. It is clearer than ever that North-South issues are global issues. Not only do deteriorating economic conditions in the South undermine the social and political stability of the developing countries and pose threats for the entire world, but also those same conditions are usually the consequences of the North's inability to efficiently manage its internal adjustments and international cooperation. Naturally, the countries of the South are emphasizing the need to fashion a new order that will help to moderate their major socioeconomic problems in a more predictable, equitable, and efficient structure of international cooperation.[50]

The increasingly complex character of North-South relations and their growing importance requires the major countries of the North to reformulate their policies toward the developing world. Debates about Northern interests in the developing world are much less extensive in the North than they were during the Cold War, and the focus of discussions differs from region to region. In Europe, the question of the future of the developing world is examined in light of the future program of the EC, international migration issues, and the changes in Central and Eastern Europe. In the United States, discussions regarding the proliferation of weapons, the reorganization of U.S. aid programs, the redefinition of U.S. security interests, and the global processes of democratization have included consideration of the South. In Japan, the plight of the developing world has featured in debates about Japan's future global role and present status as the largest donor of international aid. However, neither in domestic political circles nor in a multilateral framework has the North engaged in prolonged and focused discussion on the future of its relations with the South.

This lack of attention is unwise, to say the least. A short list of the issues directly affecting the interests of the North in the future of the South would include the security of supplies of oil and other raw materials; nonproliferation of weapons of mass destruction; the dangers posed to international stability by aggressive regional powers; the suppression of international terrorism and drug trafficking; and the stabilization of economic conditions, which among other things would help to prevent a mass exodus from the developing world. Less directly relevant concerns would include supporting democratization and respect for human rights and discouraging environmentally damaging policies.

Given these key interests, action is required in pursuit of four goals. One is improving cooperation between global and regional security structures so that they are more effective in facilitating regional conflict resolution, undertaking peacemaking and peacekeeping operations, guaranteeing the security of individual nations, and avoiding regional arms buildups. A second goal is reformulating the norms and trade policies that guide the functioning of the global economy so that they better advance mutual interests. A third goal is restructuring multilateral trade and financial institutions to make them more relevant and responsive to regional and global problems and more helpful to national reforms and development.

The fourth goal is reformulating the conditions, aims, and priorities of bilateral cooperation on development and coordinating them more closely with the forms and structures of multilateral cooperation. With regional power centers evolving in Asia, Africa, and Latin America, the issues of the South are bound to influence the agenda of the international political system in new ways. Bilateral and multilateral relations with these power centers may open a new chapter on global power politics in the 21st century.

Part III

Conflict and Cooperation in the Changing Global Economic System

chapter 12

The Politics of the Global Economy

New Interactions between Politics and the Global Economy

Social scientists have long studied the theoretical and practical issues raised by the relationship between politics and economics, seeking to determine not just which, if either, is paramount and which subordinate, but also what is the character of the inter-relations between political processes and the economy, both on national levels and within the global system. Empirical evidence has shown that in any era interrelations between politics and economics are conditioned by both traditional and new factors. The new factors are especially important in changing the focus of political actions and the economic priorities of nations.

The Cold War profoundly influenced the main processes, insti-tutions, and interstate relations of the global economy. The arms race required a substantial and long-term concentration of material and human resources. During every decade of the Cold War, an amount equal to 50 to 60 percent of one year's global output within that decade was spent on defense. The Soviet Union spent more than twice as much as the global average on defense-related activities. Between 10 and 14 percent of the global working-age population served in the military or in defense industries and services. Approximately one-third of total R&D expenditures throughout the world were defense related. The share of direct arms exports averaged 5 to 7 percent of global exports.[1]

World trade, international capital flows, and the global technology markets were subordinated to national security considerations during the Cold War, resulting in major constraints on East-West economic relations. These constraints extended to scientific cooperation, relations between developed and developing countries, and even West-West technology transfers. Economic sanctions, trade restrictions, the freezing of assets, and other political measures were frequently used by the West against the Soviet Union and its allies. Such institutions as the Coordinating Committee for Multilateral Export Controls (COCOM), established in 1948, became important instruments of Cold War policies. The transfer of arms and defense-related funds became a constant component of international assistance programs. Cold War defense expenditures influenced economic cycles and, in some countries, stimulated the growth of investments, incomes, and employment.

The Cold War also strengthened the role of national governments in the economy. The need to redistribute the GDP within national economies and the requirements of planning and programming defense-related economic and research activities increased the presence of the modern state bureaucracy. In the context of the global political and ideological confrontation, governments came to recognize the strategic importance of domestic socioeconomic stability. Sustaining international economic stability also became a major strategic goal. Cold War political-economic conditions encouraged the moderation of economic conflict among the main competitors, which operated within an interdependent network within both alliance systems.

The Cold War, however, was only one of the political factors that influenced the global economy in the decades after World War II. The efforts of governments in various countries to boost national competitiveness by adopting protectionist measures, the progress of trade liberalization, and the U.S. withdrawal in the early 1970s from the Bretton Woods commitments all exerted a major influence on the world economy. The asymmetry of economic power and the character of the relations between the developed and the developing countries comprised another important political, and at the same time economic, factor that contributed to the state of the global economy.

The global economic consequences of the end of the Cold War cannot be confined to the impact of the decline in defense expenditures—even though demilitarization, if it is conducted on a large scale, will significantly influence the rate and patterns of sustainable economic growth. In the first place, the political changes that inspired and accompanied the collapse of the Soviet Union and the transformation of the former socialist countries of Europe will have important and long-term economic consequences. Furthermore, in the absence of Cold War conflicts, conditions may improve for the collective management and solution of such problems as environmental degradation, poverty, and debt. It may also become easier to find workable solutions to the many difficult problems of globalization that influence the functioning of the economic system at all levels and in all areas, including income growth and distribution, level of demand, rate of employment, allocation of resources, and the character of global competition and cooperation. We must recognize, however, that progress in these areas will be hard to achieve, given the persistence of deeply entrenched obstacles and the emergence of new difficulties.

Some of these new problems are caused by the fact that changes in the global economic system generally occur within different time cycles than do those in the international political system. Because the global political and economic clocks keep different time, they create significant tensions. For example, when people suddenly enjoy greater political democracy and freedom, their economic expectations change and grow. In most cases, however, political and institutional transformations cannot produce immediate improvements in a nation's economic performance or standard of living. The phenomenon of the "revolution of rising expectations" that has been observed in postcolonial countries has reappeared as a potentially dangerous problem for the states of the former Soviet bloc. Unfulfilled socioeconomic expectations, accompanied by disparities between the economic promises and the actual performance of new systems, may set back the process of political reform.

Another problem caused by the different rates of movement in the political and economic clocks is of a longer-term nature. The progress of those economic processes that generate new linkages among states and that are related to the globalization of capital, science, technology, ownership patterns, and entrepreneurship requires fewer restrictive economic frontiers and larger, freer markets. These economic processes transcend states and intensify their interactions. The political process, however, sustains and may even increase the number of states and the "length" and "height" of protectionist frontiers in an era of more intense competition.

The new interactions between politics and economics in the post–Cold War era will be different in the developing world, where nonmilitary aspects of national security have been more important in the past. In economic terms, the developing countries have remained as insecure as they were during the Cold War. Their abilities to meet the challenge of attaining an acceptable minimum standard of living for their citizens have not improved. They face the same difficulties in expanding and diversifying their production base and in reducing their commodity dependence.

In short, while the end of the Cold War was a milestone in the global political system, it did not have the same impact on the world's economic system. Because the differences between the political and economic phases and trends of development might engender new problems, we must examine the sources of longer-term change in the economic system, where the changes in the different phases are extremely complex and turning points are less apparent than they are in the political system.

Economic Changes in Historical Perspective

In all sciences, the methodological rationale for determining phases and identifying turning points is disputed, depending as it largely does on the subjective selection of factors in spite of the best efforts of scientists to arrive at objective criteria. One of the pioneers of international macroeconomic research, Simon Kuznets, defined an economic epoch as a relatively long period, possessing distinctive characteristics that give it unity and differentiate it from epochs that precede or follow it. Economic epochs, Kuznets added, can be distinguished at various levels of social life and are associated with the interplay between technological and social change. They affect a variety of social units and states, and the different communities within them.[2] Other schools of thought relate phases of development to the introduction or spread of fundamental technical or institutional innovations,[3] or to scientific discoveries of epoch-making significance. Another approach is to examine the primary technoeconomic sectors that typify an era, whether agricultural, industrial, postindustrial (service economy), or hyperindustrial (where services are transformed into mass-produced consumer goods).[4]

Many scholars consider the great shocks of history (wars, economic catastrophes, or major crises) as signals of new phases. Angus Maddison distinguishes four phases of development in the 20th century: the phase of the so-called liberal order from the 1870s to 1913; a period of conflicts and autarchy from 1913 to 1950; the "golden age" from 1950 to 1973; and a period of inflation and slow world economic development, which began with the oil crisis of 1973 and the disintegration of the international financial system. During the golden age, the liberal relations characteristic of the beginning of this century were restored, and, moreover, restored under more favorable conditions than before. Governments undertook programs that encouraged economic growth and sought to sustain full employment at the same time as the financial system was functioning relatively well, the colonial system was dissolving, and the world was becoming, generally speaking, more democratic.[5]

The theory of long waves or cycles, which has disappeared and reappeared in social science analysis for decades, is another framework for studying the historical interrelationship of political and technoeconomic changes.[6] Long cycles are usually discussed around the time of major global changes; discussion ceases once continuity sets in to distinguish a certain era. Debates about long cycles and the beginnings of new phases have become more animated since the early 1970s, particularly under the effects of the international oil crises of the early 1970s and 1980s. Those crises, as well as other developments of the 1970s and 1980s—the sudden break from the golden age of world relations, the slowing of development accompanied by rapid inflation (stagflation), the increase in unemployment—drew the attention of analysts, who set out to seek causal explanations of these phenomena.

Although the theory of long cycles may be attractive to students of historical determinism, because of differences in the causes of phase-particular developments, one cannot identify any precisely recurring cause-and-effect relationships. In fact, the causes and effects referred to in the theory are often confused. For example, innovations appear in different national and global settings under different conditions, but their frequency of occurrence in the various cycles is the consequence of different variables. The phasic characteristics outlined by Christopher Freeman and Carlota Perez are so diverse that little cyclicity can be identified.[7] Nevertheless, Freeman and Perez's criteria are suitable for characterizing various phases in economic and technological history.

While agreeing that different stages of development may be identified for nations and for the global economy, and that well-defined phases may succeed one another within economic epochs, this book interprets the phases of world economic development differently, using five interrelated aspects or features of ongoing economic changes. Those five features, here termed "regulating forces" of the economic system, are as follow:

- *Changes in the conditions and patterns of economic development*, resulting in a deceleration and growing diversity of economic growth, increasing unemployment, and structural problems and imbalances. These changes were the consequences of a number of factors, including demographic trends, a slower and unequal increase in demand linked with major shifts in national and global income distribution, debt problems, the difficulties faced by countries in managing technological and structural changes, the collapse of the commodity markets, and the crises in Central and Eastern Europe and the Soviet Union. Changes in national economic priorities (notably, declining defense expenditures), economic philosophies, and macroeconomic policies—characterized as the "new market revolution"—have also played an important role. The changing goals and instruments of macroeconomic management have transformed the economic role of governments in the growth process. In many countries, the government's role has become more indirect and less relevant to key economic and social problems.

- *The transformation of international political and economic power relations* as a consequence of the erosion of U.S. hegemony, the disintegration of the Soviet Union, and the emergence of new global and regional power centers. These changes have resulted in major shifts in global competition and upgraded the role of factors that determine or influence the competitive position (the market power) of countries in the new era, such as a nation's innovative capacities and technological capabilities, the flexibility of its institutions to respond to change, and the quality of its labor force.
- *New scientific and technological developments*, which have resulted in the transformation of the technological foundations of the world economy. At the center of the transformation is the transition to production and services based on information systems, the spread of biotechnology (based on the achievements of the biological revolution), and the use of new materials and energy sources.
- *The evolving relationship between global economic development and the environment.* The otherwise adaptable ecosystem has been approaching the limits of its life-sustaining capabilities, at least in certain areas, because of the impact of such global effects as a thinning ozone layer, pollution of air and water, and global warming. This accelerating degradation of the ecological system jeopardizes the future of development.
- *Changes in the needs, character, and conditions of international economic cooperation* caused by the intensification of globalization and the interdependence of states, the establishment of regional integration groups, the radical increase in the importance of international capital movements, the integration of capital markets, and the emergence of global problems. Transnational corporations (and forms of cooperation) play a particularly important role in this process.

Each of these regulating forces has political, economic, and social components and combined and cumulative effects. These forces determine the character and scope of changes and the emerging opportunities and problems in the global economy.[8] Although the role of the regulating forces is analyzed in this book in the context of the economic transformation currently under way, on the basis of their past cumulative effects one can identify three phases since the end of World War I: the period between the two world wars; the post–World War II phase, which ended by the 1970s; and the new phase, which has been evolving since the 1970s.

Critical Questions

The five regulating forces are analyzed here not with the theoretical aim of identifying phases, but rather with the intention of finding answers to a number of crucial questions concerning the future of the world economy.

1. What will be the most direct international economic consequences of political changes (from the viewpoint of economic interests, growth potentials and dynamics, microactors and macroactors, and the integration of the transforming states into the global economy)?

2. To what extent are the dominating policy models relevant in the new era, especially with respect to changing patterns of demand for labor, problems of national and international inequalities, the creation and utilization of economic opportunities, and the strengthening of international cooperation?

3. How could the growth rates of global economic development be increased in the new phase and the development process sustained to better satisfy global needs within a reasonable period of time?

4. What are, and what will become, the sources and consequences of major international economic conflict that will threaten to disrupt markets and cooperation regimes?

5. Is a more coordinated process of global economic development feasible or even desirable for achieving a harmony of interests and mechanisms for international economic conflict management in the late 20th century? Is the market a more efficient instrument for this, or is the best method a combination of both the market and global coordination? On which level (regional or global) can competing countries become more predictable, rational, and cooperative international economic partners in a multilateral framework?

6. Could the search for economic security at national, regional, and global levels become the source of collective initiatives to

improve the functioning of the world economy and the efficiency of international cooperation and to facilitate the use of existing and future multilateral organizations and informal structures to guard against major human and environmental crises and catastrophes? Could it produce rational, responsible, and predictable national economic policies?

The search for answers to these questions will help us not only to understand the new opportunities and risks that governments, businesses, and international organizations face, but also to recognize the needs and possibilities of collective risk management in the new era. Global political stability will depend largely on the collective capacity of the international community to cope with existing and future economic problems.

chapter 13

Changing Regional and Global Conditions of Economic Growth

Trends in Global Economic Performance

The experiences of the post–World War II period proved that a system of sustained and widespread growth in demand and output is a fundamental condition for the maintenance of a high level of employment, the satisfaction of social needs, the alleviation of poverty, and the solution of the major problems facing the world economy. In a slow-growing or stagnating economy it is highly likely that the many opportunities offered by the end of the Cold War and the global wave of democratization will go unrealized. But how realistic is the possibility of reviving economic growth and sustaining the development process in the coming 10 to 15 years?

There are actually two important questions here: One, can the economic growth potential of the world be improved in the coming decades without major policy changes and institutional reforms? Two, which countries and sectors may be the engines of such growth? Neither of these questions can be answered without understanding the primary driving forces and consequences of quantitative and qualitative changes that have occurred since the 1970s, which marked the end of the postwar phase in the international economic system.

In recent decades, fundamental spatial and structural changes have occurred in the world economy. The developed industrial countries have built up highly productive and increasingly knowledge-based economies with new high-tech industrial sectors and a large, rapidly expanding modern service sector that responds to changing needs. Radical changes have characterized the life-style and consumption patterns of the population of the developed countries. Elsewhere in the world, new industrial regions have been created in areas that earlier had depended on imports to meet their demands for manufactured goods. The development of industry and the establishment of these new industrial regions have increased demand for capital goods, materials, and technologies. The growth of output in these regions has corresponded to the opening of new markets. The ratio of trade to GDP has increased in almost all countries. Financial markets have expanded very rapidly.

The faster global spread of new technologies on which a widespread industrial development has been based has both required and promoted a transformation of transportation and communication services. The communications infrastructure has been massively expanded; many harbors, railways, and roads have been constructed; and an air transport system now spans the globe. This transformation has also reduced transportation and communication costs. Industrial development has facilitated the global reach of transnational corporations, while intensifying international competition. By the mid-1990s, a global "information superhighway" has been created, with profound effects on the functioning of the international system.

Although the share of agricultural production has decreased in all countries, agriculture continues to be of worldwide importance as a source not only of food supplies but also of income, export earnings, and taxes—especially in the developing countries. In the developed countries, significant labor and capital reallocation has occurred from the traditional light and heavy industries to the high-tech and modern service sectors. Reallocation of resources has been both a condition and a consequence of the information revolution.

As a result of economic restructuring, new production and service blocs (in microelectronics and biotechnology, for example) have appeared as growth sectors, and their role in the global economy has increased steadily. A "material revolution" has resulted in better alloys and compounds and in new synthetics. One outcome of this revolution has been the decline of energy and material needs per output unit. Structural changes have been accompanied by major changes in the map of global production, with a few developing countries increasing their production and international competitiveness significantly not only in the global output of various traditional industries (textiles, iron, and steel), but also in a number of high-tech industries (computers and consumer electronics, for example).

The major spatial and structural transformation in the world economy during the past 30 to 40 years has been accompanied by the growth of production, incomes, and consumption on a global scale. According to UN estimates the value of the world's gross product (total goods and services) in 1990 at current prices amounted to $22,400 billion. This represented an increase of about 300 percent in the volume of the global product since 1950. In per capita terms, the global output was slightly above $4,000.[9]

While there has been a converging trend in the technological levels and economic performances of the major industrial countries of the three economic poles of the system (North America, Western Europe, and Japan), enormous disparities have developed among the economic performances of different parts of the world. The average per capita product of industrial countries in 1990 was more than 14 times higher than that of developing countries. The gap has grown larger not only between the developed and the developing countries but also among developing countries.

With their improved production capacities, income levels, and economic structures, some of the newly industrialized countries (NICs) or territories such as South Korea, Singapore, and Taiwan have graduated into the higher middle-income category, while others such as Malaysia have reached its frontiers. At the same time, some countries have been downgraded in the world market-place. Since the 1970s, gaps in the levels of technology and productivity and in standards of living have grown significantly, especially with respect to the former Soviet Union and Central and Eastern Europe. By and large, these nations have remained outside the international technological-industrial and service revolutions (the chief exception is in the military sector) and have not participated in the transnationalization process that adjusts products, production processes, and management practices. Similarly, most of the developing countries, especially those dependent on the production and export of raw materials, have been marginalized by world market forces.

Although overall global production has increased substantially since World War II, the rate of economic growth has been decelerating for the past 30 years. In the 1960s, global output expanded by over 50 percent; in the 1970s, the figure fell to 45 percent; and in the 1980s, output expanded by only 30 percent. This slowing of growth is of even greater magnitude when per capita global production is considered. The annual average growth of per capita global production was 3.2 percent in the 1960s, 1.9 percent in the 1970s, and 1.3 percent in the 1980s. During the 1980s, per capita GDP actually declined in Latin America, Africa, and the Middle East.

As indicated by table 1, the inequalities among the main regions of the world in per capita income has increased. The decline in per capita income affected 1.2 billion people during the 1980s, or about 23 percent of the world's population. After stagnating in the 1980s, per capita income growth in the Soviet Union and in Central and Eastern Europe has also declined, adding another 360 million people to this crisis-ridden group.[10] At the same time, parts of Asia, especially East and Southeast Asia, experienced a relatively large growth of per capita GDP. Although per capita income growth has slowed in many industrial countries, it has still permitted the maintenance of a high standard of living. Personal expectations concerning living standards and the satisfaction of social needs have also remained high despite the deteriorating economic performance of most parts of the industrial world.

As these changes indicate, the international economic system has become increasingly polarized. Indeed, some experts characterized the situation at the end of the 1980s as a "two-track" global economy.[11]

By the end of the 1980s, the competitive positions of countries and the character of changes in the global economy were determined by a few key industries and services that are in the forefront of technological development. These industries have

Table 1. Percentage of Average Per Capita GDP of the
Developed Industrial Countries

	1960	1990
Developed Industrial Countries	100	100
Central and Eastern Europe, USSR	27	26
Developing Countries	10	7
Latin America	26	16
Africa	9	5
South and East Asia	4	5
West Asia	25	22

Note: In 1993, the International Monetary Fund recalculated global GDP data for 1990 based on purchasing-power parities rather than market exchange rates. By this calculation, the per capita GDP in the developing countries would be close to 18 percent of that in the developed industrial world. Although calculations based on purchasing-power parities better express consumption-level differences, it would be misleading (because of the uncertain foundations of those calculations and the qualitative differences in goods consumed) to use those figures to compare the global-market performance of the countries.

Sources: United Nations, *Overall Perspectives of the World Economy* (New York: United Nations, 1990); and *World Economic Survey, 1990* (New York: United Nations, 1990). The data for Central and Eastern Europe were recalculated from net material product statistics obtained from the United Nations Economic Commission for Europe.

concentrated in a small number of countries, which thus possess the bulk of global R&D capacities and play a crucial role in global output, trade, and capital flows. At the end of the 1980s, for instance, 12 industrial countries produced about 80 percent of world product. Differences in the rates of development over the last 90 years among leading industrial countries are shown in table 2.

The key countries of the global economy, which in many ways determine the character and scope of technological changes, the directions of structural shifts, and the functioning of the markets for knowledge, technology, and capital, are also the main sources of revitalization and sustainability of economic growth. The spillover and global demonstration effects of their economic policies are also crucially important in influencing trade and development patterns.

Table 2. Average Annual Growth Rates

	1950–1980	1900–1990	1980s
Japan	7.1	4.2	4.2
China	6.5	2.9	10.4
Brazil	6.0	4.8	1.9
Germany	4.4	2.8	2.7
Italy	4.4	2.8	2.3
Canada	4.3	4.1	3.3
Australia	4.0	3.1	3.2
France	4.0	2.4	2.1
USSR (Russia)	3.9	3.3	1.0
India	3.8	2.1	6.0
United States	3.2	3.2	3.0
Great Britain	2.5	1.8	2.7

Source: Angus Maddison, *The World Economy of the 20th Century* (Paris: OECD Development Centre, 1989).

Structural and Systemic Determinants of the Economic Changes

The global growth process is necessarily uneven. Figures showing the deceleration of economic growth on the global level are averages that reflect the deteriorating conditions of economic development in general but mask growth in particular areas. Problems are by no means identical in all parts or sectors of the world economy. The simultaneous presence of overproduction and starvation, and of increased production and declining incomes, reflects a long-lasting structural crisis in the global agricultural sector. (Agricultural protectionism in most of the industrial countries has been both a cause and a consequence of this crisis.) The global raw material and fuel economy also faces significant and lasting structural problems caused by rapid technological changes and major shifts in demand. These problems generate considerable uncertainties, major fluctuations, and a decline in prices and producers' incomes. Manufacturing industries are likewise experiencing structural problems caused by rapidly growing new productive capacities, improved competitiveness in many semideveloped countries, sluggish demand, and the persistence of managed trade in important sectors of the industrialized countries.

In the mid-1990s, all these changes must be understood in relation to the ongoing structural transformation of the global economic system caused by the transition to knowledge-based economic activities and the emergence of Asia as a new growth center in the world economy, and to the capabilities of countries to manage the socioeconomic consequences of the changes. These latter capabilities are determined by country- and region-specific economic-institutional factors shaping the leading systemic models. Some systems or models concerning resource allocation and adjustment have proved more efficient within a dynamic technological, socioeconomic, and competitive environment than have others. Although the leading models have converged since the 1970s (as illustrated, for instance, in the progress of deregulation and the privatization of the public sector in many different parts of the world), the various models have retained many of their specific characteristics.[12]

The character of any country-specific economic systemic model is largely determined by the structure of ownership—specifically, by the degree and patterns of state and private ownership, the diffusion of ownership and nationalization of productive assets, and the relationship between ownership and control of property. Another important determinant of systemic models is the character of motivation—what types of incentives, societal norms, and corporate or state goals encourage more efficient performance and greater competitiveness? Three other key systemic factors are the source of information available to the main economic actors (whether they receive their information directly from observing and testing the market or from central directives issued by governments or other hierarchies); the role of information networks, which connect economic actors horizontally and vertically;[13] and the quality of institutions, which is a reflection of management and governance cultures.

In the post–World War II era, three main economic-institutional models—the American regulated free market model, the European social market model, and the Japanese coordinative corporate model—have emerged, each representing specific patterns of development with differences in innovative capacities, resource allocation, production and consumption patterns, international competitiveness, and attitudes toward globalization and interdependence. These models were not rationally conceived in advance of events; rather, they evolved as events unfolded, social learning progressed, innovations appeared, and the international demonstration effect exerted its influence. Social and economic theories like Keynesianism and liberalism also helped to shape the models. Although the interconnectedness of national economies has engendered similarities in organizational forms and policies, national historical, cultural, social, and institutional environments have markedly influenced the development and performance of these economic models.[14] Understanding these differences, as well as the dynamics, strengths, and weaknesses of the models and their implications for competition and international cooperation, is a key requirement of more successful international risk management, policy coordination, and reform in international organizations and regimes.

The American Regulated Free Market Model

The American pluralistic market economy model has greatly influenced the global economy because of the significant power of the United States. Although this model has undergone several changes, it still retains some of its fundamental characteristics: a more limited role for the state in the economy than the state is permitted in other industrial countries; a foundation in risk-taking and flexible entrepreneurship; a symbiosis of small, medium, and large firms; the simultaneous protection of competition and competitors; a sophisticated and competitive money market; a profit-oriented business perspective; and a mass-consumption orientation (by the end of the 1980s, the United States was ahead of Western Europe and Japan by about 40 percent in per capita consumption, although close to Western Europe and behind Japan in per capita investments).

Several nonsystemic factors account for U.S. economic power and dynamism. One is the size of the U.S. economy, which remains the largest concentration of wealth in the world, with 23 to 25 percent of global gross national product. It is also the largest single market in the world, made extremely diverse by the large number of actors, income groups, and tastes. Another source of U.S. power is the critical mass of U.S. R&D resources in science and technology, coupled with the largest venture capital market in the world. This "economic opportunity" base has long and successful experience in innovative entrepreneurship and a high degree of competitiveness. U.S financial markets, with all their disincentives in promoting a high level of savings, are very efficient at allocating funds toward higher-yielding uses, especially over the long term. U.S. economic power is also sustained by the ability to adjust to changes in a relatively flexible way because of the mobility of capital and labor and relatively few government regulations influencing resource allocation.

The American model is especially efficient in the presence of strong demand factors generated by growth of income or income redistribution promoted through the federal budget. However, the strong reliance on the market as the main instrument of adjustment (achieved through layoffs and bankruptcies, as well through the maintenance of competition and an entrepreneurial culture) has exposed a large segment of the population to the uncertainties and risks of the marketplace. Although the transnational giants of the U.S. economic system are able to combine long-term technological and development strategies with short-term profit goals, the predominantly short-term view of the less powerful actors has made economic performance increasingly vulnerable in areas where long-term strategies, programs, and commitments are necessary. Other vulnerabilities include long-term adverse changes in savings-investment ratios, the deterioration of the country's physical infrastructure, declining long-term trends in productivity, and the deteriorating quality of the U.S. educational system.

Shifts have occurred in the functioning of the model in the post–World War II decades. The government assumed a larger role after World War II in demand management and regulation,[15] spurring the economy by means of large defense expenditures and creating "built-in stabilizers." In the 1980s, "Reaganomics" represented a move in the opposite direction, bringing deregulation, supply-side economic policies, and tax reductions, but also increasing defense expenditures and the volume of the federal budget, which led to major macroeconomic imbalances.

The problems of the U.S. economy were reflected in the rapid increase of both the internal and the international indebtedness of the United States. By the late 1980s, individual debt accounted for nearly two-thirds of Americans' disposable income, corporate debt was close to 60 percent of business revenues, and government debt was about 190 percent of government revenues. The net U.S. investment position that had secured a $106 billion claim on other countries in 1980 had been converted into a $700 billion foreign investors' claim on the United States by the end of the decade.[16] In this environment, the stability and reliability of the capital market became, and has remained, especially important to the overall stability of the system. The increasing weaknesses of the American model in the new era were made more apparent by the long recession of the early 1990s. Unemployment grew, and a large part of it became structural. Large as well as small firms suffered, many going bankrupt. International challenges increased.

A relatively liberal, market-oriented model with strong profit incentives stimulated the internationalization of the U.S. economy during the past 40 to 50 years. The large U.S. firms became increasingly multinational and their use of foreign investments as an instrument of global sourcing contributed to the redeployment of major U.S. industries abroad. Exports, which represented 5 percent of gross national product (GNP) in 1950, rose to account for about 12 percent of GNP by the end of the 1980s.[17] Between 1950 and 1970, U.S. imports of goods and services increased from 4.2 percent of GNP to 6 percent. By the end of the 1980s, imports accounted for approximately 13 percent of GNP. Import penetration in manufacturing as a percentage of apparent consumption rose from 5.5 percent in the mid-1970s to above 13 percent by the late 1980s.[18] Although all categories of consumption saw greater import penetration, it was most pronounced in automobiles, consumer electronics, textiles, and shoes.

The "double deficit" (that is, both domestic and external) turned into large internal and external debts, which grew to total $4,000 billion by the end of 1992. This process was accompanied by increasing instability in the U.S. banking system in the 1980s. Yet, the performance of the U.S. economy was strong enough to secure a lead of about 30 percent over West European countries in per capita GNP in 1992. In purchasing-power parity dollars, the U.S. per capita GDP ranked first in the world, 8 percent above Canada, 25 percent above Japan, and 35 percent above Germany.[19]

However, the U.S. global position has been declining in key areas of the world market. The erosion of U.S. leadership has been especially painful in certain high-tech branches, since the United States is still first in R&D globally. The U.S. share of the international market for high-tech industries declined from 30 percent between 1970 and 1973 to 21 percent between 1988 and 1989. At the end of the 1980s, the United States had positive trade balances in only two high-tech areas, aerospace and computers, and both of those industries were experiencing relative declines. There are indications, however, of some improvement in the early 1990s.[20]

The interconnectedness of the U.S. capital and technology markets with global markets has increased rapidly. Earlier facilitated by the postwar Bretton Woods system, U.S. involvement has since grown because of the important role played by U.S. transnational corporations in international investments, an expansion in the operations of the large U.S. commercial banks in the main financial centers of the world, and a substantial increase in the U.S. import of capital during the 1980s, when the United States borrowed heavily abroad.

Although U.S. trade policy has been in general more liberal than the policies of other actors in the global economy, the United States has maintained a number of protectionist measures against its competitors. U.S. trade policy has been excessively short term in orientation and has seldom been related to longer-term policy goals. Furthermore, the U.S. constitution gives Congress responsibility in trade policy matters. The detailed elaboration of legislation covering trade and investment is a slow and tortuous procedure at the best of times, and is ill suited to an era of rapid changes that require fast and flexible responses. For instance, the 1988 Omnibus Trade and Competitiveness Act, a 1,128-page document, took three years to complete and is remarkably wide-ranging. The debate over the North American Free Trade Agreement (NAFTA) has offered further evidence of the procedural difficulties that confront the framers of U.S. policy.

The insistence on reciprocity from trading partners that receive policy concessions has been a traditional element of U.S. policy. The pursuit of "effective reciprocity" has been characterized by some non-American experts as "aggressive unilateralism," whereby the U.S. government seeks to determine the fairness or unfairness of another country's trade policy. While the United States is still an advocate of an open international trade policy within a multilateral framework, it also seeks increasingly to manage its economic relations with other countries on a bilateral basis. By 1991, the United States had 3,600 product quotas; some of the tariffs it imposed on imported goods ran as high as 458 percent.[21]

With global competition intensifying and NAFTA ratified, international trade issues may become increasingly politicized in the United States. Caught between domestic protectionist pressures and international calls for more open markets, the position of the Clinton administration seems certain to grow more difficult.

The increased interconnectedness of the U.S. economy with the rest of the world has two very significant consequences. First, the international effects of U.S. domestic problems and policies are stronger than in the past. This is particularly important in capital markets, where past experience proved that large-scale U.S. borrowing, through the medium of the interest-rate mechanism, increased the debt-servicing burdens borne by many countries. Other countries were "crowded out" of the investment market, being unable to compete with the attractive profit opportunities offered by the United States. Second, some of the main traditional partners of the United States, like Japan, are searching for ways to reduce their dependence on the U.S. market or for instruments to enhance their competitive presence in the United States.

The policies of the Clinton administration represent another shift in the functioning of the U.S. model. The 1990s will be a period of national economic adjustment for the United States. Making that adjustment in the face of inevitable domestic political opposition and numerous domestic economic difficulties will not be easy. Increasing investment in such areas as new technology, manufacturing, and education requires an increase in domestic savings. This, in turn, may require a further reduction in defense expenditures and, over the long run, a modification of the spending habits of the U.S. population. U.S. citizens, however, have become less tolerant of government actions (such as the imposition of higher taxes) that affect their quality of life.

If the U.S. market mechanism is to function efficiently in the new domestic and international environment, the deficiencies of that mechanism will have to be corrected by government involvement in areas like education, health care, and the provision of employment opportunities. Support seems to be growing in the United States for greater government investment in physical infrastructure, education, and sciences, and even for further regulation of banking and industry.

With growing competition for international markets and capital, the United States has strong incentives to establish a more secure and larger market by encouraging regional integration in North America—and subsequently in other parts of the hemisphere. NAFTA is an important step in that direction. It remains to be seen if NAFTA will become an economic bloc or a loosely knit free trade area. This will depend on the impact of NAFTA on the levels of output, trade, employment, and income of the United States, Canada, and Mexico, and on the character of competition with other economic blocs. Conceivably, NAFTA could become an instrument of new trade wars

The Social Market Economy in an Integrated Europe

The West European economy model can be characterized in the mid-1990s as a variant of a social market economy combined with the remnants of the post–World War II welfare state. In some countries, like the Benelux nations and France, the model has preserved many elements of the welfare state. In other countries, and especially in Germany, the model has become a corporate version of the social market economy, which combines the advantages in efficiency of decentralized economic guidance with the benefits of central corrective mechanisms for dealing with market failures.

This model has been shaped by a number of international and regional factors: the division of Europe; the strategic interest of the United States in the reconstruction and stability of Western Europe; the establishment of the EC; and the influence of competitive market forces. Among the internal regional factors, the European political tradition of representative democracy, which presupposes intensive interactions between social groups and the state in a delicate and pragmatic balance of market forces and state interests, has formed the model's socioeconomic framework. Within the social market economy model, certain countries have proved to be efficient in maintaining or restoring macroeconomic and sociopolitical equilibrium, and also in coordinating policies on a national scale in such areas as savings and investments, research and education, and improvements in the quality of government. Other countries, faced with a more difficult domestic political balance, have experienced less success. The corporatist version of the social market economy has placed particularly heavy demands on the ability to sustain a balance of interests among entrepreneurs, trade unions, and government bureaucracies.

In the post–World War II period, the European model better protected firms and citizens from the major shocks of structural adjustments than did the American model, but in doing so the European economic system acquired much inertia as interest groups sought to protect the positions they had obtained. The power of the central governments increased because the concept of a social market assumed governmental responsibility for the correction of market deficiencies and imperfections and the provision of various public services. Such services were uniquely interpreted and implemented by each country. The majority of West European countries continued to maintain a relatively extensive level of state intervention even though, in many cases, the state-owned firms that had earlier dominated the economy were privatized.

In their external economic relations, West European countries—dependent on external supplies of raw materials, fuel, technology, and capital, and facing increasing global competition—have had to accept the realities of competitive interdependence. Their response to the conflict between the globalization process and the constraints created by national political and economic boundaries has been international economic integration, the most notable results of which are the cooperation regimes of the EC and the European Free Trade Association (EFTA), which, on January 1, 1994, combined to form the European Economic Area, a new free trade regime in Europe that facilitates the free movement of goods, services, capital, and people.[22]

The EC has formed the core of the integration process. Because of limited national markets, members of the community searched for options that went beyond the concept of a traditional customs union. The development of the EC has involved harmonizing national policies, liberalizing the flow of goods and people, and building institutions—all of which have bolstered cohesive regional forces. The supernational structures of the community have become important in managing the problems of the region and in elaborating plans and programs that accommodate national perspectives in the integration process.

European integration has contributed to the economic development of countries through its trade-creating and trade-diverting effects. Trade among EC countries has increased more rapidly than has trade with countries outside the community. Integration has also created greater markets that allow for a more rational allocation of resources and greater economies of scale. The proportion of the total trade of the EC member states that is conducted with other EC countries grew from 55 percent in 1980 to 62 percent in 1990. During the 1970s and the 1980s, all the countries of Western Europe went through a difficult period marked by the two explosions in the price of oil, high raw material prices in the early 1970s, rigidity of the labor market, and increasing international competition. Europe's response was to establish a single market that would function as the largest market in the world. Six percent of the world's population lives in EC member countries. Their combined share of global output (on the basis of GDP) in 1990 was 23 percent, and close to 40 percent in global merchandise exports and imports. Twenty-five percent of global trade occurs within the community—accounting for about 60 percent of the total trade of its members. The EC has certainly become the most introverted region of the world in terms of trade patterns.[23]

The single market represents a liberal economic approach that allows for the mobility of market forces within the community, including the free flow of capital, commodities, services, and people. The smooth functioning of the single market, even when all member countries finally implement the domestic measures necessary for its full introduction, will not be easily achieved, however, given such problems as the high level of structural unemployment, increasing competition in slow-growing markets, the specific interests of agricultural producers, difficulties in sustaining domestic social balances, and differences of interests in further progress toward monetary union.

When the community was founded in 1958 by France, Germany, Italy, and the Benelux countries, shared interests rooted in the Cold War division of Europe facilitated compromises and made it relatively easy to reformulate the specific interests of each member state and to link those interests to the common goals of creating larger markets, harmonizing national interests and policies, and establishing common instruments for protection against the rest of the world. In the early 1990s, the reformulation and harmonization of interests and policies is more difficult to accomplish.

On a microeconomic level, the single European market will promote major structural changes in terms of mergers of firms, rationalization, and reorganization. There will be more competition, especially in the financial market, which, however, may result in more efficient resource allocation. Important gains can be expected from economies of scale. A key issue is macroeconomic management. Progress toward economic and monetary union, including a single currency, implies the increasing convergence of macroeconomic policies, fixed exchange rates, and ceilings on budgetary deficits. These changes will impose new requirements on member states, including the need to coordinate their monetary policies. In fact, almost all of the institutions of the EC will have to be redesigned.

An economically integrated Europe will inevitably face problems concerning national priorities and institutional and policy differences. For instance, one of the most difficult aspects of the integration process will be implementing the concept of a "Social Europe." The main social security structure that has been sustained by political forces in one form or another in many parts of Europe is the welfare state, which is based on the principle of compensating the disadvantaged section of the population. However, the welfare state can only function effectively within national boundaries, where it is safeguarded by the domestic balance of social forces. It is, in fact, an anti-international system. Social legislation enacted by governments as a means of securing support from their electorates and sustaining political stability effectively places upper limits on comparative labor costs and thus hampers the creation of a competitive Europewide labor market. If national welfare systems are to be prevented from harming competitiveness by being Europeanized, then answers must be found to such practical questions as which country should set the norms of a Europewide social market system and according to which sociopolitical-economic structures.

Progress in establishing the single market is bringing other problems to the surface. The enlargement of the EC has created important new regional disparities in terms of income, employment, productivity, and infrastructure. The practical responses of member countries to measures contained in the single market program will depend on their regional competitiveness. The increased flow of goods and people and the intensification of communication will place new demands on the establishment of regional, national, and European infrastructural networks. The physical space of Europe, presently managed primarily nationalistically, will have to be reorganized; this will be an enormous undertaking. Another area where changes will have to occur is in the labor market, where the present regional and sectoral rigidity of wages is increasingly incompatible with the idea of a single market.

Plans that go beyond the single market—that are, in fact, the logical consequences of a unified market—include the creation of a European Monetary Union with a single currency and a European Central Bank to determine European monetary policy and the achievement of political union. Progress toward political union will encounter many obstacles, most of them related to the differing interests within and among member states regarding the extent of national political independence from centralized institutions in matters such as fiscal policy.

The EC will also have to face the potentially serious conflicts caused by progress toward supranationality in monetary matters. The reformulation of national political-economic interests of member states as they respond to such developments as the unification of Germany or the expansion of the community's membership may give rise to new problems. The EC will have to take into account the implications of the association and membership of the emergent democracies and market economies of Central and Eastern Europe and the former Soviet Union. Moreover, there is also the challenge of immigration from Eastern Europe, the South Mediterranean, North Africa, and other parts of the developing world with which Europe has historical ties and on which it depends for much of its raw materials. All these problems will have to be managed in the context of an increasingly competitive world.

In such an environment, strengthening the cohesive forces of the community will depend on its ability to improve the competitive position of member states—especially in high-tech sectors—and to establish a sound social and environmental base for sustaining economic growth in the region.

Nonetheless, the opportunities offered by successful progress toward a more integrated Europe centered around the EC are promising—more promising, to be sure, than the possibilities of European states enhancing their competitiveness through unilateral measures. A region with a population of more than 500 million (excluding the successor states of the Soviet Union), a combined GNP in excess of $6,000 billion, and a large scientific research potential can become a major global center of growth in the 21st century. However, Europe must take care to avoid seeing itself as a closed fortress. Most of the major European countries have deeply vested interests in international openness (including a well-functioning system of international economic cooperation) because of their dependence on the rest of the world for raw materials and markets. Under these circumstances, rather than progressing in the direction of a "Fortress Europe" inspired by neomercantilism or regional autarchy, the countries of the region are likely to develop politically and economically into an increasingly cohesive economic bloc, one that remains relatively open and decentralized.

The Coordinative Corporate Model of Japan

From the perspective of economic growth and the expansion of economic power, Japan has been the most successful industrial country of the post–World War II period. Japan's share of global output grew from less than 1 percent in 1950 to above 12 percent in 1990. In world exports, Japanese output grew from almost zero to about 10 percent during the same period. This was accompanied by a tenfold increase in Japan's per capita GDP. In 1990, on the Human Development Index (which ranks countries according to their citizens' life expectancy, adult literacy rate, mean years of schooling, educational attainment, and per capita GDP) Japan was the highest among the 160 countries indexed. The United States occupied seventh place and Germany, fourteenth.[24]

The Japanese coordinative corporate economy model, with its system of administrative guidance and industrial cooperation, has several important characteristics, some of recent origin, others rooted in Japan's history. The historical element is especially influential in the development of high standards of education, a strong work ethic, and a diligent labor force. The emphasis placed on long-term development in the Japanese model has been widely recognized as another key element of Japan's success. The Japanese have long understood that the dynamism of a market economy in a world of strong competitors is not created by textbook competition between many independent producers, but by the application of the most up-to-date technology by firms wielding extremely strong market power. To the government and nongovernmental actors of Japan, modern competition is a prolonged, comprehensive battle in which education, technical development, resource accumulation, competitive pricing, quality manufacturing, and market-penetration strategies are all important weapons. (A similar outlook has also inspired the economic success of the Asian NICs, especially South Korea.)

This perspective has been manifested in Japan's approach to many issues influencing economic development and social change, such as education, technology, and production. Measures taken in these areas have reduced ecological and external economic vulnerability and enabled the industrial restructuring of industry through the redeployment of some productive phases to East Asia and through trade-related direct investments in the United States, Europe, and elsewhere. The long-term approach has facilitated the strategic integration of cooperation and competition among firms, which have established special relationships to share risk, access capital and technology, and avoid "excessive" competition. Another advantage of the corporate model is its multidimensional cooperative approach that unites the government and the business sector on all-important issues so that each can rely on the other in global competition and in the realization of national goals. The flexible coordination of macroeconomic and microeconomic policies is facilitated by a system of constant consultations through different committees and other groups centered around the Ministry of International Trade and Industry with the aim of achieving consensus on a wide range of industrial and trade policy issues.

An historically rooted component of the Japanese model is corporate loyalty. Cohesion between employers and employees is
also fostered through guaranteed lifetime employment (an innovation of the 1950s intended to quell labor unrest), as well as
through other management instruments, such as the use of both
material and nonmaterial incentives and the maintenance of a
respected seniority system. Unemployment in Japan has remained
the lowest among major industrial countries. Even during the
deepest recession of the post–Cold War period in the early 1990s,
only 2.8 percent of the Japanese labor force was unemployed.

For more than a millennium, Japanese society has been oriented toward absorbing, digesting, and reproducing foreign learning and new technology. After the Meiji restoration in 1868,
strenuous efforts were made to create a modern industrial society,
including the encouragement of very high levels of savings and
investments. These efforts were intensified after World War II,
and achieved remarkable success. For example, during the 1980s
gross domestic investments amounted to about one-third of GDP,
and gross domestic savings to about 34 percent. The proportion
of private savings was 25 percent of GDP. Gross domestic investments in Japan during the same decade were roughly one-third
larger than the average for the entire industrial world. From the
end of World War II, Japan took advantage of the favorable
global situation and the support of the United States to develop
an export-oriented policy and exploited all its human, technological, and institutional advantages in adjusting to the changing
international economy.[25]

A frequently cited factor in the Japanese success story is
Japan's limit on defense expenditures (1 percent of GDP). While
Japanese industry has become a major supplier of technologies—
such as microchips and sensors—needed by other countries for
their sophisticated weapons systems, and while Japan has a modern, high-tech army, its military spending has remained relatively
low compared to that of the United States, Great Britain, France,
and Germany. Furthermore, Japan has profited from the growth
of defense expenditures in other countries through its sales of
strategic items and the exploitation of the military R&D achievements of other countries by Japanese civilian industry.

The Japanese capital market has stimulated a high rate of
savings and provided major sources of financing for economic

growth and structural changes, as well as for foreign investments and loans. However, the capital market has helped to create a "bubble economy"—an economy created from inflated gains in real estate, stock price increases, and large bank lending operations not necessarily supported by corresponding growth of output and productivity in the real economy.[26] The bursting of this bubble contributed to recession in Japan in the early 1990s and initiated a process of structural changes in Japan's domestic capital market and financial operations abroad.

The Japanese model and similar economic systems that concentrate on increasing domestic economic power and international competitiveness have often been judged against the paradigms of globalization and interdependence and have been pronounced neomercantilist by some experts. Japan has been criticized for protectionist tendencies that have resulted in a considerable trade surplus (the cumulative surplus amounted to about $600 billion in the 1980s). This trade surplus has been a source of serious international imbalances, reflecting the structural deficiencies of the trading system.

Since World War II, the Japanese economy has become internationalized in a different way than have the economies of the other major industrial countries. Japan, of course, has remained dependent on the export of primary products, but to a declining degree. By the late 1980s, Japan's share of world imports was only around 6 percent, and import penetration in manufacturing in Japan was a mere 7 percent, compared to 30 percent in Germany and about 12 percent in the United States. Even after the Tokyo Round of the General Agreement on Tariffs and Trade (GATT), Japanese tariff rates remained very high in each product group: 9.7 percent in food products, more than twice that of the United States (4.1 percent) and the EC (3.7 percent); and 11.9 percent for manufactured goods, again more than double that of the United States (4.2 percent) and higher than that of the EC (10.2 percent).[27] The issue of openness in the Japanese economy will remain a major source of friction between the main industrial powers and a key problem area in the international trading system.[28]

The internationalization of the Japanese economy has been taking place through export orientation and foreign direct investments. Some of those investments have been related to the international marketing strategies of the large Japanese corporations. In the automobile and machine-building industries, Japan's share of the world market climbed to between 22 and 23 percent in the early 1990s, but the share of exports in Japan's GDP remained relatively stable at around 10 to 11 percent. Private direct investments of large Japanese firms increased threefold (in terms of yen) during the 1980s, and by the late 1980s foreign production by Japanese firms accounted for 6 percent of Japan's domestic production. Although this percentage was low in comparison with the United States (25 percent) and Germany (17 percent), Japan is eager to increase the rate of foreign production to around 20 percent of its domestic output by the end of the first decade of the 21st century.[29] Japanese direct investments are highly concentrated in Asia. Many Japanese firms would like to redeploy all labor-intensive production to Asian countries that offer cheap labor (and expanding markets), concentrating domestic production on value-added goods.

Although not all host countries greet this expanding Japanese involvement in Asia with enthusiasm, partly because of their unhappy memories of Japanese imperial adventures earlier this century, other countries welcome it as a source of technology, employment, and trade opportunities.

Japan has already become the leading integrating power in the region, having done so without any formal commitment to regional integration. Japan's trade with Asian countries has increased rapidly, doubling between 1982 and 1992 and surpassing its trade with the United States in 1989. The yen has become the key currency among Asian countries in financial transactions, and is an important reserve currency. Japanese private direct investments are growing and are rapidly creating new technological and trade ties. By 1990, Japan had invested about $25 billion in Asia, twice as much as the United States. As columnist David Sanger has observed, "Piece by piece corporate Japan has created a startling replica of itself, not only in look and feel but also in culture."[30]

Among the overseas subsidiaries of Japanese firms (which numbered close to 7,000 in 1989), about 2,500 are located in East Asia, together employing about 600,000 people. Japan has transformed a large part of Asia into its own industrial and trade backyard, and has done so through a unique form of partnership that takes into account diversity in the stages of development and in market practices. Thus, the subsidiaries of Japanese firms in Taiwan, South Korea, and Singapore produce high-tech and knowledge-intensive goods; in countries such as Thailand and Malaysia, they manufacture labor-intensive and intermediate products; and in Indonesia and the Philippines, where labor is cheap and abundant, they concentrate on the traditional sectors of manufacturing. Japan is showing increasing interest in Indochina and its relatively skilled, disciplined, and low-cost labor force. In China, where Japanese direct investments have risen especially rapidly, Japan is represented at all technological levels.

This diversified approach is profitable to Japan's partners in the region. Diversification has been fueling a high rate of growth in Asian countries where the political and business leadership has, in many cases, patterned its economic development after the Japanese practice of jointly targeting and financing strategic industries. At the same time, Japanese experts are anticipating the formation of a loosely structured and open region in Asia that would attract new investments from leading industrial countries and ultimately would become the largest global production and export base for goods of mass consumption.[31]

Despite its formidable strengths, however, the Japanese model also contains a number of weaknesses. Japan's dependence on foreign markets and external resources is a constant source of vulnerability. Japan may reduce its dependence on U.S. and European markets in the future, but Japan can only partly compensate for such reductions by an increase in intra-Asian trade. Within the GATT trade negotiations, external pressures on Japan to open its markets to imports are a key issue. The character of hierarchical (vertical) relations in the Japanese system could become an impediment to technological progress, which requires horizontal relations among different firms and other economic actors. The North American and West European mass-consumption societies are increasingly influencing the consumption patterns of the Japanese middle class and undermining support for such key elements of the Japanese model as a high level of savings. Commitments to lifetime employment may not be sustained under pressure from external competitors. Demographic problems, especially the aging of the population and the consequent shrinkage in the size of the working-age population, may exert an adverse influence on the performance of the Japanese economy in the coming decade.

Although Japan will retain its prominent position in the global economy, it will have to go through an adjustment process, including industrial restructuring, infrastructural modernization, and movement toward a more liberal policy in international trade relations. The rapid and widespread increase in the use of the yen as an international currency necessitates further steps in liberalization, with greater flexibility and openness required in the Japanese money market if it is to function effectively as an international market. According to calculations performed by some Japanese economists, the country needs at least 4 percent annual growth in GDP to sustain the domestic balance that ensures the smooth functioning of the Japanese model. The recession of the mid-1990s has proved very painful for all the traditional actors in the Japanese economy because it has exposed some of the weaknesses of the model in the new era of the world economy. In an era of slower economic growth, tougher competition, and increasing regionalization, the Japanese model may not be able to carry the country toward economic might as reliably and efficiently as it did in the past.

The Mixed Economies in the Rest of the World

The "rest of the world" is an admittedly imprecise term for the vast area of the globe in which the majority of people live. In part II of this book, it has been noted that most of the expected sources of instability and risks are to be found in that area; it has also been pointed out that nonmilitary sources of instability will be particularly significant in the future. The economic systems of the countries in the rest of the world have, therefore, great political as well as economic importance.

The three main market models—the regulated free market economy of the United States, the social market economy of Europe, and the coordinative corporate economy of Japan—characterize the economies of the developed industrial countries and several of the NICs. In Central and Eastern Europe, the CIS, China, and various developing countries in Africa, Latin America, and Asia the present economic models are hybrids, composed of elements that have endured from the Soviet model of a centrally planned economy and of features copied from the various market economy models or developed under a variety of domestic and international pressures and influences. Like North America, Europe, and Japan, the rest of the world is facing major economic challenges.

Central and Eastern Europe and the Commonwealth of Independent States

The historical failure of the Soviet Union and the Central and East European countries to establish an efficient and competitive economy was largely due to the inherent deficiencies of the model of central planning, the roots and most important elements of which were developed in the war economy of Soviet Russia in the early 1920s, and then further elaborated in the 1930s.[32]

The reasons for that economic failure cannot be understood in isolation from political factors and forces present in the communist system: the totalitarian bureaucratic state; the one-party system; and the politicization and bureaucratization of economic processes. The central planning model enshrined the ideological principle and practices of state ownership in a hierarchical economic system, where development goals, priorities, and output and distribution targets were defined by the central authorities. Economic information was communicated to producers and consumers through central directives. The model was inward-looking and sought to maximize economic growth in physical terms, based on quantitative targets. International economic cooperation was considered merely a balancing item in economic plans, and even among the members of the Council for Mutual Economic Assistance (CMEA)—established in 1949 and better known as COMECON—such cooperation rarely went beyond relatively simple forms of trade relations.

The centrally planned economies were able to achieve fast growth and major structural changes at the early stage of their development. This period was later characterized by Soviet economists as "the era of extensive growth," because it was based not on the increase of productivity and efficiency, but on greater factor inputs (capital and labor). The costs of development were very high even at that early stage, and became insupportable later on. Those costs, together with other deficiencies of the system (like its distribution orientation and neglect of wealth creation), prevented the transition to a more developed economic stage in which the sources of growth should have been rapid technological changes and increasing productivity and efficiency. The fact that the system lacked the capabilities to make fast and efficient structural adjustments also became increasingly apparent.

The need for reform of the system was recognized at various times within the Soviet bloc. The New Economic Policy of the 1920s, a brief encounter of the Soviet system with market forces, is widely considered the first attempt at systemic reform. After the death of Stalin in 1953, measures to change the way in which the system functioned were introduced in all the socialist countries, but the foundations of the model were left unchanged. The most far-reaching reform measures were introduced in Hungary, but even those reforms proved inadequate to the task of changing some of the fundamental systemic characteristics of the command economy. In the Soviet Union, reforms were aborted either because of bureaucratic resistance or because their partial and irrational nature created economic chaos and led to stagnation and then to decline.

Central and Eastern Europe had problems of their own. The post–World War II political landslide in the region resulted in the introduction of the Soviet model regardless of the historical characteristics and level of development of individual countries. The establishment of communist regimes in the countries of the region served to isolate them from their traditional Western trade partners, which had also been the main sources of modern technology. Instead, the region was tied to the Soviet economy, which was less developed than some of the countries in Central and Eastern Europe, and which could not provide the new technology and managerial expertise needed for their modernization. Countries like Czechoslovakia, East Germany, and Hungary were not only locked into the level of economic development they had reached at the time of the socialist takeover, but also their technological capabilities were downgraded in relative terms in an era of fast global technological changes. The Central and East European countries became at the same time dependent on the Soviet market and Soviet shipments of raw materials and energy supplies; that dependence, though it facilitated the attainment of full employment and offered a certain security of supplies and sales, contributed to the development of relatively outdated, globally noncompetitive economic structures.

The technical and institutional problems connected with the systemic character of the socialist economies were compounded by other sources of economic difficulties. The subordination of the Soviet economic system to the pursuit of ideological goals and national security interests resulted in the militarization of its economy at an unprecedented rate in a period of peace. A large part of the human, R&D, and material resources of Soviet society were wasted, and its industrial structure was distorted. The acceleration of the development of strategic weapons in the 1970s, the intervention in Afghanistan, and the high-tech arms race of the 1980s overburdened a relatively weak and inefficient economy. Meanwhile, the costs of supporting friendly regimes and sustaining large armies outside the country were growing. A great number of internal conflicts—social, ideological, political, and ethnic—increasingly undermined the domestic structure of Soviet regimes in the post-Stalin era. During that period, popular support was courted not so much through oppression and intimidation as through promises of constant improvements in the standard of living; as these promises were broken and standards of living stagnated or actually declined, so new sources of discontent and conflict were created.

Although popular uprisings occurred at a relatively early stage in the life of the communist regimes of Central and Eastern Europe, they were crushed by Soviet forces. In those years, the domestic political structure of the Soviet Union was relatively stable. That stability, however, gradually eroded under the impact of external and domestic political and economic failures, prolonged economic stagnation, and a decline in the standard of living. The policy of glasnost introduced in the mid-1980s by Mikhail Gorbachev in an attempt to change the character of the regime and replace the rule of the party bureaucracy with various democratic forms, like greater freedom of expression, opened the floodgates to the tide of popular dissatisfaction and swelled conflicts within the ruling elite.

The transformation process now in progress in the countries of Central and Eastern Europe and the former Soviet Union is very difficult and painful. These countries have had to undertake the tasks of changing inherited, distorted, and obsolete production structures, modernizing underdeveloped infrastructures, and trans-forming formerly state-run systems into market-oriented and efficient economies. Neither a shock-treatment nor a gradualist approach to the implementation of reforms has produced spec-tacular success. There have been, however, some spectacular failures, the most notable being the ineffectiveness of Russian microeconomic stabilization policies. Moderate success has been achieved in some countries, such as Hungary, which has the advantages of unambiguous domestic political support and a more tolerant population and better-trained managers than exist in the states of the former Soviet Union.

In all countries, the most disturbing aspect of attempted reform has been the very high human costs. Not only is there a pervasive sense of insecurity throughout the region, but also unemploy-ment, poverty, and crime (including the emergence of organized crime) are fast growing. Mass unemployment, together with other consequences of the economic transition such as inflation and declining standards of living, have aggravated the ten-sions among different groups within the societies of the former socialist bloc.

All those problems suggest that the transition to the market system will be longer and more costly than has been anticipated by the countries themselves, as well as by the outside world. With a great diversity of political and economic, and external and internal influences at work, significant differences are certain to appear among countries in terms of the pace of the transition process and the character of the evolving economic system. The privatization process, for example, may be creating a peculiar pattern of ownership that features a large small-business sector, a considerable number of state-owned firms, and substantial and highly concentrated foreign ownership.

In Russia and the other republics of the CIS the evolving economic model is likely for many years to resemble the mixed economies of the developing world. In Central and Eastern Europe, and especially in those countries that want to become members of the EC, the domestic economic model will have to be shaped to conform with the market system of the EC. But even in countries like Poland and Hungary it is highly probable that while the role of the state will have to change, it will none-theless remain strong for some time, shaping, and to some extent managing, the transformation process in areas like privatization, market building, the development of a new legal framework, and the moderation of the adverse social consequences of the transition process. In this context, the quality of macro-management and micromanagement and the commitment and pragmatism of the political leadership are crucially important conditions for success.

Success also depends on the evolving economic model facilitating the structural integration of the former socialist countries into the global market system. By the same token, however, the global economy must itself adjust to accommodate those countries. Is this adjustment likely to occur at the required speed and to a sufficient degree? Clearly, a slow-growing and increasingly competitive world economy is not an ideal environment for facilitating the integration of, and encouraging an open and relatively liberal economic system in, the countries of the old Soviet bloc. Yet, those countries need strong supportive measures, including not only foreign direct investments or other forms of resource transfers but also trade opportunities, massive technology transfers, and, in most cases, assistance to improve their managerial capabilities.

Two questions arise, neither of which can be definitively answered for the moment: Are the members of the global economic community sufficiently motivated to help the transformation and consolidation process succeed? Are there sufficient external resources available for that purpose?

The first of these questions is the more important. Although its answer cannot yet be fully known, we have good reason to hope that the transformation process will receive adequate external assistance. In the first place, the interests of the international community will be ill served if political instability, civil wars, and human suffering are allowed to sweep across the former socialist bloc, in the process threatening the safety of neighboring states and undermining respect for human rights and norms of nonviolent international behavior. In the second place, few countries can look with equanimity at the spread of nuclear and other weapons of mass destruction (and of the knowledge to build such weapons) from the former Soviet military-industrial complex. Third, in economic terms, all countries stand to gain if the Central and East European countries and successor states of the former Soviet Union can be transformed from a global economic liability into sources of effective global demand. Indeed, a number of experts consider the large-scale modernization of Central and East European countries and the former Soviet Union as an opportunity to accelerate global growth.[33]

China

Predictions that China will be the next economic superpower may be premature as of the mid-1990s, but certainly China has the potential to attain that status.[34] Chinese human resources are plentiful. The Chinese population is already over 1.2 billion and is projected to reach 1.3 billion by the early 21st century. Its active working-age population will be 647 million by the year 2000. Although the size of its agricultural population of 333 million will remain largely unchanged, its industrial work force is set to grow rapidly. In the 1980s, China created approximately 100 million new jobs in modern and small-scale industries.

China's natural resources are equally immense. The country possesses substantial oil, coal, and iron ore reserves and contains a large area that has the most fertile soil in the world. The nominal GDP of China in 1992 was $444 billion, and its per capita GDP was $378. A "Chinese economic area" is evolving that encompasses China, Hong Kong, and Taiwan. Within 20 years, this area may account for 12 percent of global GDP and 20 percent of world trade, with high-tech commodities, mechanical-electrical equipment, chemical products, light-industrial products, and textiles being chief among the area's exports. As such, the Chinese economic area will be a major source of international competition for middle-income developing countries and some industrial nations, although it will also offer those countries opportunities to increase their exports because of its growing market.

The Chinese political leadership maintains firm central control in political matters while pursuing a pragmatic economic development policy. Although that policy retains significant elements of central guidance, it also encourages major steps toward economic reform. Such reform is no easy task, especially within the state-owned sector. Nonetheless, China's economic reforms, which began in 1978, have been successful overall. The economic system of China has been reshaped in several ways:

1. A large and increasing proportion of China's economic activities are no longer under direct state control exercised through the central planning process. China has chosen a policy of rapid development of a nonstate sector instead of the privatization of state enterprises. The nonstate sector consists of collectively owned enterprises (owned by local governments and/ or workers), individually or privately owned enterprises with paid workers, and partially or entirely foreign-owned enterprises. The proportion of enterprises owned by the state fell from 76 percent in 1980 to 53 percent in 1991. During the same period, collectively owned enterprises increased their share from 24 to 36 percent, individually owned enterprises rose from zero to 5.7 percent, and foreign-owned enterprises from 0.5 to 5.7 percent. Only 40 percent of the retail sales sector is state owned. Seventy percent of the new jobs created in the 1980s were created by rural enterprises.[35]

2. Marketization implied subjecting all production units to market forces, regardless of their ownership. The marketization process has followed several guidelines: prices must be stable enough to avoid politically motivated state price-fixing and to prevent speculation; goods must be made available through the market rather than through administrative allocation; prices must reflect relative scarcities; there must be competition if there are to be gains in productivity; and decision makers in charge of firms must behave according to the rules of the market.

The process of marketization has been state controlled and gradual, and, as of the mid-1990s, is still at a relatively early stage. Most markets are highly imperfect: product markets are highly segmented; no real labor market exists; and the capital market is still in an embryonic state. Competition is still restricted. State-owned enterprises operate under soft budgetary constraints, and their top leadership is appointed by the government.

3. Initially, economic reform focused on the rural areas. Reform in the agricultural sector involved dismantling the communes, introducing the responsibility system, and encouraging new forms of cooperation. Farmers were allowed to engage in non-agricultural production; leases on farms became transferable, thereby allowing agricultural specialization; and agricultural markets were liberalized. The development of collectively and privately owned rural enterprises, which behave according to the

rules of the market, was a major component of the policy of economic reform and absorbed a large number of unemployed or underemployed farmers, whose existence had been "hidden" in the collective system. Agricultural output has increased substantially. Between 1978 and 1990, rural incomes increased over 10 percent annually, and consumption by the agricultural population increased 126 percent over the period. Agriculture has become a major source of domestic demand and investments. Rural economic growth has had favorable effects on nonagricultural industries.

4. Parallel with the agricultural reforms, the system of foreign trade has been undergoing reform. A gradual decentralization of foreign trade, which was accelerated after 1985, has permitted direct exports by enterprises; the retention of a proportion of foreign-exchange earnings from exports, which has in turn allowed increased imports of new technology and the introduction of new products; and the establishment of market exchange rates. Official exchange rates were successfully devalued in order to reflect market rates. A managed floating rate was introduced in 1991.

Emphasis has been placed on increasing international competitiveness and export-based, outward-oriented production. A major shift away from the export of natural resources has been accompanied by an increase in the export of finished industrial products (the latter accounted for 52.5 percent of exports in 1992). Policy regarding foreign direct investments has been progressively liberalized since 1979; in the 1990s, liberalization has been extended from manufacturing to finance, commerce, and infrastructure. Until 1992, attention was heavily focused on the development of coastal zones. The success of the coastal development strategy has, however, fostered tensions between the coastal regions and the more backward regions of the country, and since 1992 more attention has been given to the internal areas of China.

All these measures have led to a rapid economic growth rate of 8.5 percent annually between 1978 and 1990. That rate is expected to be 7 percent for the rest of the 20th century. Even so, it should be noted that in terms of GDP based on market prices the Chinese economy will only be about one-fifth or one-sixth the size of the Japanese economy by 2000.

Chinese exports have also grown substantially, rising at 15 percent per annum between 1980 and 1992, or from $9.7 billion to $52 billion. During the same period, the percentage of China's GDP accounted for by exports increased from 4.7 to 14.3 percent.

China will, however, have to face a number of problems in the coming years: the slow pace at which its institutions are adapting to economic reform; inadequate infrastructure, especially road transportation; possible water shortages caused by population growth and industrialization; and increasing soil, air, and water pollution. Periodic macroeconomic imbalances and inflationary pressures will also be important issues. The inefficient functioning of the state sector has been, and will continue to be, a cause of bottlenecks in the growth process, creating deficits, frozen loans, and debt defaults. China's achievements in the field of exports may be endangered by its overdependence on a few trade partners—namely, Hong Kong, Japan, and the United States— but it will be very difficult for China to diversify its export markets because of structural and institutional problems.

Growing differences among regions in terms of their conditions for development are generating social strains. Absolute poverty is concentrated in areas with limited resources; these areas contain about 10 percent of the nation's population. Rich provinces are reluctant to share their incomes with poorer parts of the country. Throughout the country, poverty has not been reduced by higher growth rates. Furthermore, market forces are spurring the growth of income differences in both rural and urban areas. These trends will further aggravate problems with the political and social stability of a number of provinces, municipalities, and autonomous regions. At the same time, Tibetan separatists and minority groups in various other regions are pressing for greater autonomy.

The Chinese economic model will probably undergo further change as a result of the influence of market forces within the country and its increasing participation in the global economy. Some Chinese economists anticipate a growing convergence of the Chinese model and the systemic model of the economically successful countries of Southeast Asia. However, it remains to be seen whether Chinese political forces will block such a convergence or whether economic changes will encourage political adjustment.

Asia

The economic transformation of China is an integral part of the changes that are affecting all of Asia. Asia is evolving as the development region of the global economic system. Almost 60 percent of the world's population, over 3,300 million people, live within the sprawling continent of Asia. On its western edge lies the oil-rich Middle East, which through its exports of oil and gas is closely tied to the industrial world. The countries of the Middle East have developed an economic model in which, typically, large state monopolies connect the region to foreign oil consumers while small private entrepreneurs are the key actors in the domestic market. Middle Eastern countries that do not export oil tend to be poor and underdeveloped and have mixed economies. Western Asia is, however, on the periphery of Asia both geographically and in terms of the economic transformation of the continent. A peripheral position is also occupied by the newly independent Asian republics of the former Soviet Union, which remain closely tied to Russia and are undergoing economic transformations similar to those experienced by many other former Soviet republics.

The rest of Asia can be divided into two parts in terms of economic characteristics: impoverished South Asia (the countries of the Indian subcontinent) and fast-growing East and Southeast Asia. Both areas have a population of about 1,500 million, but their growth rates differ widely. Over the past 40 years, South Asia has experienced an annual growth rate of between 3 and 3.5 percent, whereas the figure for East and Southeast Asia has been between 7 and 10 percent. These differences in economic performance, though partly caused by geostrategic, historical, and human factors, are chiefly the result of differences in systemic models and economic policies. Until the mid-1980s, the South Asian economic model was less open and market oriented. For example, the largest country in that region, India, developed a planning model with a pronounced socialist character. The countries of South Asia relied heavily on direct government control of the economy and a noncompetitive public sector that dominated large parts of the economy.

Whereas the South Asia economies have been relatively closed and inward-looking, those of East and Southeast Asia have adopted a model that has been heavily influenced by the Japanese experience. At the risk of oversimplifying, it could be characterized as a managed corporate market model. Typically, the state has played a key role in defining the direction and main goals of, and the legal framework for, economic development. The state has also promoted improvements in infrastructure, rapid improvements in education and training, and technological development directly through subsidies and indirectly through such means as the transfer and diffusion of new technologies. While protecting the economy from external competition, the state has also ensured the autonomy and efficient management of enterprises in both the public and the private sectors.

The East and Southeast Asian model has been strongly export oriented and has been conceived in such a way as to facilitate flexible adjustment to the changing needs of the global market. The model has permitted economies to upgrade rapidly. South Korea, which in the 1950s was on the same level as Senegal in terms of per capita GDP, belongs in the mid-1990s to the group of higher middle-income countries.

Since the early 1980s, the countries of South Asia have gradually begun to change their economic model, moving toward liberalization, privatization, and increasing openness. Major reforms have been introduced to increase efficiency in the public sector. In East and Southeast Asia too, the economic model is being reshaped as a consequence of growing domestic social problems, external pressures to liberalize import policies, and difficulties in the world market caused by slower economic growth, protectionism, and sharper competition. The role of the domestic market is increasing and new giant firms are demanding from the governments that helped cultivate them less protectionism and greater liberalization of the financial markets.

Latin America

Economic systemic and policy reforms have also been implemented in Latin America since the 1980s. Steps toward liberalization, a somewhat reduced role for the state and state-owned firms, and a larger role for the private sector have altered the character of the mixed market model that is dominant in Latin America. Although these changes have by no means been dramatic—and the countries involved have certainly not been radically liberalized—they have widened existing institutional and policy differences between the more- and the less-developed parts of the region.

In general, the symbiosis between the public and private sectors that has characterized the typical Latin American model has been advantageous to the private economy. The private sector has been supported by protectionist measures and the purchases made by state-owned firms and other public institutions from private firms. Some countries have taken important steps toward restructuring their public sectors, deregulation, and the liberalization of conditions for foreign direct investment. Growing social problems, environmental degradation, and macroeconomic imbalances (inflation and budget deficits) may require further adjustments and systemic reforms in most countries of the region.

Africa

Within the developing world, Africa is the most fragmented region. With a population of 640 million, Africa has 52 independent states, 35 of which have a population of less than 10 million, and 15 of which are landlocked countries. The combined GDP of 25 countries south of the Sahara was $215 billion in 1990, less than that of South Korea; South Africa alone had a GDP of $65 billion. When the Organization of African Unity, at its 1991 summit, decided to establish an African Economic Community by 2025, it was responding to real needs. Only two countries in sub-Saharan Africa are able to develop their economies in an economically sustainable way: South Africa and Nigeria. Other countries tend to be too poor and too small to develop efficient infrastructures and to attain a scale of output necessary to increase their competitiveness. Today, the majority of countries in the region are in a state of crisis. Population growth is 3.1 percent annually, an unprecedented rate for a major region. Poverty is omnipresent. Per capita GDP and food production have been declining since the end of the 1980s. Africa has been adversely influenced by the global debt crisis and worsening terms of trade. Without major external assistance, the internal policy reforms of most countries will fail. By all indications, Africa will find the 1990s to be a very difficult decade.[36]

In view of the problems, possibilities, and needs of the developing countries, and in spite of the increasing roles being played by the market and the private sector, the dominant economic models of the South are, and probably will continue to be, characterized by strong state involvement, a relatively large public sector, and government intervention and regulation.

Notwithstanding the similarities among its members' economic models, the developing world is an extremely heterogeneous complex of countries differentiated not only by their respective development levels but also by the size of their countries and their roles in the global economy.

The gaps between the North and the South have increased in almost every significant indicator of the distribution of wealth, income, investments, and technological development since World War II. Between 1960 and 1990, for example, the developing countries' share of global population increased from 68.5 percent to 77.1 percent, while their share of global GNP decreased from 15.9 percent to 15.8 percent.[37]

Nevertheless, the South as a whole experienced relatively rapid economic growth during the 1960s and 1970s, both in general and in per capita terms. Although growth slowed substantially during the 1980s, it remained relatively high in those countries that, because of geographical proximity, enjoyed good economic relations with the developed countries. Some larger countries of the South, such as India and Brazil, were able to develop modern and relatively large industrial and service sectors that have been able to sustain domestic economic growth in dualistic economies, where modern and traditional sectors coexist. A number of these countries have become increasingly important participants in the global economy, especially as exporters of industrial products, and have changed the patterns of international trade flows as the pace of economic structural change has accelerated. Having overcome the initial difficulties of industrial development, some countries have been able to tackle even highly complex technological projects. Substantial industrial productive capacities and export potentials have been established that are on a par with the standards of the developed world.

In parts of the developing world, this economic growth has transformed economic institutions. In the public and private sectors, huge industrial corporations have been established;

national banking systems have been created; scientific research has been strengthened. Despite their structural weaknesses, a number of developing countries today possess the economic organizations and infrastructure that enable them to deploy state power effectively to guard against adverse external influences such as exchange-rate fluctuations or even protectionist measures.

The majority of the developing countries, however, are in a parlous condition. They are growing further adrift from the developed world in terms of per capita GDP, productivity, and consumption. Furthermore, most developing nations remain highly vulnerable to external developments, not merely because of their traditional role as raw material producers and exporters, but also because of their exposure to rapidly changing production and consumption patterns, and, in some cases, because of adverse trade policies. It is becoming ever more apparent that only rationality and pragmatism, not dogma and ideology, can effectively define the roles of the state and of nonstate actors in mixed economic models.

The economic difficulties of the developing countries inescapably affect all nations of the world. Aside from the fact that the developing countries purchase about 30 percent of the goods and services produced in the industrial world, the internal economic instability of the developing countries creates sociopolitical unrest, which increases the numbers of refugees and emigrants to the developed countries. The difficulties of the developing world may also lead to the disruption of supplies of oil and other raw materials, thereby endangering the stability of the global economic and political systems.

chapter 14

New Global Priorities: An Agenda for Cooperation

The expansion of the global economy and the process of internationalization under way since World War II have brought a variety of new worldwide problems and risks. These problems share certain characteristics:

- Most problems are caused by unforeseen consequences of technological, economic, and social developments and policies.
- The problems are, in general, complex and multidimensional, result from several factors, and have wide-ranging effects.
- The dangers brought by the problems may already have been demonstrated (as, for example, in the case of environmental degradation).
- These problems may broaden into major global crises if countries are unprepared or unable to deal with them.
- The solution, mitigation, or management of these problems requires multifaceted and concentrated international efforts.[38]

Even when there has been general agreement on the character and importance of given problems, it has been extremely difficult to implement common international policies and undertake national actions for the management of the risks involved. The analysis of different economic models presented in the preceding chapter illustrates the difficulties in formulating a global agenda, especially in setting common priorities for the future.

The 1990s, however, are witnessing the evolution of a consensus[39] that three interconnected areas should be accorded the highest priority on the agenda for global action:

1. The revitalization of the global economic development process and the creation of conditions that will make economic growth sustainable, more balanced, and equitable.
2. The demilitarization of the global economy.
3. The establishment of global conditions for ecologically sustainable growth.

Revitalizing the Development Process

The policies formulated and implemented to address the economic problems caused by political changes at the end of the 1980s, the conclusion of the Cold War, the dismembering of the Soviet Union, and the global recession of the early 1990s will be decisive in shaping the global economy. These policies will have to influence the direction and intensity of global economic growth while accommodating major structural changes to avoid stagnation or very slow growth. These policies must increase employment, moderate the problems of the developing countries, assist the integration of Central and East European countries and the successor states of the Soviet Union into the global market, and safeguard or increase the present level of openness in international economic relations. Economic social and environmental sustainability will also be of major importance.[40]

Although a positive and efficient response to these challenges is not, at least in principle, beyond the capacity of the main actors in the international political and economic system, it will require close international cooperation on a wide array of issues, including more efficient coordination of national economic policies, improvement of the international financial system, a more liberal global trading regime, and increased international assistance. Due to the sheer diversity of interests, ideologies, and values involved and the intensification of global competition, the internal policy changes necessary to produce a more effective cooperative relationship among the major industrial powers can only evolve slowly. Rising economic and social pressures, accompanied by converging interests in making global economic development sustainable, will impel nations to take some form of collective action, at least with regard to the most pressing issues. However, while every country may be involved in this endeavor to some extent, the economically powerful nations share special responsibility for developing the necessary environment.

Economic development within a global framework is not an abstract concept, even though real economic growth takes place only within national frontiers. The majority of countries can no longer control many elements of their national economies; international capital movements, for example, are now indivisible parts of a global economic system. Instead, most countries today must adjust to, and accommodate, external changes. Global interconnectedness requires a high level of international coordination of national policies and the harmonization of national actions in many areas.

Slow global development may adversely influence the global economy, resulting in high levels of unemployment and underemployment, thus increasing national pressures to protect job opportunities against foreign competition. Directly or indirectly, slow global growth may stimulate demands for subsidizing ailing national industries and increasing the "subsidized advantages" of global competition. Sluggish demand may reduce investments and increase the obsolescence of capital in a number of countries. Sluggish growth limits demand for imported raw materials and discourages foreign investments. Thus, countries have a common interest in stimulating economic development in a rational manner when market forces are no longer sufficiently strong to power the global economy.

In the past, "locomotive" countries have driven global growth, in the process benefiting both themselves and the marketplace.[41] The locomotive effect, which has never worked perfectly, may be significantly diminished in today's more competitive and regionalized system where flow imbalances (deficits and surpluses) turn into stock imbalances (large debts) that reduce the impact of the locomotive countries on others in the marketplace.

In the future, growth-stimulating national policies may again become necessary, although they must be implemented in an internationally coordinated framework that possesses more efficient multilateral organizations, especially in the fields of trade and finance.[42] The absence of such policies in the economic environment in the 1990s may destabilize many countries, including some leading actors. Higher rates of growth and structural changes in the post–World War II decades in developed countries facilitated social stability and increased employment, and the steady increase of real resources made it easier to achieve a broad consensus about the social order. These positive consequences of faster growth were, though, accompanied by negative effects, such as the exacerbation of global inequalities and the degradation of the environment.

Demilitarization and the Global Economy

The prospect of demilitarization, especially in some of the Western industrialized countries, as well as in Russia, China, and developing countries with relatively large defense sectors, is directly related to political change and has profound implications for the future of global stability and economic growth.

Militarization is, of course, not primarily an economic process, being driven by national security considerations. Nonetheless, the process does have many economic aspects, including its implications for macroeconomic changes and its consequences for labor markets, taxes, national budgets, and levels of national debt. During the Cold War, militarization influenced the structure of manufacturing industries, the character and the structure of R&D expenditures, and the pace of technological changes. International economic cooperation was influenced by militarization not only through the arms trade and related activities but also by the subordination of international economic relations to national security considerations. The defense sector was the core of the militarization process. Because of the diverse and sophisticated product groups and the complex requirements of armies, the defense industry in the post–World War II era has become interconnected with almost all other branches of industry and thus has acquired a significant role in the global economy. The structural changes that emerged as the result of defense expenditures stimulated the high-tech industries. Military spending also influenced structural changes in the economy through direct purchases of goods and services consumed by national armies or exported abroad; through investment activities engaged in directly by governments or generated by defense-related R&D expenditures; and through the investments of those firms that had government backing.

Defense-related industries can be divided into three groups according to their character and relation to the rest of the economy: the first group is strictly limited to meeting military needs in high-tech areas, such as missiles, nuclear warheads, "smart" weapons, and specialized military aircraft; the second group is the conventional weapons sector; and the third group produces goods and services that are consumed by civilians as well as by the armed forces.

In the aftermath of the Cold War, military expenditures have declined. Between 1987 and 1992, global defense spending decreased from about $1,068 billion to about $700 billion. The decline was steepest in the former Soviet Union, Central and Eastern Europe, and the United States. In the developing world, military expenditures fell about 20 percent. In addition, the global arms trade started declining during the 1980s, experiencing a nearly 40 percent decline between 1987 and 1990.[43]

In those countries where the size of the armed forces in relation to the size of the working population is relatively large, the reduction of armed forces is bound to affect the labor market. Where a substantial proportion of government spending is represented by defense expenditures, their reduction will alter the complexion of the national budget. And where defense-related industries are sources of large sales, employment, and exports, the restructuring and conversion of the military sector will be difficult, especially if the rest of the economy is in stagnation and decline (as in Russia) or is not expanding with sufficient speed (as in the United States). The scientific community will feel the shock of reduced defense-related expenditures acutely—during the Cold War, about 25 percent of research expenditures in the United States and 40 to 50 percent in the Soviet Union were directly related to military requirements.

If defense expenditures grow faster than GDP, and if unused material and human capacity are simultaneously present in the economy, they can have a substantial economic stimulation effect. In the United States, for example, real defense spending for goods and services increased by nearly 60 percent between 1979 and 1987, and was responsible for a 12 percent growth in final sales.[44]

The reverse is also true. In a stagnating economy, reduction of defense spending can exacerbate economic problems, at least temporarily. Thus, demilitarization cannot occur at the mercy of market forces if countries wish to avoid severe economic shocks.

Disarmament and demilitarization call for changes that are likely to be achieved only slowly and at great cost. The industrial and service sectors will incur significant adjustment costs. The retraining and employment of personnel released from the armed services will present organizational and financial difficulties. Demilitarization must be planned and implemented gradually, taking into account changing security needs and its socioeconomic consequences, including its effects on purchasing power. By downsizing military sectors gradually, a greater share of resources can be devoted to infrastructural investments, international assistance, or other resource-hungry areas such as health and education.

Beyond the technical and financial issues, however, lies a formidable and omnipresent obstacle: the political and economic interests and coalitions that have gathered around the defense sector. With declining defense expenditures, alternative business and employment opportunities will have to be created. Defense conversion requires a decentralized approach. Governments can facilitate the process by aiding industries until they are restructured and providing assistance in retraining and relocating employees. In countries like Russia, where demilitarization has coincided with major domestic problems, more international support will be needed. International agreements on economic demilitarization, international loans for facilitating conversion, and international controls on the arms trade will have to assist the transition to an integrated global economy.

Toward Globally Sustainable Development

Of all the issues on which a consensus exists regarding the need for international cooperation, environmental degradation has received the most attention and generated the most action. The increasing awareness of such risks as stratospheric ozone depletion, global warming, desertification, deforestation, soil erosion, and pollution has resulted in major changes to the agenda of international risk and conflict management and cooperation. Since the 1960s, the deteriorating life-sustaining capacity of the Earth and the possibility of environmental problems provoking political, economic, and social conflicts have drawn much attention from governments, intergovernmental agencies, and the academic community.

International concern has been stimulated by several specific factors:

- The noticeably accelerating degradation of the ecosystem is seen as endangering the life-sustaining capacity of the Earth; its effects on the biosphere are believed to be irreversible in some areas.
- Major environmental catastrophes have occurred in India, Japan, and the Soviet Union, signaling the worldwide scope of environmental dangers.
- Interdependence among political, economic, social, and environmental issues has become more complex as the world's population has grown and pollution worsened.
- Conflicts of interest among countries have become clearer and better articulated, and the difficulties of harmonizing those interests have become more apparent.
- Knowledge about environmental problems and their dangers has spread fairly rapidly. A new multidisciplinary area, environmental studies, has emerged that examines the interaction of complex environmental systems, national and international policies, and human behavior.
- The spread of knowledge has increased concern and mobilized millions of people at the grass roots level in many countries. More than 1,200 nongovernmental organizations participated in the 1992 Rio conference on the environment and development.

Three areas represent the international dimensions of the ecosystem: the management of the global commons that lie outside national territorial jurisdictions; the emission and transmission of environmental pollution from one country to another, the control of which requires new forms of international cooperation; and the regional and global implications of national policies that endanger the environment, such as major losses in biodiversity

(140 plant and animal species are condemned to extinction each day), desertification, deforestation, and pollution of oceans and international waterways. International cooperation in rehabilitating the damaged environment and managing globally sustainable development is indispensable in all three areas.[45]

In spite of the positive approach to environmental issues taken by governments and the fact that a broad coalition of nongovernmental actors supports common international action, real progress toward a globally or even regionally implemented environmental policy is still slow because of diverging interests and priorities. This divergence is most marked between the North and South. Because the developed industrial countries generate about 80 percent of total global pollution, developing countries are loath to sacrifice their development—thus mitigating some environmental damage—to manage the problems caused by the industrialized countries. Some political figures of the South even accuse the North of environmental imperialism, and insist that environmental issues cannot be dealt with in isolation from questions of economic and social development.[46] However, the South is not unanimous on this issue, and important differences exist among the developing countries with regard to resource management, natural resource pricing, and the commercial utilization of resources such as forests.

The countries of the North are divided in their willingness to assume responsibility for environmental safeguards in areas such as carbon dioxide emissions or release of chlorofluorocarbons (CFCs). The history of the Montreal Protocol, a multilateral agreement on issues pertaining to CFCs, is a revealing case study of how microinterests and macrointerests can influence disputes and their resolution. The disputes surrounding carbon dioxide emissions and other sources of global warming are extremely complicated. The uncertain accuracy of available data, the difficulties of monitoring compliance, and the reluctance of countries to commit to unilateral measures and accept the costs of replacing existing technologies (because such costs would increase production costs and/or divert funds from other investments) are some of the stumbling blocks to achieving cooperation and implementing common policies. The diversity of interests connected with traditional sources of energy is aggravated by systemic factors, as the great variety of national economic models hinders the implementation of multilateral measures, including those mandated by international agreements already concluded.[47]

Although many of those agreements were not ratified by national legislatures or implemented by national governments, the influence of pressure groups in some industrial countries has led to significant steps being taken. In The Netherlands and Germany, for example, stringent policies have been enacted against the pollution of air and water. There has also been marked progress in the development of pollution-prevention technologies and in waste tracking, accounting, and management. However, differences between national policies and practices have increased, even within a regional framework like the EC.

An analysis of the environmental policies of the major industrial countries reveals a three-stage development process that follows similar patterns in different countries.[48] First is a phase of environmental inaction or negligence (preceded by ecological ignorance), in which the bureaucracy remains passive in spite of proven risks to health and the natural environment. Relevant information is ignored and social protest is disregarded, or even oppressed. The second stage is an era of symbolic activity, when environmental strategies are formulated and programs and bills are issued, although their implementation is often at best half-hearted. The third stage is the beginning of active technocratic environmental management with selective but increasingly efficient measures being taken, although the measures tend to ignore the interdependence of an ecosystem's component parts. The transition from one stage to the next requires not only better education among policymakers, greater research, and increasing interaction among experts, parliamentarians, and government officials, but also changes in public priorities, attitudes, and the level and operational efficiency of international cooperation.

Clearly, different parts of the world are at different stages of this process. Taken as whole, the global community has yet to advance beyond the second phase.

If environmental policies are to be enacted and concrete measures undertaken on the global level, several conditions must be met. First, leadership is needed to advocate the cause of environmental protection. Second, international financing is required by those countries that lack the necessary funds to implement environmental policies. The annual funding requirement for achieving the goals set forward at the Earth Summit in Rio has been estimated at about $125 billion. Only a small fraction of this will be available from external assistance to countries that cannot afford the expenditure; most of that assistance has been promised by Japan. Third, technical assistance is needed; a bilateral or multilateral framework could help to supply such assistance. Fourth, institutional machinery is required to oversee environmental work; sanctions against those nations that ignore internationally concluded agreements might also be effective. (As proposed at the Rio conference, the newly created Global Commission for Environment and Development should be given sufficient power and resources to ensure its effectiveness.)

Environmental policies influence economic interests because the problems they seek to solve are rooted in traditional patterns of production and consumption. Because economic interests are strong, national environmental policies and actions, through which international policies are in turn enacted, must also be strong. Unfortunately, the Rio conference left unresolved most of the issues concerned with the interrelation of national and international institutions. Even so, the conference stimulated new research activities that may help to produce a better global framework for cooperative environmental governance in the future.

chapter 15

The Human Dimension of Change in the Future Global Economy

In the past, consideration of the human dimensions of international change was usually confined to cultural issues and value systems, with moral and behavioral problems receiving much attention. In today's international life, with mounting population pressures and growing levels of unemployment and poverty, a broader understanding and clearer articulation of the human dimensions of international change are required; they are especially important to the analysis of the transformation of the global economy. The interrelatedness of economic and human factors has reached the extent where economic change, especially at a global level, cannot be separated from the very survival and quality of existence of the human race.

Human beings are multidimensional actors. People are elements of the global biosphere, exposed to all the forces determining the conditions for global biological existence. Human beings have reached a stage at which they can consciously influence not only the ecosystem and the frontiers of biological existence but also the biological and genetic characteristics of life.[49] Human beings are, concurrently, "economic animals," consumers and producers guided by their needs and interests who are continually developing or reordering their economic environment on different levels and within different frameworks and networks.[50] As objects and subjects of management, humans carry out a multiplicity of tasks, from inventing and innovating to "creative destruction." Furthermore, human beings, while divided into different ethnic, religious, national, and other types of communities and societies, are at the same time part of the larger culture and civilization of a given era. In this dimension, they are sources and managers of their achievements and problems, and are accountable for their actions. Human beings are also agents of conflict, even as they are agents of conflict management and resolution.

The problems related to human needs and their satisfaction, though of growing importance, lie beyond the scope of the present work. Here, attention is centered on three areas in which human behavior influences the international aspects of economic change: the global consequences of population growth (including issues that are connected with production, consumption, and the ecological consequences of growth); international migration; and the structure and formation of the global market for labor. Developments in all three areas threaten the success of the "search for security" that will characterize global economic changes throughout the 1990s and well into the 21st century—a search that will range across such areas as food security, security of oil and raw materials, access to technology, the sustainability of the ecosystem, and the reliability of international cooperation within different frameworks.

The Population Challenge

It took 17 centuries from the birth of Christ to double the population of the world. On the basis of present fertility rates, the population will double again in 40 years. The years between 1975 and 2000 will experience the largest absolute growth in global population of any quarter-century in all of human history. By the end of 1993, the world population had reached 5.5 billion; according to UN projections, it will surpass 6.2 billion by 2000 and 7.2 billion by 2010.

The increasing number of people on Earth will pose a critical and historically unprecedented strain on the ecosystem, not only in terms of further pollution, but also with respect to increasing demand for food, water, energy, raw materials, and space. Compared with the period from 1950 to 1990, the growth rate of the world population is predicted to slightly decelerate over the next 20 to 25 years, dropping from 1.85 percent to 1.5 percent annually (with major regional differences). The United Nations Population Division has projected (based on the expected average changes in the replacement rate) that the global population will stabilize sometime around the middle of the 21st century at 11 to 12 billion people, or more than 2.2 times the population in 1990.[51] This size of increase might be diminished by successful family planning programs; the effectiveness of such programs, however, is often undermined by the ideological, political, economic, and institutional opposition they encounter in many countries.

Differences in the population trends of the developed and developing countries (see tables 3 and 4) are caused by a number of factors, including changes in life-styles and family patterns with respect to socioeconomic conditions, the diversity of attitudes toward family planning, and the development of health policies resulting in lower mortality rates. From 1970 to 1990, the annual rate of increase in population slowed from 0.9 percent to 0.5 percent in the developed part of the world. There was a corresponding slowdown in the developing countries (from 2.4 to 2.1 percent) during the same period; within this group, Asia dropped from 2.3 to 1.8 percent, and Latin America from 2.5 to 1.9 percent. Yet, in Africa there was an increase from 2.7 to 3.0 percent. More than 90 percent of the anticipated global population increase will occur in the developing world. Diverse growth rates have resulted in major changes in the territorial and age distributions of the population throughout many regions of the world; the continuance of these varying rates of growth will further accentuate the demographic trends.

Beyond the international and regional changes in the distribution of world population, nations have experienced internal shifts as a result of urbanization. In the early 20th century, the world was still very rural; only about 14 percent of people lived in urban settlements. According to projections, by the end of this century, one-half of the Earth's population will be urban. Seventy-eight percent of the population in developed countries and 40 percent in developing countries will be living in cities.

Table 3. Total Population (in Millions) and Average Annual Growth Rates (Percentage) by Decade, 1960–2025

Country Groups	1960	1960–1970	1970	1970–1980	1980	1980–1990	1990	1990–2000	2000	2000–2025	2025
Developing Countries											
North Africa	54	5.2	69	2.6	89	2.6	115	2.4	146	1.7	220
Sub-Saharan Africa	209	2.6	271	2.9	361	3.1	489	3.1	663	2.7	1290
South and East Asia and Oceania	842	2.4	1069	2.3	1338	2.2	1657	2.0	2012	1.3	2814
China	657	2.4	831	1.8	996	1.5	1153	1.3	1310	0.6	1540
Western Asia	47	3.0	63	3.5	89	3.8	129	3.0	174	2.6	329
Mediterranean	47	1.9	57	1.8	68	1.8	81	1.5	94	1.0	120
Latin America and the Caribbean	217	2.7	283	2.4	359	2.1	441	1.7	523	1.2	702
Subtotal, Developing Countries	2069	2.5	2639	2.2	3295	2.1	4059	1.9	4914	1.4	7003
Developed Market Economies	650	1.1	722	0.9	786	0.7	839	0.7	898	0.4	993
Eastern Europe and the Former USSR	295	1.1	329	0.8	358	0.8	387	0.4	404	0.5	460
World Total	3019	2.0	3697	1.9	4447	1.8	5295	1.6	6228	1.2	8472
Least Developed Countries	238	2.5	304	2.6	392	2.7	510	2.8	675	2.4	1215

Source: Calculated from country data in United Nations Department of International Economic and Social Affairs, *World Population Prospects—The 1992 Revision* (New York: United Nations, 1992). The projections are based on the "medium variant" projection for each country.

Table 4. Population as Percentage of World Total

Country Group	Number of Countries	1960	1970	1980	1990	2000	2025
Developing Countries							
North Africa	6	1.8	1.9	2.0	2.2	2.3	2.6
Sub-Saharan Africa	49	6.9	7.3	8.1	9.2	10.6	15.2
South and East Asia and Oceania	46	27.9	28.9	30.1	31.3	32.3	33.2
China	1	21.8	22.5	22.4	21.8	21.0	18.2
Western Asia	12	1.6	1.7	2.0	2.4	2.8	2.9
Mediterranean	4	1.6	1.5	1.5	1.5	1.5	1.4
Latin America and the Caribbean	49	7.2	7.7	8.3	8.3	8.4	8.3
Subtotal, Developing Countries	167	68.5	71.4	74.1	76.7	78.9	82.7
Developed Market Economies	34	21.5	19.5	17.7	15.8	14.4	11.7
Eastern Europe and the Former USSR	10	9.8	8.9	8.1	7.3	6.5	5.4
World Total	211	100.0	100.0	100.0	100.0	100.0	100.0
Least Developed Countries	47	7.9	8.2	8.8	9.6	10.8	14.3

Source: Calculated from country data in United Nations Department of International Economic and Social Affairs, *World Population Prospects—The 1992 Revision* (New York: United Nations, 1992). Note that under "World Total" country group shares may not add to 100 percent because of rounding.

The United Nations projects that in 2000, 77 percent of the population in Latin America, 41 percent in Africa, and 35 percent in Asia will live in urban settlements. In the developing world, most of the urban growth is taking place in already large urban settlements—in 24 "megacities" with populations that are, or will soon exceed, 10 million. The list is headed by Mexico City, which had a population of 20.2 million in 1990. Municipalities will be unable to keep up with the demand for infrastructure and services. As urban slums spread, so will their attendant lack of adequate housing, roads, health care and educational facilities, safe drinking water, and sanitation. Rapid and spontaneous urbanization will increase the numbers of unemployed, underemployed, uneducated, undernourished, and critically ill. The urbanization process is transforming the issue of the population-supporting capacity of many countries and regions from a theoretical problem into a practical concern, one that could become a major source of tensions and international conflicts. As such, it is critical that migration to cities be slowed down through rural industrialization and the provision of better educational and health services in rural areas.

Another dimension of demographic change is found in the age composition of the population. The proportion of children under age 15 reached close to 40 percent of the population by the end of the 1960s, and slightly declined afterwards. By the end of the 20th century, children under 15 will make up more than one-third of the global population. In the developed countries this proportion will remain at 20 to 22 percent. There has also been an expansion at the other end of the age scale. In 1970, the proportion of people worldwide over 60 years of age was 8.3 percent; by 1990, it had reached 9.2 percent, and by the end of the century it will account for about 10 percent. While the median age of the population is growing in both developed and developing countries, the share of the over-60 age group in total population will be close to 30 percent in the developed countries and only about 7 percent in the developing world.

Also increasing is the proportion of the world's population that is of working age (that is, people aged between 15 and 64). The proportion of this age group increased on a global level from 57 percent in 1970 to 62 percent in 1990, and will reach

64 percent by 2000. In the developed industrial countries, this proportion has remained relatively high (close to two-thirds of the population); in the developing countries, it will increase from 54.4 percent in 1970 to over 60 percent by 2000. Between 1970 and 1990, about 1,140 million persons were added to this group, amounting to more than 1 billion in the developing countries. According to UN projections, the number of people of working age will increase by about 620 million in the 1990s and by 740 million in the first decade of the next century. Of this increase, only 4.7 percent will be in the developed world, with more than 95 percent occuring in the developing countries. In the developing regions, the most rapid rates of increase in people of working age will occur in the Middle East, South and Central America, and in certain African countries. In terms of total numbers, the largest increments will occur in South Asia and China.[52]

Before entering into a discussion about the global economic implications of population changes, several qualifications must be made. First, although population projections have proved to be the most reliable data in anticipating or predicting changes on a global scale, some projections have been wrong. Population increases have been overestimated, for example, both globally and regionally. Second, population changes are important, but they are by no means the sole determinants of changes in the global economy. In a global economic context, demography is interrelated with such other processes as the availability of natural resources, the influence of technological transformation, the role of economic growth patterns, and the impact of social policies. Third, the pressure of demographic forces on the functioning of a society or economy is often indirect, manifesting itself only gradually and through a variety of problems. Fourth, interrelations between demographic and economic changes are more complex on the level of the global economy as a result of increasing global demographic diversity. For example, because population growth is concentrated in low-income countries, high-income countries will be affected through repercussions on the environment, increasing migration, and the development of regional sociopolitical tensions and crises. Fifth, attitudes toward population issues, especially toward family planning, are influenced by multifarious values and ideologies. Sixth, while population problems are potentially very dangerous from a global viewpoint, they may not influence national public attitudes and government decisions, which are usually only prompted by shorter-term concerns.

Although many countries do have national demographic policies, there is no well-conceived and coordinated international activity. As the following discussion suggests, collective policies and actions could help to reduce or avoid many potential dangers associated with demographic trends.

The increase in global population will entail a greater demand for resources and a heightened emphasis on particular areas of the global resource economy and ecosystem. Resources connected with food, especially soil, water, and fuel (energy), are the most directly involved both as components of a complex, interrelated framework and as discrete problem areas. Agricultural land shortages are becoming widespread in many parts of the developing world. Projections have drawn attention to the global consequences of deforestation (in Latin America and Africa, 17 to 20 millon hectares annually), desertification (in Africa), and soil degradation (in almost all regions of the world) resulting in the loss of about 24 billion tons of top soil annually. Urban growth is also likely to diminish the amount of land available for agriculture, and urban pollution will contribute to soil degradation. A large increase in water withdrawal for irrigation and industrial and domestic use will create water scarcities that may prove especially dangerous to international stability in the Middle East, North Africa, and Central and South Asia.

Because the problems differ by region, the identification and management of the international consequences of these issues can best be achieved in a regional framework. Some aspects, however, require global cooperation, especially those regarding carbon dioxide emissions and the dangers of global warming.[53] Population growth will also influence the supply and demand of nonrenewable natural resources.

Demographic factors directly influence the functioning of countries and the international system in many ways. Size of population can be a key variable. In about 60 microstates and ministates, the low number of people can make it difficult to create and maintain an adequate and efficient infrastructure and domestic market for many economic activities. In other countries, by contrast, the population is too large and unmanageable. Ideally, countries with large populations should enjoy the economies of scale offered by a large market and develop a large and highly diversified economy, such as that of the United States.

The shifts in age composition of the world population represent another dimension of demographic changes with international consequences. The aging of the population in the developed industrial countries reduces the proportion of the age group belonging to the labor force. This may impel some countries to phase out and redeploy labor-intensive activities to other countries and concentrate instead on value-added production and services (as Japan has done). In countries where the shrinking of the size of the working-age population is a serious problem, there is a push to encourage immigration or to increase productivity by innovation and an accelerated mastery of new technology. An aging population increases the need to restructure social expenditures to meet the particular needs of older people. Some countries already devote more than one-half of their social and health expenditures to services for the elderly.

In developing countries, the increase in the number and proportion of the working-age group is reducing demographic dependency ratios (in other words, the proportion of the population dependent on the working-age population is diminishing). This trend could stimulate economic and social development, but only if a sufficient number of new jobs are created to accommodate the expanding labor force. The optimistic expectations of developing countries regarding the favorable impact of industrialization and urbanization on employment opportunities have proved to be exaggerated. Although the rise in industrial employment has been rapid in developing countries (4.0 to 4.5 percent during the past 25 years, albeit with large regional differences), only 22 to 24 percent of those in the working-age group have been employed by industry, with the remainder working in agricultural or service sectors or left unemployed or underemployed. This stands in stark contrast to the historical patterns of the developed industrial countries, the industries of which were able to employ 40 percent of those entering the labor market in the last century.

Some countries, such as China, have been able to create employment by combining the development of modern high-tech industries with small-scale, labor-intensive rural and township industrialization. This approach has served not only to ease the pressures of unemployment or underemployment but also to prevent migration to the larger cities and to produce cheap industrial goods to satisfy local demand. In most of the developing world, however, the picture is much less encouraging. Around 400 million people worldwide are unemployed, and this number is increasing. If the unemployed were able to contribute to the growth of GDP according to the average per capita output figure in developing countries for the early 1990s, they could increase the product of their countries by about $300 billion.

About 60 percent of the population in developing countries is employed in agriculture and low-productivity services, including the "informal" sector. The increase in the informal sector is closely tied to the urbanization process. Because the informal sector serves the local population, upgrading that sector in terms of productivity and income depends on an increase in the purchasing power of those people. Upgrading informal sectors would thus require the creation of more stable and sustainable employment and skill-intensive production. This, in turn, would require substantial capital outlay. The investment needs for new jobs in the modern industrial sectors of the economy are large. The range of gross investment per potential new worker varies from $1,090 in Bangladesh to $10,660 in Thailand.[54] (Of course, the "modern" industrial sector of Bangladesh is somewhat of a misnomer, as it lags significantly behind the technological modernity of Thailand's industrial sector.)

Technological and structural changes and the slowdown of economic growth are certain to increase tensions in the global labor market. Countries will deal with employment and unemployment in different ways, some by reducing working hours, others by instituting retraining programs or parceling out part-time employment opportunities. The labor market experienced high growth in the postwar period—full employment, job openings that compensated for job losses connected with technological change, and positive conditions for vertical mobility (upgrading the labor force) and horizontal mobility (moving in the direction of more productive sectors). Under the new economic conditions of slower growth, however, the labor market can only adjust at low speed. Such change is always painful, and those who are most affected are seldom reasonably compensated. Through the pledges made by UN member states after World War II not to allow a return to the mass unemployment of the 1930s, sustaining employment has to some extent become a global commitment.[55] Over the next 10 to 15 years, the creation of new employment opportunities and the moderation of unemployment may become the most important socioeconomic challenges.

The Nomads of the 21st Century

> Seeking to escape from their desperate fate, millions will attempt to leave behind the misery of the periphery to seek a decent life elsewhere: they will be the nomads of a different kind, a new version of the desert nomads migrating from place to place looking for a few drops of what we have in Los Angeles, Berlin, or Paris, which for them will be the oases of hope.[56]

Insufficient and inefficient responses to the increase in unemployment will contribute to pressures for international migration, especially from much of the land belt south of the developed industrial world. North America will feel the effect of such pressures from Latin America, as will Europe from Africa, and the Arab-Islamic hinterland and Russia from South Asia and China. The net effect of these mass movements of economic nomads will be to place severe stress on the global economic and political systems. International migration, much of it illegal and unrecorded, has always had greater importance than has been indicated by official statistics. It has also become self-generating insofar as ever more immigrants are attracted to the settlements established by earlier migrants. Furthermore, with most migrants being relatively young, they have contributed significantly to population growth in their host countries.

Most of the great population movements in the first few decades after World War II occurred as a consequence of political change. Since 1947, for example, when India and Pakistan became independent, an estimated 40 million people have moved across the borders of these two countries. The establishment of Israel has likewise prompted mass emigration of Palestinians and immigration of Jews from throughout the world. In every continent, wars, revolutions, and other political upheavals have caused major outflows of people. It is quite possible that the disintegration of the Soviet Union will also result in a mass migration.

In the mid-1990s, though, most emigration is likely to be economically motivated, with immigrants from the South seeking to share in the relative prosperity of the North. In 1992, the World Bank estimated the number of international migrants of all kinds to be 100 million, with refugees accounting for around 17 million. Although immigrants still play an important role in the functioning of the labor market in a number of countries,[57] emigration cannot mitigate the problems of today's developing world as it did for an overpopulated 19th-century Europe, which exported 10 to 15 percent of its labor force to North America and Oceania between 1850 and 1914. The sheer size of the increase of population in the developing countries make emigration pressures and the number of potential emigrants much greater than they were in 19th-century Europe. Furthermore, the modern economies of countries receiving immigrants have less need of an influx of labor than did the labor-intensive industrial economies of 19th- and early 20th-century North America. During the post–World War II years, for example, Asian countries were able to export less than 0.1 percent of their labor force. Japan has been the only advanced industrial country in the region to be a target for migration.

If the development process is left to socioeconomic forces, people will be uprooted by poverty and their migration will provoke international and national conflict. In the developed world, concern over the effects of mass immigration are growing. Responding to the need to protect their own labor markets, industrial countries are likely to impose strict quotas on the numbers of emigrants they will accept. Instead of an iron curtain separating the East from the West, a golden curtain may be drawn between the North and the South. The developed world is also increasingly hostile to immigrants from the developing countries because many bring with them a distinctively different political and cultural identity. In Europe, for instance, the influx of Muslims from North Africa is engendering either violent opposition or a more muted but nonetheless substantial discomfiture among various sectors of a traditionally Christian and liberal European society.

Internationalization of Labor Markets

The impact of international migration on the labor markets of host countries depends not only on the quantity of immigrants but also on the quality of their education and vocational skills and their ability to adjust to new technology, changes in demand, and the specific character of each country's labor market. National labor markets are extremely heterogeneous in terms of their openness, forms of organization, and supply and demand conditions. However, global processes like technological change and structural shifts in output and consumption do tend to generate certain uniform trends in demand patterns.

The internationalization of labor markets has been promoted in some areas by institutional arrangements, such as those within the EC, that liberalize movements of labor across national frontiers. In the relatively liberal international trading system, transnational corporations have also become an integrating force, connecting their production units and marketing and distribution operations in different parts of the world, while profiting from differences in the relative costs of labor. Through the transnational corporations, the labor markets of industrialized countries are now more directly linked with the labor markets of the developing world than they were in the past, affecting the demand for labor, the level and structure of employment, and wages and working conditions.

Because of the constraints on the mobility of the labor force, labor markets are still less internationalized than are the markets for goods, capital, and technology. The degree of international openness of labor markets varies from country to country, depending on short- and long-term employment and unemployment trends. In some countries, both unions and government regulations act to restrict entry into labor markets. Internationalization also influences the incentives offered to labor. The patterns and the extent of that influence depend on the role of such international actors as the transnational corporations, as well as on the scale of international migration. Even unemployment compensation programs and training and retraining mechanisms can be affected by the internationalization process.[58]

In the advanced industrial countries, however, converging occupational patterns, similar educational and skill needs, and narrowing differences in wage rates are both causes and consequences of the internationalization of labor markets. Although the internationalization of labor markets reduces certain national advantages that arise from differences in levels of wages, skills, and productivity, improving the quality of the labor force has nonetheless remained important to enhancing national competitiveness.

The human side of a nation's international competitiveness has many aspects, including the national capacity for the efficient utilization of skilled people and the ability of workers to adjust to changes in technology and the demand for labor. These are functions of a nation's investment in human resources to achieve organizational, managerial, and technological competency in the labor force. Since the close of World War II, and particularly since the advent of the technological era, investment in the long-term improvement of the quality of the labor force (through better education and greater access to health care, for instance) has become increasingly important to international competitiveness.

The post–World War II period has seen a qualitative improvement in the educational levels of all countries of the world. One can measure this improvement in several ways: changes in literacy rates, mean years of schooling (of the population over 25), and number of years of free, full-time compulsory education. In 1950, only one-third of the adult population of developing countries was literate; by 1980 the figure for literacy was 56 percent. Although on an international level it is difficult to find comparable and consistent data, from the sources that do exist one can conclude that free and compulsory education has increased everywhere, albeit with differences among countries. Developing countries typically require 5 to 11 years of compulsory education, and developed industrial countries 8 to 11 years. Nonetheless, the picture is not wholly encouraging. In the developing world, the dropout rate at the primary school level is 44 percent. Furthermore, in many parts of the world, social and cultural traditions dictate that girls receive fewer educational opportunities than do boys. According to UN data, more than 100 million children worldwide (about 5 percent of the total child population) receive no primary education and 200 million receive no education beyond the age of 12.

As a result of economic difficulties and constraints, the quality of educational services varies widely—not only among but also within countries. In some nations, most pupils barely attain functional literacy, whereas in others the school system prepares students to participate in the information revolution, even to the extent of teaching them computer literacy. In 1990, the global average of the mean years of schooling in the population over 25 years was 5 years—10 years in the industrialized, and 3.7 years in the developing countries. Tertiary enrollment ratios (the proportion of a given age group in colleges, technical schools, and other higher educational institutions and universities) also attest to the educational divide between the North and South. Although the number of university students throughout the world increased rapidly between 1950 and 1980, with the developing world showing twice the rate of growth of the developed world, by 1987–88 tertiary enrollment was only 6 percent in the developing countries, compared to 34 percent in the developed industrial countries.[59]

These averages were exceeded in the developing world by such countries as South Korea, Argentina, and Uruguay and in the developed world by nations such as the United States and Canada (which had figures of 59.6 and 62.6 percent, respectively). In Central and Eastern Europe, however, the relatively low and declining tertiary enrollment ratio (21.5 percent) suggests a disregard for the importance of investment in human capital that may seriously hinder reintegration into the global economy.[60]

By the end of the 1980s, the total number of people with university and other higher education degrees in the industrial countries was about 60 million and about 30 million in the developing countries, more than twice the number of 30 years earlier. A relatively large concentration of highly skilled people was to be found in developing countries that had implemented national policies to improve educational levels. In countries such as South Korea, China, India, Egypt, Thailand, and Indonesia, numbers reached the critical mass necessary for creating and sustaining modern industries. The internationalization of the labor markets probably has been most pronounced among this group of highly qualified people, whose knowledge is readily applicable to almost any industrial and technological environment.

Human Resource Development in a Competitive Global System

Successful competitors in the international economic system will increasingly shift their attention from the efficient management and combination of resources—particularly technoeconomic resources—to the management of human resources. Emphasis will be put on sustaining and improving the ability to utilize appropriate knowledge, to mobilize the will to work in a competitive and cooperative framework, and to maintain voluntary social discipline. Those nations that presently neglect these areas will fall ever further behind in global economic competition unless they rethink their priorities immediately. It takes decades for a nation to develop the experience, education, expertise, technological and managerial cultures, and formal and informal relationships that promote the intellectual interaction necessary to produce a reservoir of qualified people able to solve the complex problems of socioeconomic development and to be technologically innovative.

The quality of the knowledge possessed by those people involved in national decision-making processes plays a significant role in creating an environment conducive to human resource development. Beyond determining employment creation, unemployment compensation, and welfare payments, these people must pursue three other objectives in the development of their nation's human resources. The first is optimizing the quality of the labor force and human resources generally. This entails stimulating or implementing reforms in the educational system, retraining the labor force, and promoting scientific awareness and progress. The second objective is creating sociopolitical and economic conditions that favor economic development, including working conditions and incentive systems that encourage the attainment of desired levels of education and skill through both pecuniary and nonpecuniary (for instance, social status) rewards. National policies regarding human rights (such as declarations of the right to work, freedom of education, and freedom of movement) are also related to this effort. The third objective is developing policies for managing the human dimension of structural change, economic adjustments, and the related inevitable shocks. In this regard, policymakers need to develop measures to buffer the adverse impacts of economic change on individuals and to assist workers in adjusting to a new technological, psychological, and organizational environment in which old skills are degraded and new abilities demanded.

How these objectives are accomplished will vary from country to country. For example, countries that are open to the world market and depend on exports must sustain a highly flexible and adaptable economy and society. The more vulnerable a society is to rapid structural changes, the stronger its internal discipline and the higher its tolerance of shocks must be.

Transnational markets for goods, capital, and technology are becoming increasingly integrated and interconnected with labor markets. Technological breakthroughs that save labor and create new competitive capacities emerge quickly. If the expansion of economic activities and the growth of incomes occur at the expense of large numbers of the work force, powerful protectionist pressures may develop. Sustaining a relatively liberal global market system depends on the appropriate management of the human dimension of development, both nationally and internationally.

chapter 16

Technology and the Global Economy

Global Security in the Era of the Information Revolution

In the next century, the size and quality of the R&D sector, innovative capacity (the flexibility and efficiency of an economy and its ability to promote change and adaptation), and technological and scientific capabilities will become even more important in establishing the positions of countries within the shifting global hierarchy of political and economic power. Already, in the late 20th century, science and technology influence the scope and intensity of economic growth, the character of global markets, and the operations of multinational firms at a global level. Indeed, the role of science today is more widespread, pervasive, and multidimensional than ever before.

Science and technology are not independent variables. They function within a socioeconomic environment. Technological change is the result of several factors: the quantitative and qualitative differences between existing and emerging technologies and, from a macroeconomic perspective, the speed of substituting old technologies and diffusing new ones.[61] Substitution and diffusion are influenced by the capability of socioeconomic systems to manage the creative destruction process. This process involves structural transformations in political, economic, and labor sectors.

Microeconomic factors such as entrepreneurship, the availability of capital, and markets have always determined technological change. In the 1990s, the process of transition to a new technological era is occurring in a diverse and increasingly two-tracked global economy. Over the past 15 to 20 years, most industrial countries and a small group of developing countries have been able to support technological transformation. The vast majority of developing countries, however, struggling with grave social and economic problems, have been unable to develop practical measures for sustaining technoeconomic progress. They have become increasingly marginalized in the global economic system, especially in scientific and technological areas.

The concept of technology encompasses much more than tangible assets or physical capital. The increase of knowledge through the growth and influence of science as seen in universities and research centers is an intangible asset, as are other institutions for innovation, for adding value to human skills, and for advancing the capacity of industry and the service sector to absorb, use, adapt, and market new technologies.

The concept of a "technological era" shares many commonalities with the theory of long cycles.[62] A technological era is defined by the technologies that serve as the foundations of a social production system. These technologies shape output and consumption patterns and help determine productivity. Their logics and postulates influence skill and employment patterns and investment needs. Dominating technologies influence the style and quality of life, transform organizational systems and sociopolitical infrastructure, and provide a framework within which entrepreneurs operate and social choices are formed. These technologies cause major changes in the patterns of the international division of labor and in the functioning of global markets. They can have major consequences for national security policies and military doctrines.

The five sectors that have shaped the modern technological era are microelectronics (the foundation of information technology), materials technology, biotechnology, propulsion and space technology, and power technology. All are generic, multi-purpose technologies. Their development and global diffusion are at different stages in different nations. The use of these technologies is a factor in the speed and spread of economic growth in the major industrial countries.

New technologies have expanded the productive frontiers of individuals, firms, and countries at an unprecedented rate. Their global spread has been significantly faster than that of the key technologies of earlier periods for several reasons, including greater access to education; the internationalization of science; the information revolution, with its effects on consumption and production; and the part played by transnational corporations in diffusing technology.

Despite the unprecedented rapidity of the spread of new technologies, the transition to the new technological era on a global scale is a long-term, complex, and uneven process. This is partly because sources of the new advanced technologies have economic interests in maintaining oligopolistic positions and using their market power to influence the forms, speed, and costs of the diffusion process. There is also a high threshold of entry for latecomers. Building the necessary technological infrastructures and the capacities to support modern industries and services costs a lot of money and takes a long time. Even the developed industrial countries are encountering difficulties in adjusting to rapidly changing requirements, particularly in the fields of scientific infrastructure and education.

The NICs illustrate the problems involved in becoming a player in the new technological era. Although they are able to import advanced technologies to upgrade certain economic sectors and have developed export industries on the basis of their cheap and relatively skilled labor forces, NICs must make greater strides in upgrading their technological capabilities or they will fail to graduate into the category of developed industrial economies. Specifically, these countries must improve their human capital and create national R&D infrastructures and socioeconomic support systems.

The former socialist countries are still outside the mainstream of global technological transformation. In the past, their entry into the new technological era was been slow, uneven, and distorted by political-strategic and economic-systemic factors. For

instance, the Soviet Union's concentration on military technologies resulted in a closed and costly scientific and technological
military-industrial sector, with little or no spillover to other sectors. In spite of the relatively large number of university gradu-
ates within their labor forces and their relatively well-developed
scientific infrastructure, the former socialist countries have a
long way to go in creating the structural conditions necessary
for their integration into the world market. To bridge the gap,
they must learn entrepreneurship, gain access to financing,
and participate in those institutions (transnational firms, intergovernmental structures, and scientific cooperation networks)
that play a crucial role in global science and technology. Still,
their human resource base and R&D infrastructure are valuable
assets that can accelerate the catching-up process, at least within
some segments of their economies.

In those former socialist countries that possess the human
resources and scientific-technological assets compatible with
the requirements of the industrial world, concern is growing
that many highly qualified people will be tempted to work
abroad. In all the former socialist countries, government subsidies and demand for technology are diminishing, and R&D
is facing grave difficulties. As a result, many researchers in
Hungary, Poland, and Russia have abandoned scientific research
and have been employed by foreign firms; a greater number
have simply left their countries for R&D positions abroad. The
R&D sectors in Central and Eastern Europe might yet be saved
by wise government policies and support, internal restructuring, and efficient participation in the global system of science
and technology.

Because the transition to the new technological era is proceeding in an uneven way, economic opportunities are also distributed unevenly. The process is resulting in geographic, functional, and social polarization; new technology gaps; new patterns
of interdependence with varying degrees of asymmetries; and
new forms of competition and cooperation.

The Technoeconomic Dimension of the Global System

Four dimensions of the transition to the new technological era
are important to the process of global economic transformation.

1. *A new interrelationship has developed between science, technology, and society.* Because the inventions resulting in new technologies are scientifically based, science is instrumental in shaping the competitive positions of countries and firms in the global economy. National science policies are now much more important than they were in the past and must seek to create a critical mass of engineers and scientists in both pure and applied fields.

The technological capabilities of a country, which are reflected in its potential for innovation, its ability to supply national technological needs from domestic sources, and its role in the global market as a supplier or purchaser of new products and processes, have always helped to determine relative international competitive positions. There are two traditional interrelated components of technological capabilities. One is made up of a nation's cumulative technological culture, its stock of knowledge, and the patterns of its information flows.[63] The other component is connected with the national economy and market and includes macroeconomic and microeconomic factors and their interaction—that is, the incentives and opportunities for innovation, the volume of savings and investments, the degree of entrepreneurship, the character and scope of competition, and the efficiency of government policies.

In the new technological era, these components help a country generate or acquire new knowledge; apply multiple new technologies rapidly and efficiently; make the necessary social adjustments; create high-quality scientific and technological infrastructures (including educational and research institutions and government agencies); reduce the gap between the requirement for new skills and the potential of the educational system to provide them; improve governance; improve the quality of entrepreneurship; and expand the scope and flexibility of the capital market. The three centers of science and technology— North America, Western Europe, and Japan—are far from equal in all the areas constituting technological capacity. The strength of the United States is based on the size and universality of its R&D sector (the United States has significant R&D capabilities in all important areas of science) and its long experience in commercializing new technologies within a highly competitive environment. Europe is strong in research and the creation of new knowledge. European secondary education is superior to that of the United States, and Europe has many excellent universities that are increasingly interconnected with industrial firms. The strength of Japan is explained by its social and institutional capabilities for rapid structural adaptation and its efficient system of innovation.

2. *The impact of the technological changes is pervasive across a wide variety of production processes and in a large area of product families.* The diffusion and application of new technologies have altered the structure of the economy in the industrial world and induced changes on a global scale in output and consumption patterns, skills, life-styles, and institutions. Science-based sectors have emerged and become important in the restructuring and growth of the global economy. Both product and process innovations are directly linked to science. New, high-tech production processes have prompted major changes within traditional industries. A highly productive, high-tech service sector has emerged that is integrated with high-tech manufacturing and is spurring change in traditional industries, and in agriculture as well. The changes themselves have facilitated the rapid growth of small firms with highly specialized knowledge. In the past, economies of scale were important. Today, economies of scope are increasingly significant and have resulted in the creation of flexible manufacturing systems able to respond rapidly to changing market needs.

New technological gaps have appeared among sectors, firms, and countries. At the same time, however, the information revolution has facilitated the faster dissemination of knowledge and technological know-how. Although scientific and technological inventions, innovative capacities, and the bulk of ownership have been concentrated in three or four countries, the ability to copy new products and processes has increased. The global system of science and technology has become directly associated with, and organized by, transnational corporations. Despite the difficulties they face in retaining their oligopolistic positions in some key high-tech sectors, these corporations continue to exert a strong influence over the global distribution of costs and benefits of innovations through the use of instruments like licensing agreements. The global sourcing activities of the transnational corporations, which once focused on raw materials, cheap labor, and relatively inexpensive capital, are now increasingly focused on knowledge—

or intellectual capital. On average, about 18 to 20 percent of the research activities conducted for or by a transnational corporation takes place outside that corporation's home country; the proportion of external sources of research is growing rapidly, particularly in U.S. transnational firms.

3. *The diffusion of the new technologies and the spread of the information revolution have become major sources of internationalization.* Science and technology have always been international in the sense that scientists and inventors have been able to draw upon a stock of internationally available knowledge. In the new technological era, however, R&D activities have become more interconnected globally.

Information technologies play an important role in the internationalization process. These technologies have overcome the traditional barriers of time and space. Modern societies need access to vast amounts of information. In the economy, information represents power and opportunity. Information is also vital to national security. Worldwide demand for information has risen sharply, and the new information technologies have facilitated its rapid collection, processing, and dissemination. Data-compression technology allows huge amounts of information to be transported within very short periods of time. The process of internationalizing information has been furthered by the creation and operation of vast information systems connected by telecommunications networks through which an enormous volume of knowledge flows among countries. Nations that do not participate in these networks inevitably fall further behind in the technological race.

The process of internationalization is highly asymmetrical and unequal. For example, in the second half of the 1980s about 80 percent of telecommunications equipment was concentrated in the developed industrial countries. The number of installed telephones per 1,000 people was 20 times higher in the developed than in the developing countries. The city of Tokyo had more telephone lines at the end of the 1980s than did the entire African continent.[64] Interestingly, while the modern sectors of the developing countries are becoming integrated with global information flows, the other sectors of their economies are being increasingly marginalized.

The spread of new information technologies has facilitated the interconnectedness of markets. The capital and money markets have been greatly influenced by the new telecommunications networks. Fundamental changes have occurred in the developed industrial world, presenting new challenges to corporations and government policies. The interconnectedness of the Far Eastern, European, and American financial markets has created a global capital market operating around the clock, spreading the shocks of regional disturbances throughout the system within 24 hours. Interconnectedness has also been an important instrument in the globalization of competition.

International education has intensified the internationalization process. Although the degree of internationalization of higher education is still much lower than it was in medieval times, when often the majority of a university's students and professors were foreigners, higher education is rapidly becoming internationalized. Calculations based on UNESCO and national statistics show that 3 to 4 percent of the student population of the industrial world studied abroad—usually in other developed countries—in the early 1990s. The United States alone had almost 400,000 foreign students.

The number of foreign students is much larger at the postgraduate than the undergraduate level; this helps diffuse the scientific foundations of high technology, especially among the developing countries. Tens of thousands of experts, engineers, and doctoral students from the South have studied at the leading R&D institutes of high technology in the North over the past 25 years; the knowledge they have taken back to their countries has contributed to the establishment of eminent institutions of higher education and technology in many developing nations. About 20 developing countries now have the critical mass of experts needed to assimilate the most up-to-date technology, especially in defense-related areas. Further, the information revolution, through the establishment and spread of computerized databases, has made new developments in high technology more widely known and more easily available to scholars and governments in many countries. All these changes have contributed to an increased potential for understanding and utilizing new technology, and have given developing countries the ability to copy many of the achievements of the more developed countries. Less positively, these changes have also laid the scientific and technological foundations for the proliferation of the most destructive weapons.

The diffusion of the new technologies has changed the patterns of the international division of labor. The global map of comparative advantages has been radically altered by the spread of new technologies and the transformation of production and consumption structures. In replacing labor and materials, the new technologies have often undermined and eliminated a country's comparative advantages. Developments in information, communication, and transportation systems have reduced the importance of distance in production location. New technologies have facilitated the emergence of integrated production systems and a functional deployment of production phases. These changes have influenced the functioning of the global economy and the relative positions of the actors in international economic relations, bringing forth new imperatives and patterns in competition and cooperation among the global technological and economic centers.

4. *Science and technology have influenced the functioning of the international political system.* Because almost all new technologies in the Cold War era had dual purposes—military as well as civilian—they exerted an especially strong influence on national defense policies and the arms race. The arms race fueled technological change even as new technologies fueled the arms race. According to calculations based on national statistics, 8 to 10 percent of global military expenditures was spent directly on R&D during the 1970s and 1980s, when military R&D accounted for 18 to 20 percent of total R&D expenditures.[65]

Science and technology (especially information technology) have had other political consequences. They have contributed to the opening of traditionally closed societies and brought the people of the world closer together. National and international agendas are increasingly being set by the media, itself transformed by new developments in science and technology. This has changed the process of national political decision making. The political process today often bypasses traditional information channels; through television, citizens can follow events not only in their own countries but also in distant regions, practically as they happen. Thus, people are able to react swiftly—more swiftly than their governments are able to react officially—to vivid reportage of violations of human rights, violence, environmental disasters, and so forth.

By enabling the same television programs and movies to be seen throughout the world, and by reshaping consumption patterns on a global scale through the demonstration effect of the life-styles depicted, new technology has encouraged the emergence of a new global culture based on shared values and concerns. Such a culture threatens the gradual destruction of local identities and cultural diversity. At the same time, though, the information revolution brings nations closer together and facilitates a better understanding of the common problems and concerns of humankind in critical areas such as the environment, poverty, peace and war, drug abuse, and AIDS.

As science and technology influence the functioning of the international political and economic systems, so do those systems help determine the process of technological transformation. Of the major trends and developments currently under way in global politics and the world economy, four will be especially influential in this regard:

- the end of the Cold War and the evolving political patterns of the post–Cold War era;
- the slowing of economic growth in the major industrial countries, stagnation and decline in other regions, ongoing and new national and international economic imbalances, and structural disturbances;
- the emergence of new forces and forms of global competition resulting from the convergence of technological capabilities and economic potentials and ever-widening gaps in national capacities to respond to the socioeconomic imperatives of the new technological era; and
- the growth of environmental concerns linked to the global spread of new technologies like nuclear energy and biotechnology.

These trends will have significant consequences in several areas: upgrading national, regional, and global capabilities for the efficient management of the human side of technological transformation; restructuring the global technology market; and progressing toward a sustainable model of world development.

The Rationalization Process and the Human Dimension of Technological Change

Success in the global economy has always required the rationalization of production processes—that is, the more efficient use of science, technology, and human skills and the reorganization of production and services with the aim of increasing productivity and profitability. The speed of contemporary structural changes, in combination with sharpening competition and the deceleration of economic growth, has made rationalization even more important in international competition. In the recession of the early 1990s, rationalization in manufacturing and service sectors contributed to an increase in structural unemployment in all the industrial countries.

With the growing emphasis on rationalization, the diffusion and multiple uses of new technologies, and adjustment capabilities, several conditions for success in the international economic system are changing. The proper management of human factors has become critical, with the new relationship between technology and employment being the foremost problem.

Although new technologies are labor saving, their impact has thus far been selective. The occupational groups that have been affected most are clerical and secretarial workers, middle management, skilled craftspeople, and unskilled labor. The recession in the early 1990s and the technological structural changes connected with the rationalization process have produced significant changes in the service sectors, where a great number of people in banking, retail trade, and transportation have been replaced by technology. The introduction of new technologies may cause substantial unemployment in other sectors. Long-lasting unemployment rates of above 6 or 7 percent of the labor force would impose large burdens on welfare systems and threaten social stability. High rates of unemployment may also inspire moves toward protectionism.

The dangers created by employment problems can be avoided only through prudent and internationally coordinated policies. New policies are needed to reduce working hours, to create a flexible and organized retraining system, and to adopt a more human-centered approach in designing and introducing new technologies.

Another requirement for more efficient management of the human dimension is the modernization and upgrading of the national reservoir of skills. Achieving these goals hinges on making the educational system, especially at the secondary and higher levels, more relevant to the needs of modern industry and adjusting incentive systems and labor conditions to match the requirements of the new technological era. The kinds of changes necessary include introducing early retirement, shorter working weeks, and retraining programs. The economic difficulties of many countries in the 1980s and 1990s, particularly the developing countries, have weakened their capabilities in this area.

Most countries, especially the smaller ones, will not be able to manage the human dimension of global technological development efficiently on a national level. Instead, they will increasingly depend on regional and global cooperation. Even the larger countries will face problems in the absence of carefully conceived human developmental policies and major reforms, as the transnational markets for goods, capital, and technology increasingly interconnect with national labor markets.

Science in the Post–Cold War Era

All the political, socioeconomic, and institutional changes forming the new global system are also altering the position and character of science. The drive for greater efficiency and economic rationality is reshaping the role of science and making national science policies more pragmatic and market oriented. Several components of those policies, such as the selection of research priorities and the integration of science policies with other social objectives (for instance, environmental protection and economic development), are being redefined to secure higher yields. The R&D policies of large corporations, which formulate objectives to correspond to future changes in demand, are also being influenced by these changes.

Some experts have characterized this situation as the "end of the era of great science." However, this is an overly pessimistic view. The role of science in global production and competition will only increase. New knowledge will be the basis of the most innovative technologies, and any jump in technology will depend on a jump in knowledge. Expenditures on science will have to increase in those countries that want to increase their economic competitiveness and improve their citizens' quality of life.

The single most important source of change in the position and structure of science is the end of the Cold War. The Cold War fueled innovative efforts in military technologies. By 1992 it was evident that even in the absence of full demilitarization of science and technology in the United States and Russia, less money would be available for military-related R&D. Defense-related research in the coming years will probably focus more on the application than on the generation of new technologies. (Space research may be an exception.) Less emphasis may be placed on developing mass-destruction weapons systems and more on developing "smart" weapons, sophisticated ammunition, and communications, reconnaissance, guidance, and command-and-control technologies. Changes in the defense industries of developed industrial countries will likely lead to the establishment of smaller but increasingly efficient high-tech armies.[66]

In the successor states of the Soviet Union, and especially in Russia which has inherited the bulk of the Soviet military research potential, the oversized research capacities in defense-related areas will have to face up to economic realities. Russian scientists with expertise in nuclear, biological, and chemical weapons and missile-delivery systems may seek work abroad and thus contribute to the global proliferation of weapons of mass destruction. Even a partial conversion of defense industries in the former Soviet Union will be a formidable task that cannot be undertaken without extensive international cooperation and assistance.

Despite the fact that the research infrastructure will remain concentrated in the developed industrial and former socialist countries, the internationalization of science is destined to increase. The process may advance along two divergent paths. One is greater cooperation in reducing global gaps and managing and solving global problems. The other is the coalescence of science into three regional economic fortresses. However, bridges may be built between these two paths in the form of an expansion of existing international networks of scientists and scientific institutions and an increase in institutionalized cooperation (for example, through joint or parallel research or shared research contracts in the EC). International interconnectedness will increase further as a result of the global sourcing policies of the transnational corporations. Strategic R&D alliances among transnational firms already account for about 15 percent of their R&D activities.

The growth of scientific bases in the developing world and their participation in international networks is becoming an increasingly important conduit for internationalization. The research and higher education institutions within the developing countries vary in their R&D capabilities and opportunities to participate in global R&D networks. Such opportunities are better in areas where the developed industrial countries have political and economic interests in intensifying cooperation.

The internationalization of science will be promoted by eliminating restrictions previously imposed on contacts between scientists from the former Soviet bloc and their colleagues elsewhere in the world. There will also be mounting pressures in the developed industrial world to increase the internationalization of higher education and to establish a system of internationally recognized and accepted standards of scientific education, which will enhance the international mobility of scientists and technicians.

Structural Changes in Global Technology Markets

Technology markets are heterogeneous and complex structures that involve the sale and purchase of licenses, know-how, embodied knowledge in modern machinery and equipment, and high-tech services. Technology markets are made up of several interrelated structures—or "frameworks of relations"—the most significant of which is the relationship between the three main global centers of technology. Here the transnational corporations play an especially important role. About two-thirds of all technology-related transactions—trade, capital flows, and direct payments for new technology—takes place in the main global centers. This part of the technology markets is characterized by major shifts in competitiveness between the three main centers and by intensified competition and new forms of cooperation structures. Another framework of relations is the North-South component, which is characterized by a diversity of patterns and relations, and in which the NICs play an increasing role. This market segment accounts for about 20 percent of all technology transactions.

The East-West and East-East components of the global technology markets have been affected by the political and economic transformation of the former Soviet bloc. Political constraints on sales of technology have ended and market considerations have risen to the fore. In the 1990s, the technological relations of the former socialist countries have been dominated by the problems of transition to a market system and the implications and difficulties of their reintegration into global technology markets. The outcome of these changes is unknown. Will they result in a dualistic technology and market structure composed of small and highly competitive niches closely connected or integrated with the transnational corporations and coexisting with a backward and poor sector that serves the domestic market? Or will the modernization process result in a slowly expanding and broadly based modern industrial and service sector with a modern infrastructure? The latter outcome will depend on the fulfillment of a variety of domestic and external conditions such as an increase in the efficiency of governmental economic and innovation policies, a growth in entrepreneurship, a rapid improvement of human capital, an availability of investments, and an improvement in marketing and managerial capabilities. These conditions will be difficult, but not impossible, to satisfy.

The international markets of technology (goods and services) constitute approximately 27 to 30 percent of the world market of goods and services. Through their growing volume and share of the world market, these technology markets have become the key forces acting to increase world trade and foreign direct investments during the past 25 years. Structural and other changes in these markets have major impacts on international trade and the global economy as a whole. They influence access to innovations, changes in corporate strategies, and institutional conditions (including government policies) through their interconnectedness with goods and services. They also have a major influence on the scope and character of competition. Due to the dynamics of technological change, it is increasingly difficult to maintain or strengthen the competitive positions of even the largest firms and strongest countries without constantly upgrading their technological capabilities and marketing operations.

Further expansion of the information technology market depends to a large extent on changes in the production and use of these technologies, improvements in product performance, and lower prices. U.S. firms have achieved breakthroughs in some areas of information technology, especially in micro-chip manufacturing, out-innovating and out-investing their major Japanese competitors by focusing on multimedia chips, which increase the audio, graphics, and video-processing capabilities of personal computers. The world market in these areas of new technology will become more competitive and its structure may change yet further. Even large companies such as Philips and IBM have already been forced to introduce major innovative technologies and restructure their systems. An array of specialty companies has come into existence, each focusing on a differ-ent segment of the chain: chips, disks, distribution, database software, customer service. On the whole, these small com-panies have proven to be more efficient than the large inte-grated producers.[67]

The Industrial World and Changes in the Technology Markets

The global markets of technology have always been hierarchical structures. In the mid-1990s, the leading positions in those hierarchies are occupied by the developed countries, which are the main exporters and importers of the new technologies and the key sources and hosts of technology-related investments. Recently, however, changes have been occurring that are dimin-ishing the developed nations' lead over the rest of the world. Most notably, over the past 10 years the NICs have increased their share of the international trade of new technologies faster than any other group of countries.

The United States, which still possesses the most diversified R&D establishment, retains its preeminent position in global technology markets. That position has been eroding, however. Whereas in 1970 U.S. factories supplied 95 percent of home market needs in high-tech products, in the second half of the 1980s this proportion dipped to about 80 percent. In the 1970s,

U.S. factories produced 51 percent of the high-tech products of the industrial countries; by the end of the 1980s, the U.S. share was down to 40 percent. As mentioned above, there has been a similar decline in the U.S. share in world trade of high-tech products, from 30 to 22 percent.[68]

While U.S. firms are trying to sustain or even restore their positions in certain high-tech industries and markets, all relevant technological and economic indicators, such as the volume of R&D expenditures for civilian use, the number of new patents, and the number of scientists and engineers, show a convergence among the performances of the United States, Western Europe, and Japan. However, a fragmented pattern of advantages in different sectors and an increasing degree of specialization exists. Per capita R&D expenditure in the mid-1960s was 100 in the United States, 21 in the European Common Market, and 10 in Japan. At the end of the 1980s, the U.S. level was still 100, but the figure was 67 in the European Community and 107 in Japan. Total U.S. R&D expenditure in 1964 was 3 times the combined R&D outlays of Western Europe and 20 times larger than that of Japan. In 1989, the Japanese figure was 60 percent of U.S. outlays while the combined expenditures of West European countries were 73 percent of U.S. outlays. In the early 1960s, close to three-fourths of new products and processes were of American origin. By the late 1980s, the U.S. share had declined to about 40 percent, although this figure is somewhat misleading because many of the non-U.S. technologies are often based on American licenses and know-how.[69]

All such changes indicate that Western Europe and Japan are catching up with the United States in terms of technological capability and performance, resulting in sharper competition and turbulence in the market. In this new era, the technological strategy of the most advanced countries is not to aim for overall global technological leadership but to target the best position in the international technological division of labor and in the technological market. They often target the same industries, however. Industries that are the sources of U.S. strength, such as aerospace, defense, and some areas of electronics and telecommunications, are also targeted by Western Europe, which is strong in machinery, chemicals, and nuclear power stations. Japan, while sustaining or increasing its advantages in engines, motor vehicles, machinery, and semiconductors, is targeting the electronics and electrical industries and pursuing breakthroughs in areas such as robotics, artificial intelligence, and biotechnology. Russia, having inherited most of the technological potential of the Soviet Union, retains an important position in the technology market, especially in space technology. Its slow transition to the market system may result in changes in the structure of global technology markets.

The Asian NICs have reached the limits of their competitiveness based on imported technology and low-cost production. Some NICs are entering a new stage of technologically based competitiveness by developing domestic R&D in segments of the information technology markets. Some firms are striving to increase their global R&D sourcing activities in Europe and the United States. The process of upgrading technological capabilities and entering into a higher stage of the global technology markets is being duplicated by countries in Asia and Latin America. The success of these countries depends not only on their abilities to upgrade their R&D infrastructure, but also on their capabilities to make adjustments, on changes in marketing structures, and on the availability of financing.

Technological transformation is rapidly changing the functioning of the markets, especially the forces of supply and demand, at least from a technological point of view. As already noted, the spread of flexible manufacturing systems is increasing the flexibility of supply and allowing economies of scope to replace, in some areas, the economies of scale valued by industries in the past. The integration of sales, design, and production with telecommunications systems has facilitated the spread of "just-in-time" systems and a more rapid response to changing demand patterns. The choice between horizontal diversification and vertical integration (a key managerial problem of the past) is further complicated by the existence of a flexible network of independent subcontractors.

The relationships among the actors in the global technology markets are also changing. The post–Cold War world no longer justifies the imposition of strategic controls on international technology sales to former adversaries. The phasing out of most restrictions on sales offers new opportunities to suppliers, both large and small, and will dramatically increase the availability of technology to Central and Eastern Europe and the former Soviet Union. The intensification of the technology flows to the former Soviet bloc may improve the production and export potential of that region and increase the number of competitors in the global technology markets.

The advent of the single European market will compel most firms active in the field of technology to reevaluate their technological competence in a large competitive framework. While the single market will provide new opportunities for European firms, it will also threaten many of those businesses that once enjoyed local preferences and protection. (Sectors that are already highly internationalized—electronics, aerospace, and car manufacturing—will be less affected.) Future technical standardization, a key target of the single market process, will be problematic in light of the absence of agreement on common standards and the likelihood that the way in which standardization will be introduced will favor the largest business groups.

The increasing internationalization of technology markets, the higher costs of R&D, and the intensification of the creative destruction process—especially the shortened life cycles of new products—have forced the business sector to focus on reducing costs, increasing productivity, and improving the performance and quality of products. One result of these efforts has been the spread of "technoglobalism" in the transnational sector. This term is understood to mean that transnational enterprises employ the research capacities of many different countries in their corporate systems. Another aspect of technoglobalism is the spread of strategic alliances among transnational firms. The increasingly expensive R&D process stimulates the development of different cooperative arrangements, specific-purpose joint ventures, and cross-licensing arrangements (especially in areas such as aerospace, biotechnology, computers, telecommunications, software, and new materials). Within the scientific and technological triangle of the United States, Western Europe, and Japan, 90 percent of technological cooperation agreements are concluded at intergovernmental and company levels.

The implications of technoglobalism and the efforts of European countries, particularly EC members, have stimulated the progress of international programs involving cooperation among businesses, governments, and academics. The common regional scientific and technological development programs (for example, the European Strategic Programme for the Research of Information Technology—ESPRIT—or the Research of Advanced Communication in Europe—RACE) include dozens of research institutes, universities, transnational corporations, and small and medium-sized enterprises. This form of cooperation is characterized as "technoregionalism" and is developed not only in opposition to, but also often in tandem with, technoglobalism. It represents a collective regional response to the pressure from many firms for the support and protection of their governments in the cut and thrust of international competition. Of course, the spread of these new cooperative programs does not mean an end to government policies aimed at protecting and supporting national R&D. Regional or national technoprotectionism may widen into a global trend if competition becomes sharper in a slowly growing global economy.

The Developing World and the Technology Markets

In the field of technology imports, the failure or success of developing countries depends on the local environment: its technological culture; the level of economically motivated demand; the quality of the host economy; the supportiveness of the infrastructure; the appropriateness of specific technologies; and the terms of the economic and business conditions attached to the sale and use of the imported technology.[70]

In developing indigenous R&D capabilities, the most significant problems of developing countries are rooted in their weak technological capabilities and bargaining positions, slow growth in the world economy, the debt problem, and specific difficulties with trading partners. Despite these difficulties, a number of large developing countries, such as India, Brazil, and China, have made progress in the establishment of scientific and technological capabilities. Some developing countries have advanced rapidly in world trade and have been able to erode the competitive positions of the developed industrial countries; NICs such as South Korea, Singapore, and Taiwan have combined their relatively well-qualified and cheap labor forces with highly developed technologies, organizational methods, and marketing systems adopted from industrial countries. In the future, however, many of the advantages of cheap labor will diminish as the result of automation or flexible manufacturing systems through which traditional labor-intensive industries are transformed into knowledge-intensive industries, a process that may reintroduce comparative advantages to international competitiveness.

Another area where the market position of the developing countries has been strongly influenced by technological changes is raw materials. This sector experienced difficulties in the 1980s and was hit hard by the global recession in the early 1990s. The declining material intensity and increasing knowledge content of finished goods, the production of cheaper and more efficient substitute materials and better alloys, and the reduction of waste will further reduce the importance of the traditional global raw material economy. The ratio of aggregate mineral and metal consumption to industrial output declined by an average 1.9 percent annually between 1970 and 1989, creating completely new demand patterns for raw materials. In addition, the introduction of high-tech equipment has made the production of fuels and minerals more capital and knowledge intensive. All these changes have contributed to a decline in raw material prices, leaving many traditional producers and exporters of raw materials with mounting economic difficulties, not least a growing indebtedness.

The growing demand for more effective protection of intellectual property rights is also of particular significance to developing countries, which, as the followers in technological development and the net importers of new technology, often copy technology to minimize their costs. The rising importance of knowledge in global production, the growing costs of R&D, and the role of technological capabilities in international competition have made the protection of intellectual property not only a legal issue but also a political one. The issue was one of the main sources of contention between developed and developing countries in the GATT negotiations that were concluded at the end of 1993. Know-how and trade secrets are, of course, assets to high-tech firms. In an era of information technologies, it is no longer difficult to copy products, and some countries have made technological piracy a common practice.

In response to calls from the developed world for greater protection against this kind of piracy, developing countries have noted that the owners of new technologies often enjoy oligopolistic positions and price the new technologies unfairly high. More often than not, restrictive conditions are attached to the use and export of technologies. Such practices are considered by some developing countries to be components of a global strategy to sustain oligopolistic power and increase the technology rent.

Even after the 1993 agreement in the GATT, finding a broadly acceptable and workable solution to the question of intellectual property rights will not be easy. Owners of intellectual property regard protection of their rights as a key condition for future transfers of technology. But many political figures and experts in the developing world resist such demands while pressing for freer access to new technologies.[71]

Technology and Ecology in the New Era

The global technological transformation and the diffusion of new technologies has prompted both concern and optimism regarding the management of the global ecosystem. On the one hand, through their use of dangerous chemicals, biogenetic manipulation of living organisms, or potential for increased emission of radiation, some new technologies create ecological problems. On the other hand, most of the new technologies have actually facilitated the reduction of the amount of energy and materials needed to produce a given quantity of a product. In many instances, new products and processes are "friendlier" from an ecological viewpoint than were earlier technologies. Furthermore, many global problems (industrial pollution, nuclear waste, and depletion of the ozone layer, for instance) can probably only be solved by the application of new technologies.

Their introduction as instruments of environmental protection will be difficult to accomplish, however. The problem lies not so much in the development of appropriate technologies (many potentially useful technologies already exist) as in their distribution and use. The price of technology, the conditions for its international transfer, the ability to adapt it to different systems, the capacities for assimilating it, and the creation of international mechanisms to organize and oversee the process: all pose formidable obstacles to the application of technology for the benefit of the global ecosystem.

An Interim Balance

Any conclusions about the future effects of post–Cold War changes on the global technology system would be premature. It is evident, however, that the transition to a new technological era will continue to be a complex and uncertain process, subject to future innovations, shifting market forces, and a changing global sociopolitical environment. In an era of slower economic growth, many firms have found it especially difficult to cope with the rapid pace of technological change and the greater flexibility that new competitors enjoy.

The process of social adjustment to new technology seems likely to become yet harder and more painful in the future, requiring more supportive national policy measures and more efficient international cooperation. Institutional, legal, and regulatory frameworks for dealing with the consequences of the technological transformation are still in their formative stages and cannot yet cope with the new and evolving problems. New ethical principles, legal approaches, educational forms, and political mechanisms are urgently needed.

If the world is to master the capabilities of new technologies to achieve a more equitable, safe, and ecologically sustainable global order, it must embark on a process of dialogue that has a broader scope and a larger number of participants than that conducted at GATT meetings or international conferences on the environment and development. The international community should seek to convert military R&D capacities to civilian use in the pursuit of new knowledge with which to moderate global problems and manage risk collectively. The dangers posed by new discoveries, especially in such areas as nuclear research and genetic manipulation, should be brought under international control.

chapter 17

Trade and Capital Markets in the Changing Economic System

Among the sources of instability and risk in the international economic community, those connected with economic issues, especially trade and monetary issues, will become more difficult to manage in a world of increasing competition. The relatively free access to markets, the availability of external resources under reasonably stable and predictable conditions, and the governance of the global trading and financial system will all attain unprecedented importance.

The Changing Role of International Trade

International trade has played a major role in the increase of interconnectedness and interdependence in the post–World War II world. Global trade has created unprecedented opportunities for economic growth, but it also has become a medium for the international spread of disturbances caused by national policies, imbalances, and changes in competitive positions.

Since World War II, significant changes have occurred in the relations among world output, international trade, and the factors shaping competitive positions. The growth of world trade has surpassed the increase in world output. Between 1950 and 1973, world trade increased by 7.2 percent and global output by 5 percent annually. During the 1970s and early 1980s, the growth rates of world output and trade converged temporarily, but the more rapid increase of world trade was resumed in the mid-1980s. Whereas world exports represented only 10 percent of world output in 1950, by 1980 they had surpassed 20 percent, and in 1990 they were close to 24 percent. These changes have been especially noticeable in industry. Between 1950 and 1990, world trade in industrial products expanded almost twice as fast as the output of manufacturing industries.

The national economic importance of foreign trade increased not only in those countries that formerly had been heavily dependent on exports and imports—that is, where foreign trade continuously accounted for a substantial proportion of GDP—but also in countries such as the United States or the Soviet Union, where 30 or 40 years ago exports and imports were of a negligible magnitude.

An analysis of factors responsible for the growth of trade in the post–World War II period reveals their long-term technical and structural causes, as well as their short- to medium-term conjunctural components (like temporary bottlenecks in supplies from one country to another).[72] Many factors have been related to technological change, associated transformations in competitiveness, and consumption and output patterns. The share of manufactured products in world exports grew from 60 percent in 1970 to 69 percent in 1990. The share of high-tech products in world trade rose from about 3 percent in 1970s to nearly 18 percent in 1992.

The comparative positions of countries have undergone major changes. As noted above, these changes have been especially marked in the area of high technology, where between 1970 and the end of the 1980s the overall trade surplus of the United States became a deficit in many high-tech goods, while the surpluses of Japan, Germany, and France increased dramatically.[73] There also has been a decrease in the U.S. share of global raw materials and agricultural products, declining from 14.7 percent to 9 percent for foodstuffs, from 6 percent to 3.5 percent for agricultural raw materials, and from 7.3 percent to 3.3 percent for ores and metals. A slight increase in the U.S.

share of world trade has been experienced for fuel, rising from 9.2 percent to 11.0 percent.

The increasingly knowledge-intensive character of the global economy, especially in the industrial and service sectors, will reduce overall dependence on raw materials.[74] Imports of raw materials will nonetheless increase, as will the number of importing countries. Presently, one-half of global industrial production depends on imported raw materials. Only a handful of states are able to meet their raw material and energy requirements from domestic sources. In 1925, only 14 percent of all energy sources crossed national borders; by 1990, the figure was 37 percent. In certain cases, fuel and raw material imports are cheaper than domestic production would be (as in the United States); in other cases, there are simply no alternatives (as in most West European countries and Japan). As the industrialization of the developing countries proceeds over the coming decades, so import needs will increase globally. Most of the Soviet Union's successor states will have to rely on imported fuel and raw materials, mainly from Russia and the Central Asian republics.

The structural problems are different in the agricultural markets, which have been even more depressed and unstable than the raw material markets. There has been a tendency toward self-sufficiency everywhere. In the developed industrial countries, the ratio of imports related to food consumption declined from 6 percent in 1960 to 4 percent in 1989. The most dramatic changes have taken place in Western Europe. Its share of global agricultural imports dropped from above 50 percent in the 1960s to below 40 percent in the 1980s, and its proportion of agricultural exports increased from 30 percent to above 40 percent. There is also a declining trend of imports in developing countries. All told, in the 1980s only 10 percent of total global food and grain production entered world trade.

Another aspect of structural changes is the expansion of intrasectoral, or intraindustry, trade in the form of transnational product development, design, production, and marketing. This trade has grown much faster than world trade; by the late 1980s, it constituted about one-half of total world exports. Its growth has been stimulated by the spread of transnational firms and their global sourcing strategies, which have contributed to the deepening division of labor while offering large cost reductions.

Intraindustry trade will remain important in the future, especially among transnational corporations, interconnected as they are by ownership, strategic alliances, cross licensing, and long-term contracts. The ability to compete in the global economy will increasingly depend on a country's capabilities (meaning primarily the capabilities of its firms) to realize the potential gains derived from the globalization of supporting industries and to concentrate on value-added aspects of industrial and service activities.

The information revolution, as we have observed above, has dramatically decreased transportation and communication costs; facilitated the instant transmission of technology blueprints, fluctuations in stock prices, and changes in marketing strategies; and altered the traditional character of intraindustry trade. The informational revolution will also permit the future integration of output and sales through the use of computer systems. Although national governments can disrupt the integration process with protectionist measures and regulations, to do so would be to risk global chaos and incur losses (in terms of declining trade and output, shrinking incomes, rising unemployment, and so forth) on a far greater scale than protectionism brought in the past. On a regional level, the functioning of the single European market and the expansion of the EC toward Central and Eastern Europe, Japanese policies for the establishment of more structured relations with many Asian countries, and the development of the North American free trade area will help spread the new forms of intraindustry trade. Another factor in the expansion of world trade has been, and will remain, the increasing internationalization of the service sector, especially financial services and telecommunications.

World trade patterns have also been influenced by the decline in the "smokestack" industries, especially in the traditional metallurgical and light industries of many countries. Although smokestack industries are increasingly redeployed to certain developing countries (where their comparative positions are often improved through modernization), their continuing presence in the developed world, and the socioeconomic difficulties associated with phasing them out, are a major problem for the world economy and a constant source of protectionist pressures.

Conjunctural components that are connected with the cyclical development of the global economy and/or other factors of temporary growth and decline, like the investment boom in China in the early and mid-1990s, may also have lasting structural effects on international trade and promote long-term relations among countries and regions.

While both structural and conjunctural factors in the post–World War II period contributed to the increasing international division of labor and the rapid growth of world trade, the slow-down of economic growth and the various ways in which structural changes occurred (contributing to an increasing fission in the world economy) created major new structural imbalances in world trade, adversely influenced the functioning of the international trading system, and were largely responsible for the increase in global debt and the debt crisis of the 1980s.

Structural disturbances and global and regional imbalances are, in fact, permanent characteristics of global economic development. Their intensity and significance may be the result of several factors: changes in international competitiveness; economic policy and adjustment failures; and mismanagement of national economies. Their consequences may vary greatly, depending on the nature of the sources of the disturbances, the character of the countries affected, and the ability of the international market and institutional mechanisms to correct imbalances and manage related problems. These issues are, of course, influenced by the functioning of the international multilateral trading and financial system.

In the mid-1990s, the international trading system arrived at a new turning point with the conclusion of the Uruguay Round of GATT negotiations.[75] The agreement reached, which will alter the international trading system more dramatically than did any of the previous GATT rounds, has three key elements: the reduction of tariff duties on manufactured goods by about one-third; the partial extension of world trading rules to cover agriculture, services, foreign direct investments, and intellectual property rights; and an increase in the power of GATT to supervise the fulfillment of agreements under its aegis and settle disputes between member states. As with all GATT agreements, the process of national ratification and the bilateral elaboration of specific details will be long and arduous. Despite differences of opinion about the future impact of the agreement on the global economy, three consequences do seem evident: the global trading system will become more open and competitive, which will favor the stronger countries; poorer nations will be compelled to make more concessions toward liberalization than they receive; and "marginal producers" (the least efficient producers, that is) will be forced out of the market in a number of industrial and developing countries if agricultural subsidies and other protective measures are reduced.

The Globalization of Capital Markets

The smooth functioning of the global economy in the late 20th century depends on the state of global finance. Since the late 1960s, the increasing financial integration of national economies has taken place in an environment of growing speculative money flows and inefficient macroeconomic management. In the absence of effective multilateral constraints on national policies and effective international supporting mechanisms, major imbalances have developed in some countries. Disorder has been manifested in unpredictable and dramatic shifts in interest and exchange rates, international flows of capital, and the prices of financial assets, which have all had an adverse effect on global economic growth. Severe strain has been placed on creditor-debtor relations, capital markets, and the banking system. The increase of instability has raised the dangers of global financial collapse, a more dangerous risk than in the past due partly to the increased role of international money and capital markets in financing production, consumption, and trade and partly to the growing interconnectedness of financial institutions and flows. The ability of countries to avoid financial crises by collective action has become a leading concern for global risk management.

The international financial system is probably the most complex and the least transparent factor of the global economy. It consists of interstate organizations (the International Monetary Fund, the World Bank, and the Bank for International Settlements), formal and informal interstate groupings, money exchanges, stock exchanges, state and private banks, various other types of financial institutions (insurance companies, investment funds, and so forth), and regional concentrations of these financial institutions that are represented by closely interacting international money centers. The money markets have become internationalized to a much greater extent than have the commodities markets. This is reflected in the internationalization of banking operations.

Banking can be divided into wholesale (or investment) banking and retail banking. Wholesale banking serves the larger members of the corporate sector; retail banking serves smaller business and individual customers. Wholesale banking has become very internationalized. The Bank for International Settlements estimates that the stock of international financing reflecting international banking activities increased from $1,500 billion in 1983 to $3,200 billion in 1988.[76]

Retail banking has remained largely local, although interbank relations have extended international interconnectedness. The international spread of credit cards has played an important role in this process. By 1990, for example, Visa had more than 160 million customers in 80 countries. Other financial institutions have also become more internationalized, although this is seen more in the global spread of large insurance firms than in the cross-border supply of services. The liberalization of the insurance business within the EC, which accounts for about 25 percent of world insurance premiums ($406 billion in 1987), will certainly contribute to greater internationalization of insurance services. There has also been rapid growth in the internationalization of the securities trade, concentrated in the large capital markets of London, New York, and Tokyo.[77]

In the mid-1990s, the financial geography of the world is a complex, three-dimensional structure composed of global, regional, and national processes and institutions. The latest communications technologies facilitate the efficient combination of marketing and banking transactions on a global level. Globalization has been promoted by the growing volume of internationally tradeable products in the financial markets and the increasing number and role of global clients, which include transnational corporations, institutional investors, and the less important and less visible money launderers. Global arrangements concerning rules, procedures, and standards have been adopted by multilateral institutions to influence markets and competition and to reduce or manage risk. Rapidly developing telecommunications technology allows operations and transactions to cross continents at unprecedented speeds.

Since the 1970s, the international financial market has expanded rapidly, not least because of the impact of demand and supply factors. In the 1970s, thanks to the second explosion in oil prices, the oil-producing and -exporting countries earned a surplus income of close to $1,800 billion, a great portion of which went into the international money markets. Measured in terms of the ratio of bank credits to the global GNP, international banking activity increased from 1 percent to 18 percent between 1970 and 1990. Volumes in bond markets likewise expanded considerably, with the combined national and international stock rising to $10,000 billion by 1989. The daily volume of trading in the U.S. foreign exchange markets increased from $10.5 billion to $183.2 billion between 1980 and 1989.[78]

In the course of the 1980s, the vast surpluses of Japan and the Federal Republic of Germany permitted the outflow of a total of $800 billion to the international money markets. At the same time, an escalating demand for external sources of financing appeared in the United States, developing countries, and various Central and East European countries. In the 1980s, the United States raised more than $800 billion from external sources.[79] During the 1980s, the international money markets multiplied 6 times, with a daily volume more than 50 times as large as that of commodity markets. The pattern and direction of international money flows also changed. The leading industrial countries' capital markets were rapidly internationalized. Market positions underwent change. There was a decrease in the role of dollars in international operations, whereas the yen and the West German mark gained considerably.

In spite of the internationalization process, the regional capital markets have preserved many of their essential characteristics. The "Anglo-Saxon" markets of the United States and the United Kingdom still maintain a relatively transparent institutional system with specialized commercial and investment banks, open disclosure and reporting requirements, and highly experienced and influential rating agencies and financial analysts. The continental European markets are dominated by universal banks. Institutional capital formations are far fewer in Europe and disclosure requirements are very liberal and undemanding. The Japanese market has a large institutional and specialized system with relatively few disclosure and reporting requirements. Great differences exist in the positions and roles of the central banks and governments in the market. In Japan, the capital market system, in spite of its liberalization, is more orchestrated than are the markets of Europe and North America. The differences among these systems complicate international coordination and the implementation of multilateral risk management measures.

Institutional differences notwithstanding, fundamental, and in some ways similar, changes have occurred in the functioning of international capital markets and the structure of their operations. All are now reliant on international computer-based telecommunications systems, which have further increased the interconnectedness of the Far Eastern, European, and Anglo-Saxon financial markets. An around-the-clock global capital market has been established, spreading the shocks of regional disturbances throughout the global system within a day. Other changes and innovations have responded to the new needs of national economies and the international economic system. One innovation is "securitization," meaning the conversion of nonliquid assets such as mortgages, car loans, and credit card loans into securities that can be easily priced, bought, and sold in open markets. (Technically, the different loans have to be pooled first and used to back securities.) More than two-thirds of U.S. residential mortgages were securitized in the early 1990s. This demonstrates the use of capital markets to set prices for risks and to facilitate risk management.

The international integration of capital markets has occurred simultaneously with the integration of the money, commodities, and securities markets. This has been instrumental in the diversification of investments by international financial institutions, banks, insurance companies, investment funds, and transnational corporations, advancing yet further the globalization of operations and interests.

The regional, intersectoral, institutional, and operations-related integration of the international capital markets has improved the efficiency of investments, reduced the costs of operations, and boosted the income of financial institutions. However, new risk factors have emerged as a consequence of the fact that changes in the rates and patterns of savings, monetary and fiscal policies, regulations, disturbances, and shocks—especially in the finances of major actors in the system—can now spread rapidly from one region to another, particularly in an environment of floating exchange rates. Transmitted to other sectors first and foremost through international trade, shocks can cause large volumes of capital flight or speculative capital movements, thus destabilizing economies, especially those of the weaker countries.

The expansion and the growing internationalization of the financial system have not been paralleled by institutional changes designed to increase the system's stability. Despite helping the sectors producing and trading goods and services in the global economy weather the major shocks of the 1970s and 1980s, the international financial system itself has grown more vulnerable. Among the various sources of this enhanced vulnerability, two are especially important. One is the absence of international institutions similar to "international lenders of last resort" (such as global or regional central banks) that can act instantly in the event of default, the dangers of which have increased. The other is the presence of serious domestic problems in large money markets related to conjunctural factors (large-scale speculations, exchange-rate fluctuations, critical errors in government policies intended to maintain macroeconomic stability, or the mismanagement of external finances) that may cause financial crises.

The degree of internationalization and the large volume of the financial markets, accompanied by the spread of deregulation, require built-in stabilizers beyond those that presently exist (like the informal agreements among the G-7 states, a few structured controls imposed by the EC, and agreements in the Bank for International Settlements concerning reserves). Several experts have suggested that by uniting the International Monetary Fund and the World Bank a global institution would be created that could serve as a catalyst to growth and a bridge between international governments and private finances.

Another problem for the financial markets, and one that received much attention in the early 1990s, pertains to the increasing gap between the growing demand for capital and the actual supply of new money, which has been adversely affected by slower economic growth and a lower level of savings. The mean net savings rates declined in the United States from 10.6 percent in the 1960s to 3.9 percent in the 1980s, in Japan from 25.6 to 20.2 percent, and in Germany from 19.9 to 10.7 percent.[80] This problem became acute in the 1980s, when a number of countries chose to live with substantial deficits using high interest rates to check inflationary pressures and to attract foreign capital. The situation is projected to worsen throughout the 1990s.

According to World Bank estimates, global demand for capital will be exceptionally high—up to $100 billion annually—during the 1990s and beyond. In addition to the continuing demands of the developing countries for external financing and the regular investment needs of businesses, global capital markets will be asked to finance an array of enormously expensive undertakings: the rebuilding of the former East Germany; the reconstruction of Iraq and Kuwait; the remodeling of the infrastructure in many Asian NICs; the transition to a market economy in Central and Eastern Europe and the former Soviet Union; the replacement of the deteriorated public infrastructure in the United States, Europe, and Japan; and meeting the demands of the U.S. budget deficit. The costs of global environmental policies may also be high.[81]

These international financing needs seemed in the early 1990s to be more than sufficient to modify demand-and-supply relations in the money markets and appeared likely to create a global shortage of capital and high interest rates, which might have imperiled long-term economic growth. These problems, though, have been moderated by long recessions and slow economic growth, by increasingly cautious and selective lending policies of banks, and by government action to keep interest rates down. The shortage problem may not be over, however, even though a number of countries may ameliorate the shortage of capital by drastically reducing defense expenditures and using the savings to meet new capital needs. Another serious consequence of the rising global demand for capital may be that creditworthy debtor nations from the North will crowd out of the financial markets less secure countries from the South.

chapter 18

Toward a Transnational Economy in a Fragmented World

The Role of Transnational Corporations

Internationalization, globalization, and transnationalization are rather ill-defined concepts, often used as synonyms, that can be applied to several processes.[82] In this book, the transnationalization process in the global economic system is used to denote the interpenetration of national economies. This implies more than is commonly understood by the terms "interrelationship" or "interdependence"; transnationalization results in the increase of both interconnectedness and interdependence. Strong forces promote transnationalization, including the creation of an immense transportation infrastructure, the development of integrated international production, the intensive movement of knowledge and capital across national frontiers, and the increasing economic obsolescence and erosion of national frontiers.

In the global economy of the late 20th century, the most important forces and agents of the transnationalization process are the transnational corporations that grew out of the multinationalization of production and competition. These corporations are directly involved in the interpenetration of national economic structures

Table 5. Foreign Direct Investments Abroad, by Country of Origin
(As a percentage of total stock)

	1970	1990
United States	46	33
Great Britain	15	14
Japan	5	13
Federal Republic of Germany	6	9
Switzerland	7	6
Holland	7	6
Canada	4	5
France	4	3
Italy	1	2

Sources: United Nations Center on Transnational Corporations, *World Investment Report, 1992: Transnational Corporations as Engines of Growth* (New York: United Nations, 1992); *Economic Report of the President* (Washington, D.C.: Government Printing Office, 1992); and U.S. Department of Commerce, Bureau of the Census, *Statistical Abstract of the United States, 1991* (Washington, D.C.: Government Printing Office, 1992).

by international ownership, production, and employment, through which coporations not only share markets with host country firms but also increasingly integrate those firms into the corporations' international networks. Transnational corporations have direct access to the factors of production. They share the national income of host countries and receive incentives such as government subsidies. Transnational corporations pay taxes and wages and use national credit facilities. They have vested interests in transborder expansion. Thus, transnationalization is in fact the "microintegration" of national economies; as such, it has important consequences for international cooperation and competition.

International corporations continue to gain strength in practically all domains of the world economy. In the early 1990s, according to the United Nations, approximately 35,900 parent corporations with 171,300 foreign affiliates were working in different countries (78,200 in the industrial countries, 71,300 in the developing countries, and 21,800 in Central and Eastern Europe and the CIS). Between 1960 and 1991, the stock of foreign direct investments increased almost 30 times, with a market value exceeding $1,900 billion. By 1991, fully or partly

Table 6. Regional Distribution of Foreign Direct Investments

	1970	1990
Developed Countries		
Western Europe	40	31
United States	11	30
Japan	1	2
Others	22	13
Total	74	76
Developing Countries		
Africa	7	3
Asia	6	8
Latin America	12	11
Central and Eastern Europe, including CIS	0	1
Others	1	0
Total	26	23

Sources: United Nations Center on Transnational Corporations, World Investment Report, 1992: Transnational Corporations as Engines of Growth (New York: United Nations, 1992); Economic Report of the President (Washington, D.C.: Government Printing Office, 1992); and U.S. Department of Commerce, Bureau of the Census, Statistical Abstract of the United States, 1991 (Washington, D.C.: Government Printing Office, 1992).

foreign-owned companies produced more than one-fourth of the global product. Between 1983 and 1989, one-half of the trade of the advanced industrial nations was conducted among transnational corporations and their affiliates.[83]

Between 1970 and 1990, the world economy changed considerably with respect to the distribution of countries originating and receiving foreign direct investments. Table 5 shows the development of direct investments made by companies of the major capital exporter countries (as a percentage of the total stock in 1970 and 1990, respectively).

The most spectacular change has been in the role of Japanese transnational corporations as global investors. Between 1983 and 1989, world foreign direct investments grew nearly four times faster than world GDP; the annual increase in Japanese foreign direct investments was 62 percent. The distribution of foreign direct investments by host countries and regions likewise underwent important changes, as depicted in table 6.

The most striking features of these changes are the increasing concentration of foreign direct investments in the United States and the very small amount invested in Japan. Despite the annual average increase in foreign direct investments in the United States of about 18 percent in the second half of the 1980s, foreign transnationals accounted for only around 5 percent of total U.S. jobs and GDP in 1990. By the early 1990s, about 17 percent of the total capital stock of the United States was foreign controlled (about one-half of the consumer electronics industries, one-third of the chemical industry, and one-fifth of the automobile industry).[84] The relatively small share of the stock of foreign direct investments in Japan reflects some of the technical and economic problems for foreign investors in that country. Since the late 1980s, however, there has been a substantial increase in the inflow due to the liberalization of legislation concerning merger and acquisition activities.

In the 1980s, foreign direct investments, particularly investments by transnational corporations, became a fundamental factor of international cooperation and competition. Direct market presence in the form of production or service ventures promoted not only sales and acquisitions but also the optimal combination of factors of production. Foreign direct investments have been an important means for the establishment and operation of inter-enterprise strategic alliances. On an international scale, such investments facilitate the spread of new technology, often enabling technology owners to gain a monopolistic position. Foreign direct investments have promoted penetration into protected markets and facilitated the efficient utilization of cost differences in human resources, raw materials, and research. They have also played a positive role in host countries by adding to the national resource base, production experience, export potential, and employment level and by plugging host countries into the transnational system of strategic alliances.

Of course, capital exporters and the host countries have incurred costs. Capital exporters have been blamed for exporting jobs, promoting brain drains, reducing or undermining national competitiveness by strengthening the economic potential of competitors, and disregarding national policy priorities and interests. In host countries, the selective policies of the transnational firms have weakened the government's ability to implement national structural policies, as segments of the economy have become subordinated to external organizations, interests, and decisions concerning jobs, pricing, and levels of output.

The Transnational Integration Process

Considerable changes have occurred in the structure of foreign direct investments during the past three decades. Raw materials, agriculture, and the conventional manufacturing branches have declined in significance while the proportion of investments connected with new technology and services (particularly financial and information services) has increased. Comprehensive global figures for foreign direct investments are not available. According to figures pertaining to the main capital exporters, in the late 1980s, 30 percent of all foreign investments went to the service sector, 40 to 45 percent to manufacturing industry, and less than 20 percent to raw material production.

In the early part of the 20th century, internationalization was connected chiefly with expansion toward raw material markets. Establishing foreign affiliates or investing in international stock markets were seldom subordinated to long-term strategic goals. The international movement of capital was basically a response to direct profit opportunities. In the post–World War II international economy, the situation became radically different, particularly in the framework delimited by transnational corporations. Their comprehensive strategic goals stimulated global expansion.

The easiest way for a firm in the global economy to expand its market share and reduce competition has been to take over its competitors. To achieve this goal, a firm must have a sufficiently strong financial base and external sources of funding. The readiness of the capital markets to serve the external financing needs of corporations has been very important to this process. Most takeovers have occurred in the industrial world. However, paralleling systemic changes, takeovers have also started to occur in Central and Eastern Europe; the takeover of TUNGSRAM in Hungary by General Electric in 1990 has been an early indication of this trend.

In the new era of global enterprise, transnational business organizations have developed horizontal structures, in contrast to the vertical and hierarchical structures traditionally favored by international firms. Horizontal structures have more to do with quality and consistency within the free enterprise system than with uniformity. They give local managers autonomy, which encourages not only human resource development but also product enrichment through innovations and local market intelligence that can be utilized by the entire organization. The global company is driven by diversity. It is located in a worldwide network of local manufacturing and marketing organizations. To compete successfully, the global company must utilize international technological, capital, and marketing resources in combination with production and marketing methods that satisfy particular needs.

The efforts made by global enterprises to gain advantages from global sourcing and economies of scale, not only in raw materials but also in capital, act as an impetus to the transnationalization process. Technology is of key importance to competition, given that scientific and technological progress play a decisive role in structural transformation. Technology and the huge costs of technological development have led to the establishment of peculiar strategic alliances among competing corporations. These joint undertakings provide opportunities for the sharing of R&D costs. If R&D capacities do not exist in a company's home country, strategic alliances offer the company access to R&D facilities elsewhere. Such alliances tend to stimulate new ways of thinking in corporate strategies, including an understanding and acceptance of interdependence.

The transnationalization process and the intensification of interdependence have affected international competition in a diversified way. Many economists characterize the world economy as an arena of oligopolistic competition, strategic interactions of alliances, and different forms of cooperation. The enormous transnational corporations that are vertically and horizontally integrated are the most decisive participants in this competition. But there is also competition at the level of the national economies. The effect of that competition and its impact on the global distribution and redistribution of incomes are of great importance to national economic structures. International integration in this context can be considered as a means to improve the competitive positions of national economies in the global system.

Transnationalization of the global economy, which has proceeded faster than the ability of countries to adjust to the process, requires changes in national policies. Transnationalization weakens the autonomy of policymakers to control or influence such key economic processes as the growth and structure of national output, the increase of investments, employment, exports, and technology flows. Regulation of these processes will move, at least in part, from the national to the international arena and the sphere of intergovernmental organizations.

In the past, the rise of international regulatory agencies came as a political response to economic needs. In the more open and interconnected world economy of the late 20th century, national concern about losing industries, jobs, and sovereign control over important areas of economic activity to other parts of the world or to supranational bodies like the EC will deepen. Conflict among various national interest groups over these issues will increase. The erosion of national economic bases may also stir national security concerns. The process of transnationalization is not unilateral. It may be asymmetrical, but it is a general global tendency. However, the degree to which governments will feel compelled to sacrifice some of their economic power for the benefits that transnationalization brings remains an open question.

In the international system of the 1990s, the forces of globalization, regionalization, and fragmentation exist simultaneously. The transnationalization process, therefore, faces new challenges. Transnational corporations will have to adopt new strategies, combining various forms of coordination in their production, sourcing, and marketing activities, while taking into account regional integration, common markets, free trade zones, and changing state regulations and practices. European transnational corporations, for example, have already had to develop a multi-level strategy for dealing with the member states of the community, the EC as a unit, and the rest of the world. Transnational corporations have proved to be the most efficient microactors in moderating the recurring conflicts between the international mobilization of production factors and the existence of state frontiers. This role is likely to become even more important in the future.

In a stagnating or slow-growing global economy, in which national pressures for protectionism or greater regulation would be likely to intensify, the process of transnationalization could slow down or change. In specific regions, however, the process will be furthered by macrointegration—the international economic integration of countries. Such integration is the most effective institutional instrument for the harmonization of national economies and the forces of internationalization within a regional framework. Economic integration, which is an advanced stage of internationalization, has been more efficient in cases where it has been supported by transnationalization at the microlevel.

International economic integration suggests both a process and a condition. As a dynamic concept, it can be interpreted as the process of amalgamation of national economies. This process can further be described as an institutionalized system established for the removal of barriers to the international flow of the factors of production and for the integration of economic policies and markets; it may also be interpreted as international-level integration of the functional domains (for example, individual production branches) of national economies. In the 20th century, there has been no example as yet of voluntary amalgamation—that is, the complete integration of national economies on the basis of programs elaborated in advance. In the Soviet Union, although the economic integration of federal republics took place within the boundaries of one state, difficulties and contradictions accompanied the process throughout its evolution. The unification of the two Germanys and the amalgamation of their two economies has been driven primarily by political, not economic, considerations. In the countries of the EC, the integration process will probably result in an economically amalgamated European structure (if the process of integration does not slow down and various forces of disintegration do not gain in strength).

Transnational corporations support the integration process, which by definition seeks to dismantle national regulations within a region. Companies that belong to a well-integrated system could be favorably situated if restrictions or regulations such as import-substitution schemes were dismantled within a region in conjunction with the removal of traditional trade barriers. Outsiders would have more restricted access to the markets.

In a global environment of relatively slow economic growth, the economic system must come to terms with discontinuity, contradictions, uncertainty, confusion, and the new forces of competition and competitive cooperation. It is becoming harder for countries with weak economies to adjust to the changing needs of the markets. Governments and firms must move with greater speed in understanding the multiplicity of global challenges, meeting the new requirements of the world market, implementing appropriate national strategies, and developing efficient cooperation regimes.

If adverse effects of competition on national economies and demands for further protectionism and other barriers to trade are to be avoided, new forms of multilateral cooperation will have to be designed that can reduce political tensions by giving greater emphasis to the mutuality of gains, losses, and adjustment obligations. They might not be a panacea for the myriad problems of the global economy, but more efficient multilateral cooperation regimes would certainly be the most cost-effective method of increasing global economic security.

Part IV

Multilateralism of the 21st Century in the Making

chapter 19

Continuity and Change in Global Governance

The political structure of the global order sustained by the Cold War has disappeared, but we have yet to see the establishment of a new order built on widely shared values and possessing clearly identifiable regulating forces in all key areas of the global system. As of the mid-1990s, the post–Cold War era is essentially a period of transition—a turbulent time in which, a few positive forces notwithstanding, a great diversity of morbid symptoms are arising.[1] Only in the coming decades will we be able to discern the full character of the new order and the kinds of benefits or problems it will bring. What is clear now, though, is that if we are to expect a positive outcome of the present transition—and avoid further marginalization of nations and deterioration of cooperation—its global management must involve the collective participation of all nations.

Any comprehensive post–Cold War cooperation regime will have to be built on the foundations of existing instruments of collective international action. In so diverse a world as today's, there is no realistic alternative to using these existing institutions, which comprise the most comprehensive system of international cooperation ever established. Their reform, however, is vital, for within the economic and political spheres these instruments are largely the products of institutions and regimes that were created in the aftermath of World War II to respond to the needs of a global environment very different from our own.

Thus, before we proceed to an assessment of the requirements and character of effective multilateral risk management in the future, let us briefly review the development of the main intergovernmental economic and political institutions of the post–World War II global system. The post–World War II global order had an economic and a political institutional underpinning. Although, formally, both institutional structures functioned within the framework of the United Nations, the world organization actually had little or no operative or policy influence on the two most important agencies in the global economy.

The Multilateral Economic Institutions of the Post–World War II Order

The central international economic institutions of the global order after 1945 were the "Bretton Woods Twins," the two main pillars of the multilateral economic structure known as the Bretton Woods system.[2] The structure of the system reflected various compromises and a large degree of consensus among the major Western industrial powers on matters of common interest. All the leading Western powers shared at least three strategic goals for the Bretton Woods system. One goal was to avoid the chaotic economic conditions of the post–World War I decades and build a global economic order within the framework of which countries would behave responsibly in adjusting to socioeconomic and market changes, with multilateral institutions assisting in the promotion of trade and employment and implementation of adjustment policies and ensuring the fulfillment of mutual obligations. A second common aim was that the United States should play the role of hegemon in the system. And a third goal was to protect the North Atlantic region, especially Western Europe, from the spread of communism by stabilizing the socioeconomic systems of states on the basis of democratic values and market relations. Economic cooperation with the Soviet Union was never seriously considered when the system was designed by the Western powers. On the Soviet side, early interest in economic cooperation faded by 1946. The Soviets completely isolated themselves from the new multilateral system.

While the Western powers thus shared several common goals, they also had separate, sometimes conflicting interests. For instance, the United States, beyond its political goals, desired a large and liberal market in Western Europe; the leaders of the West European countries, however, primarily sought to regain their power positions in the postwar world. On the issue of decolonization, the United States anticipated the disintegration of the colonial empires and, by declaring its support for self-determination, promoted the process. The former metropolitan countries, though, wanted to stabilize their colonial rule with the help of the United States. This duality of interests—some specific to either the United States or Western Europe, others shared by the Western world as a whole—was to contribute to the problems, as well as to the achievements, of the Bretton Woods system.

The original blueprints for the Bretton Woods system envisaged two interrelated and mutually supportive structures: monetary and trade organizations. In the financial sphere, the functioning of the monetary order was to be aided by two institutions, both created in 1944: the International Monetary Fund (IMF), the first international monetary authority with at least some degree of power over national monetary authorities; and the World Bank, which was to help finance Europe's reconstruction (the World Bank's official name is still the International Bank for Reconstruction and Development). The new principles and rules of international trade were to be elaborated and implemented through an International Trade Organization (ITO), the charter of which was signed in Havana in 1948 by 53 states. The divergent interests of the countries concerned, however, blocked the ratification of the charter and establishment of the ITO (the U.S. Congress was particularly resistant to the idea), and as a compromise solution, the GATT was established in 1947, coming into operation on January 1, 1948.

Although various problems emerged in connection with the international monetary system established at Bretton Woods, it also had considerable merits. For instance, despite the fact that the system was based on fixed rates of exchange, and thus permitted itself a certain degree of devaluation or revaluation of currencies, the IMF was able to apply pressure to those countries enjoying long-term surpluses and those facing balance-of-payments deficits in order to harmonize their national economic policies with the balance of their current accounts.

Designed to replace the economic order that disintegrated into chaos between the two world wars with multilateral cooperation, the Bretton Woods system functioned more or less effectively until the late 1960s. Member states concluded agreements that obliged them to phase out and remove economic restrictions, promote the freer movement of goods and capital, and improve the monetary conditions of international relations.

In 1971, however, the United States discontinued the convertibility of the dollar into gold, and thus one of the supporting pillars of the system—the gold exchange standard—collapsed. In 1973 the other pillar—fixed rates of exchange—also fell.

Many explanations have been given for the collapse of the Bretton Woods system. Some economists have emphasized the domestic and international problems that beset the United States (such as its increasing balance-of-payments deficit and the high costs of the war in Vietnam) and left it unable to meet its obligations to convert official dollar claims into gold. Others have focused on the evolution of new economic power centers in Western Europe and Japan, which rendered the post–World War II arrangements outdated and unsustainable. Whatever the reasons for its demise (and no doubt there are many), the collapse of the Bretton Woods system has generated substantial problems for the international economic order. The developed industrial countries have withdrawn themselves from IMF scrutiny, and thus have essentially avoided the possibility of multilateral intervention in their economic policies. Furthermore, no new multilateral global system of cooperation has been created in the field of monetary relations. Under the Bretton Woods system, the behavior of international economic actors was relatively predictable; today, the exchange rates of many currencies are marked by instability.

At the same time, there have occurred a substantial increase in the globalization of the capital markets, a considerable expansion of international lending and security operations, and major deregulation of domestic financial markets. The development of a great number of new financial instruments—like the Eurodollar market—has made the post–Bretton Woods system more flexible and allowed the regime of floating rates to be maintained without major crises. Different currency baskets and new market arrangements help governments and companies find some degree of stability and predictability. For example, on a regional level, the European Monetary System was created by the EC in 1979 to provide greater exchange-rate stability.

Although the Bretton Woods system has collapsed, the IMF and the World Bank have not merely survived, but successfully adapted to the needs of a changing world since the early 1970s. In the case of the World Bank, it actually began a process of adaptation once the foundations of European recovery had been established in the second half of the 1950s. The World Bank turned toward the developing world and became its main international institutional lender. The bank also became a vital go-between for public borrowers and private lenders. Since the mid-1950s, the World Bank has developed a variety of new institutions for different types of financing, including the International Finance Corporation to directly assist the private sector; the International Development Agency for delivering aid to the developing world; and, in the 1990s, the Multilateral Investment Guarantee Agency, which assists in the creation of joint ventures.[3]

Following a tradition it established in the 1950s, when it chiefly served the industrial world, the IMF has become a lender, particularly to those countries, mostly from the developing world, unable to borrow reserves from markets of their choice. While its main activities are concentrated in the nonindustrial world, the IMF performs a crucial role in the wider international financial system for the majority of states in the world, which are either its borrowers or lenders.

The World Bank and the IMF have become the key institutional economic policy advisers in the global debtor community. Their attitudes toward debtors serve also as important guidelines for private investors. In most cases, their advice to debtors presents itself in the form of strict conditions for loans. The IMF has come to exert an enormous influence on the economic policies of developing countries. It also offers investors highly profitable ventures; between 1986 and 1991, service payments from debtor countries to the IMF exceeded the value of its new lending. Critics maintain that the IMF often applies its free enterprise and market-oriented philosophy in a doctrinaire way, ignoring the legitimate social and political concerns of governments. It is accused of applying standard remedies in policy recommendations irrespective of a borrowing country's unique circumstances, supporting programs that do not work, opposing economic growth, increasing unemployment and hurting the poor by imposing austerity measures on borrowing countries, and funding development projects that damage the environment.[4] Responding to these criticisms, since the late 1980s the IMF has shown itself more concerned with social and environmental issues faced by its client countries. It has also changed its borrowing patterns by introducing softer conditions for low-income members and the former socialist countries.

The operative role of the IMF in the functioning of the international monetary system, within which there are only two requirements as of the mid-1990s—that a member state should not base the value of its currency on gold and that it should inform other members how the value of its currency is determined—has diminished in importance in the industrial world. However, the IMF now monitors its members' exchange policies, an important function in a world where there are neither automatic correction mechanisms nor any reliance on guarantees that would prevent a financial collapse in the event of a serious economic crisis.

Notwithstanding all the changes made within the IMF and the World Bank, both are in need of major reform if they are to serve the world more efficiently in an era where capital flows and exchange-rate fluctuations increasingly occur outside the scope of national governments, in the process affecting the functioning, competitive efficiency, and monetary reserves of national economies.

The reverberations of the oil crisis in the 1970s and the financial shocks of the 1980s in the world economy reactivated the role of the Bank for International Settlements (BIS). Chartered in 1930 by a group of European central banks as a forum to facilitate cooperation among them and help the settlement of the debt from World War I, the BIS survived calls by the designers of the Bretton Woods system for the bank's earliest possible abolition. Since the 1960s, it has evolved into an influential monetary institution, assisting central bankers in investing monetary assets. It is essentially an institution for the cooperation of the central banks in the developed industrial countries, even though it acts as trustee for the IMF in loans to developing countries. The BIS plays an important role by holding the central clearing account of the European Currency Unit (ECU). Negotiations held in 1988 within the framework of the BIS resulted in a new set of rules concerning the division of responsibilities for the supervision of international banking activities and a new agreement on capital adequacy for banking.

Despite these developments, as indicated in part III of this book, the cooperation regime of the central banks for the support of international financial stability remains relatively weak. National monetary policies can severely constrain attempts at concerted action.[5] The increasing role of the BIS, the emergence of the European Monetary System, and the activities of the "G" structures (the G-5, G-7, G-10, and so forth) have in fact created a two-track institutional cooperation system in international monetary and financial affairs: on the one track, the system addresses, through the framework of the IMF, the problems of the developing countries and the new market economies of Central and Eastern Europe; on the other track, the industrial countries pursue cooperation among themselves.

The GATT was, in the past, unable to become an equal partner to the IMF and the World Bank in global economic policy-making. The Havana Charter had envisaged that the ITO would undertake a broad range of duties, including not only coordinating and promulgating trade policies, but also dealing with such issues as the problems of economic development, foreign investments, business practices, and commodities. Of these tasks, however, only the job of negotiating and overseeing commercial policies was incorporated into the GATT.

Within the GATT regime, eight rounds of multilateral trade negotiations have been held since 1947, resulting in a relatively liberal, though incomplete and inconsistent trade environment. The cornerstones of the GATT system have been the lowering of customs tariffs and nondiscrimination through acceptance of the Most Favored Nation (MFN) principle, under which all member states uniformly extend any favor to all of their GATT trading partners. The GATT system, however, has recognized several exceptions to the norm of nondiscrimination, not only with respect to free trade areas and integration groups and to preferential treatment shown to developing countries by the industrialized economies, but also in the way the MFN principle can be extended by certain countries.

Since 1947, the GATT system has resulted in major reductions in tariff rates, with the global average falling from 40 percent in 1947 to 4 percent in 1990. The full implications of the Uruguay Round concluded in December 1993 for the liberalization of trade will become apparent only after ratification of the agreement by national legislatures and the conclusion of bilateral agreements on implementation. During the negotiations between 1986 and 1993, several shortcomings of the regime came to the surface. First, in spite of substantial tariff reductions achieved during the past decades, tariff barriers still existed in sectors such as agriculture, in products such as textiles and steel, and in countries such as Japan and the Soviet Union and in Central and Eastern Europe and parts of the developing world. Second, during the 1980s there had been an increase in protectonist measures, which were in fact nontariff barriers (like antidumping rules, countervailing duties, and voluntary export restrictions) and thus evaded the GATT agreements. The global trading system had become increasingly tied to foreign direct investments and responsive to other regulations than those originally envisaged by the framers of the GATT. Third, the GATT's enforcement mechanism had proved to be ineffectual, slow, and cumbersome when rules were broken. Fourth, in an era of increasing regionalization, the principle of global arrangements had become more difficult to apply. State and regional interests had to be taken into account in the GATT bargaining process.

The Uruguay Round extended the sectoral relevance of the agreement to new areas such as trade in services, information, and intellectual property rights. However, the capacity of the GATT system may be inadequate to ensure the implementation and supervision of the new agreement. Furthermore, the transformation in Central and Eastern Europe, the collapse of the Soviet Union, the emergence of China as a key trading nation, and the special problems and needs of the developing countries were not taken sufficiently into account in the Uruguay Round. The new geopolitics of the trading system will require further negotiations and perhaps the creation of new institutions by the end of the century.

Beyond the Bretton Woods institutions, a number of agencies, councils, committees, and other structures have been established within the UN system to deal with global economic issues.[6] The UN system, however, with its weak and poorly coordinated structure, has only a minor role in global economic management. The industrial countries have not been interested in using the UN forum for purposes other than data collection and policy analysis for at least three reasons. First, the United Nations includes countries with very different interests and values, and the developed market economies have preferred to use organizations that are based on the values and mechanisms of the market system. Second, the industrial countries have not wanted the rest of the world to exercise any control over their economic policies. And third, the one-country, one-vote system of the United Nations is contradictory to market relations based on economic power.

Many global economic initiatives—notably, the NIEO and the notion of "development decades"—advanced in the United Nations have remained within the realm of ideas or have led merely to the creation of bureaucratic structures with little power and few resources. The impact of such initiatives on the global system has been negligible. UN specialized agencies that have had operative roles to play have been confined to specific sectors. Even within the sphere of their mandates, these agencies have tended to offer very few original and pragmatic policy options.

The United Nations and the Post–World War II Order

The United Nations Organization has been both an instrument and a reflection of the post–World War II international political order, in which it has assumed an important managerial role. Created by the Allied powers to establish firm and lasting institutional guarantees against the emergence of a new group of powers that might endanger world peace as the Axis powers had done, the United Nations quickly came to play a rather different role. The postwar division of the Allies into two hostile military alliances, each seeking to extend its influence into almost every corner of the globe, required some manageable form of coexistence, especially in an era of nuclear weapons. The United Nations, by virtue of its loose structure and its different political, economic, and social institutions, which were given a limited and politically neutral mandate and minimal operative power, was largely able to satisfy this requirement.

The disintegration of the colonial empires, an inevitable consequence of the struggle of the colonies for national self-determination in the competing bipolar system, resulted in the establishment of many new countries and the restoration of independence in formerly independent states. The need to bring these states into the international political and economic system and to establish firm guarantees of their independent existence was met by the United Nations, which formally accepted the new states as equal members in the global system. The states were able to use the organization as a forum for debate and advocacy, and had equal access to many of its facilities and equal representation in the General Assembly. Their flags were unfurled with those of the great powers. In the de facto global order, however, the great powers maintained, and even strengthened, their political, economic, and military influence and established networks of client countries in different parts of the world.

With most countries of the world as members, and with no mass exodus from its ranks such as the League of Nations suffered, the United Nations has remained the foremost instrument of global dialogue and cooperation. A system of different functional cooperation regimes has been built up around the United Nations through its specialized agencies, which deal with a wide array of issues such as food and agriculture, education and culture, health, telecommunications, civil aviation, and humanitarian relief. The norms and principles enshrined in the UN Charter have served to ensure not only the survival of the organization and its functions, but also its gradual adjustment to the managerial requirements of the global system. At the same time, however, only a few of the critical international issues of the post–World War II order have actually been managed, or even influenced, by the United Nations.

Even at its inception, no reasonable politician or scholar expected the United Nations to become a supranational institution—a world government of sorts. Such a notion flew in the face of the realities of the political world and was contradictory to the principle of sovereignty. Indeed, one of the fundamental principles of the UN Charter is the sovereign equality of states, a principle that has proved to be extremely important in the post–World War II era, not least because of the emphasis placed on its observance by the many new states carved out of the former colonial empires. However, it should be noted that the concept of sovereignty has undergone significant changes during the United Nations' existence. Throughout the 19th century and the first 40 or so years of the 20th century, the sovereignty of states implied a practically unlimited right to go to war. By contrast, UN membership places important restrictions on this right and stipulates punitive sanctions for violations of those restrictions. The acceptance of universal human rights has also eroded some of the former meaning of sovereignty.

Nevertheless, recognition of the sovereign equality of states has meant that states could find justification for policies and actions that have run counter to principles of the UN Charter and the efforts of the organization to manage international conflict. The managerial role of the United Nations has also been greatly influenced by the organization's recognition of the special role, interests, and responsibilities of the great powers. Under the Covenant of the League of Nations, the Assembly, in which all members were represented, and the Council, in which only the great powers were represented, held equal degrees of power. The UN Security Council and its permanent members (the United States, the Soviet Union—now Russia—France, the United Kingdom, and China) have, however, enjoyed greater and more exclusive power through their right of veto over all issues on the council's agenda. When the United Nations Organization was founded, it had not yet become clear what kind of a global power structure would emerge after World War II. In the face of such uncertainty, assurance of the principle of great power dominance in the United Nations, along with practical instruments for its implementation, facilitated the participation of the United States and the Soviet Union.

The special responsibilities assumed by the great powers and their power of veto have generated strident criticism. That criticism tends to focus on two areas. One is that two of the former great powers (France and the United Kingdom) have now become middle powers and owe their status chiefly to their continuing membership in the nuclear club. The other is that most of the actions of some great powers have undermined the work of the United Nations or conflicted with certain of its principles (such as noninterference in the domestic affairs of sovereign countries). Although much of this criticism is fair, the fact remains that the special status accorded to the great powers reflected the political realities of the immediate postwar period and may even have proved instrumental in avoiding another world war.

The UN Charter laid down in very concrete and multidimensional terms, and for the first time in human history, the principles of collective security. Effective collective measures were envisaged for the prevention of war, the removal of threats to peace, and the suppression of acts of aggression. Settling international disputes by peaceful means, in conformity with the principles of justice and international law, was emphasized as a common goal. The development of friendly relations among nations based on equal rights and self-determination, and the achievement of international cooperation in solving international problems of an economic, social, cultural, or humanitarian character, were also considered important in effecting collective peace and security. Within the framework of collective security principles, the security of nations and of individual citizens was promised, with specific mention made of respect for human rights and fundamental freedoms without distinction as to race, sex, language, or religion.

These principles gave the UN system a mandate for dealing with all of the complicated and emerging problems of humankind and for creating the necessary institutional framework—the machinery, in other words—to accomplish those tasks. In practical terms, the success of different initiatives depended far more on the degree of consensus among members regarding the desirability of a particular outcome than on the machinery, which has generally been underutilized. Countries have acted unilaterally in defiance of the protests of the United Nations, conscious that they will encounter only inaction or ineffective opposition from the world body. Even the Security Council has been unable to respond effectively when one or other of the major powers, or their clients, has violated the principles of the UN Charter. In other instances, groups of states (NATO and the Warsaw Pact countries, for example) have forged their own institutions for dealing with their specific security problems.

Despite its many shortcomings, the United Nations has nonetheless played a key role in sustaining the post–World War II order. No new power has emerged in the past 50 years able to threaten the violent overthrow of the postwar power structure. There has been no world war between the main powers. The 130 or so "small wars" have been confined to a local or regional area, and many have been ended as a result of UN involvement. UN peacekeeping operations (22 were conducted between 1948 and 1992) have often helped to contain violence in many different parts of the world. The United Nations has helped establish new states on the ruins of colonial regimes, states that have generally been supportive of the main goals of the world organization. In keeping with one of those goals, human rights have been accorded greater respect. The organizational structure of the United Nations has survived and expanded.

Both within and beyond the United Nations, a major expansion of international organizations has occurred since World War II. An organized network of interstate relations, typified by a comprehensive and diversifying structure of cooperation, has been established. Although only 5 percent of the agreements deposited with the United Nations are of a multilateral nature, their scope is immense. Not a single instance of international cooperation would go uncovered by the operation of some interstate organization or would be unaffected by some institutionalized cooperation program. The overwhelming majority of these organizations and cooperation programs are part of the UN system. Many non-UN intergovernmental organizations also exist.

These organizational developments, however, have not been wholly positive. Two problems stand out. First, from the viewpoint of individual states, non-UN organizations often play a more important role than do the specialized agencies and organs of the United Nations. Examples include the regional integration organizations—most notably, the EC—and the cooperation regime of the developed industrial countries, the OECD, which was created in 1961 out of the Organization for European Economic Cooperation (OEEC). Second, the development of international intergovernmental institutions has taken place in the absence of any global functional design or coordination. Consequently, parallel and competing organizations exist in many areas of international cooperation.

From this brief and incomplete overview, it is apparent that the UN system has a better record than is often claimed by hostile or ill-informed critics. Nonetheless, it is the case that the gap between the capabilities of the United Nation to help manage evolving global problems and the scale and number of those problems is widening. This gap has become all the more evident in the post–Cold War era, when expectations of effective UN participation in collective risk management have grown significantly.

The Nature of International Risks in the New Era

Anticipating, calculating, managing, and trying to eliminate risk factors have always been necessary elements in the formulation and implementation of policies in the international political and economic systems. In recent decades, transnational firms, banks, international organizations, and governments have employed highly sophisticated scientific methodologies to assess the risks associated with major decisions.[7] Sciences, especially economics, have drawn a distinction between factors of uncertainty and factors of risks. According to John Maynard Keynes, for example, the term "risk" refers to a chance occurrence of an event determined by some objectively verifiable probability distribution. Uncertainty, on the other hand, is a chance occurrence, the probability of which is not known.[8] The two terms have often been used interchangeably in the jargon of international life.

Richard Herring defines risk as a possibility of an outcome, one that is less favorable than the expected outcome, or the possibility of unforeseen developments that reduce our welfare.[9] In the international political and economic systems, and even more so in the ecosystem, where the impact and interrelationship of different processes and factors depend on a great number of changing variables that may result in incalculable scenarios of instability (even when their causes are known), Herring's definition of risk seems appropriate. In this book, international risks are defined as important, potentially disturbing and destabilizing factors or acts originating with, or generated by, various actors on different structural levels, and having spillover consequences for other members of the international community.

Given that every human activity involves elements of risk, and that risks for some groups may represent opportunities for others, to understand and manage risks in international life it is necessary to deal with concrete, unambiguous cases. As well as identifying the sources of collective risk, we must also understand and take into account the sources of risk and instability that affect individual countries. Many of these countries may require international assistance in their risk management efforts.

Five interrelated categories indicate the broad character and implications of collective future risks:

- *The risks of armed conflict*, connected with external military interventions, interstate wars, civil wars, and other forms of large-scale violence, as well as national and international terrorism.
- *Risks resulting from the political destabilization of governments*, the sources of which may be internal—like revolutions and uprisings, separatist movements, ethnic problems, and the inefficiency of national and international political institutions—or external—such as unforeseen and unpredictable political actions of governments that adversely affect other states.
- *Economic risks,* the sources of which are widespread, such as the malfunctioning of the economic system and recessions in key countries; defaults by major debtors; adverse and unexpected consequences of technological changes; errors in major economic decisions; the collapse of international cooperation regimes (especially of those vital to the global economy, like the international financial system); the sudden imposition of limitations on the availability of resources; and economic warfare.
- *Societal risks* caused by such diverse factors as large population increases; mass migrations; large-scale movements of refugees; social developments that overstretch a state's capacity to provide adequate health and educational services; and ethnic, national, cultural, and religious problems.
- *Ecological risks* engendered by the general deterioration of the environment, sudden environmental crises, and both manmade and natural catastrophes.

These five categories are often closely interrelated and even overlap. In principle, therefore, dealing with any one source of risk separately should be very difficult. In practice, however, collective risk management must be specific and deal with the principal source, or sources, of risk.

Sources of risk can, of course, be of a short-term nature (such as temporary unemployment problems, labor disputes, or short-lived disputes between countries) or a long-term nature (for instance, major wars, environmental degradation, or the economic or political collapse of countries). Sources of risk can also be distinguished according to the extent to which the dangers they present can be handled by existing means. It is easier, at least theoretically, to assess and calculate the international political risks associated with a change of government or regime than to predict the consequences of, say, ethnic conflicts that may explode into civil war or interstate violence. Social and economic sources of risk are again of a different nature. Over the short term, they may not directly affect the international political environment and thus may not be considered by governments as requiring collective action. Over the longer term, however, social and economic risks may destabilize democratic regimes, inspire protectionist pressures, and lead to the disruption of international cooperation regimes. It should be remembered that the accumulation of social and economic discontent in the 1920s and 1930s led to the rise of extremist and aggressive regimes that were responsible for the outbreak of World War II.

Critical Questions for the Future of International Risk Management

There are no universally shared definitions and concepts of international risk management. The interests and goals of governments and other international actors are in minimizing risks and avoiding risk factors altogether. Risk management, however, implies that we coexist with risks and, in doing so, seek to reduce the potential damage they may cause by employing different measures, some of which may include unilateral adjustments, others of which may entail international cooperation within bilateral or multilateral frameworks.

Even though the international institutional system has remained an essentially state-oriented structure, demands are growing for the collective assessment and management of new sources of international instability and risk and the further development of cooperation. The great majority of international risks cannot be dealt with in isolation, even by the most powerful countries. There cannot, for example, be any unilateral solution to global demographic or ecological problems, nor to the problems of international trade and capital flows in an environment of global interdependence.

Rhetoric heard in the international policy arena since the late 1980s suggests a worldwide desire to see international cooperation upgraded and intensified so that it can manage the many persistent and new sources of risks and attempt to resolve a broad range of global and regional problems. But will the community of nations, and especially those countries that have been most affected by the changes of the post–Cold War period, be able to respond to their new needs by seizing the unprecedented opportunities to intensify cooperation, or will the temptation to act unilaterally win the day? This general question encompasses five other questions:

1. What sorts of services can existing forms and institutions of cooperation provide to deal with the major global political, economic, and ecological problems affecting different types and groups of countries? Would those services best be provided within a bilateral, a regional-multilateral, or a global-multilateral[10] framework?

2. Are there sufficient incentives for nations to engage in more intensive international cooperation in the new era? How far have the interests, values, and attitudes of different countries changed since the end of the Cold War? To what extent have the interests of countries converged, inspiring a greater readiness to support multilateral cooperation to address the global problems brought about by the new structures of global power?

3. In the case of multilateral cooperation, what kind of organizational responses will be the most efficient and feasible: centralized global; harmonized global-regional; or clustered, functional cooperation regimes? To what extent can the UN system, in either its present or a reformed structure, provide collective responses to common problems? Will informal "minilateralist" structures like the G-7 group of nations be more useful in the future than the larger, more formal multilateral structures?

4. To what extent are nongovernmental actors and transnational processes (like technology and capital flows) shaping

the future of multilateral cooperation, either by their influence on government policies or by their establishment of their own cooperation structures?

5. A more general question: What lessons learned from past processes and outcomes of multilateral cooperation are most valuable for the future?

chapter 20

New Global Needs and the Network of International Cooperation

Multilateralism and National Interests

Answers to the question posed at the end of the previous chapter—that is, will cooperation or unilateral action win out?—will inevitably vary from issue to issue and country to country. Historically, the readiness and ability of nations to harmonize their diverging interests within an institutionalized framework have always been limited, as the United Nations has found to its cost. Acceptance of the realities and demands of interdependence has been irregular, and unilateral actions have frequently disregarded the principles and resolutions of multilateral organizations.

Part of the problem has had to do with the growth and diversity of intergovernmental organizations (IGOs). The network of these organizations and cooperation regimes has substantially expanded. At the beginning of this century, there were 30 IGOs. By 1950, they numbered 123. And by 1990, there were several hundred. As noted above, this growth has occurred in an unplanned and uncoordinated manner, leading to the existence of many competing organizations in almost all fields of activity.

IGOs outside the UN system frequently compete, directly or indirectly, with those within the system. Even within the United Nations, different agencies compete for mandates, tasks, and funds.

This anarchy in the system of multilateral organizations has not only encouraged institutional inefficiencies but also contributed to the "crisis of multilateralism" that has developed over the past decades, eclipsing the hopes for multilateral cooperation that arose at the end of World War II. However, the chief progenitor of this crisis has been political, not institutional, in nature. Member states have frequently pursued their own narrow goals, disregarding their broader systemic responsibilities and the needs and policies of the multilateral organizations to which they belong. One of the most visible signs of this has been the financial difficulties that multilateral bodies have faced as a consequence of their members' nonpayment of dues.

The only way to overcome this crisis of multilateralism is to address it simultaneously from three policy perspectives: global, national, and regional.

Many groups of scholars, statesmen, and organizations have advocated the adoption of a global policy perspective. Translating these internationalist views into practice has not been a simple matter, however. On the basis of general human interests, various priorities have been defined—for example, the survival of humankind or guarantees for collective security—but have only been translated into action-oriented policies on a limited scale, and then only when it was possible to identify discrete, concrete national interests that converged around these priorities.

Any policy recommendation will always have to be reconciled with the realities of a highly diverse system of states that functions at many different levels. Indeed, while the different actors in the international system—nongovernmental organizations, transnational corporations, regional integration groups, and so on—will play a more prominent role in the final phase of the 20th century and most probably in the 21st century too, states themselves will continue to play the leading roles as the fundamental political and organizational units on the globe and as the main sponsors of cooperation programs and projects, either individually or collectively.

However, with the establishment of many different multinational organizations, the international role of states has changed. International agencies and cooperation regimes now fulfill many functions previously performed by states. States are increasingly subject to legislation, binding decisions, and compulsory procedures determined by multilateral entities. Meanwhile, the abilities of states to manage their domestic problems are declining in the face of an array of very serious economic and social difficulties: inflation, recession, unemployment, environmental degradation, terrorism, rising crime, urban decay, drug abuse, and so forth. At the end of the 20th century, it is impossible to maintain the idea that states are isolated units and that their sovereignty is absolute.

Even so, the differences among states in terms of their dependence on the external environment and influence on global politics and economics will remain considerable. Furthermore, these differences may result in the disintegration or fragmentation of the global system if it is not managed in such a way as to balance, at least to some degree, the gains and losses of cooperation. Even when countries adjust to changes voluntarily and coordinate their efforts, the conflict between how the adjustment process impacts domestic interests and how it affects international interests can severely impede the progress of multilateralism. The history of multilateralism has shown that it is easier to win popular support for national participation in a cooperative undertaking when no one country incurs all the losses, or when all countries gain something as a result of their cooperation.

The international system of the late 1990s will almost certainly not develop in the direction of "unilateral universalism," where one country would dictate and enforce policies that affect the global community as a whole. Diversification, polarization, the growing importance of new centers of economic power, emerging new sources of conflicts between North and South, varying forms and factors of interdependence and its asymmetries, and the growing number of different global problems and other sources of risk will all inevitably affect the propensities for, and patterns of, international cooperation. Countries will have to maintain different types and levels of international relations. They will also need to build a greater variety of institutional structures to pursue their objectives and sustain their international sociopolitical and economic "metabolism"—that is, their complex relations, interactions, and interdependence with partners in the global system and their management of common problems.

The present network of international cooperation is already a complex web of different structures: bilateral and multilateral; multipurpose and single-purpose; subregional, regional, and global. The interrelations among these structures are certain to be influenced by the changing needs of the new era, with preferences for one or another form of cooperation motivated by the interplay of convergent interests, the initiatives of a few major powers, the practical needs of countries, and the efficiency of competing institutions and regimes. Within this complex framework of international relations, bilateralism will continue to play a key role in managing and solving problems between countries and in developing different forms of cooperation.

Bilateral Relations and Global Changes

The importance of bilateral relations in the contemporary world is illustrated by the fact that of the nearly 30,000 intergovernmental agreements deposited with the United Nations that have entered into force, only 5 percent are multilateral agreements, while 95 percent are bilateral. Most of the 750 international agreements and protocols concluded in environmental areas are also bilateral.

Multilateral cooperation has become increasingly important since World War II, and the content and techniques of bilateral cooperation have changed substantially because of the growing interaction between bilateral and multilateral frameworks, and because the norms of bilateral relations are defined and promulgated by multilateral commitments, such as those in the UN Charter. Despite the progress made toward multilateralism, however, bilateral cooperation will retain its fundamental importance for the countries of the world, especially the major powers. Furthermore, most sources of tension and conflict (such as frontier and ethnic disputes) in the coming decade will remain bilateral in nature.

Several new and traditional factors contribute to the continuing, and in some cases increasing, importance of bilateral relations. The advent of post–Cold War multipolarity necessitates a reevaluation and redefinition of the bilateral relations among those powers that are assuming much greater prominence in the international arena. Germany, for example, which is undeniably the strongest power in contemporary Europe, will play an ever more prominent role in European security matters, the future of NATO, the process of European unification, and the patterns of change in Central and Eastern Europe. Its European partners are recognizing the need to establish qualitatively new relations with Germany in both a bilateral and a multilateral context. Across the Atlantic, the United States is seeking to secure Germany's acceptance of shared responsibility for global leadership. All the major powers are considering whether it will be necessary to balance the power of the unified Germany by establishing special strategic relations with another major regional power, such as Russia.

The disintegration of the Soviet Union and the reemergence of Russia as a leading continental power present a major—and unpredictable—challenge for all of the former Soviet Union's republics, allies, and adversaries. The Soviet Union's foremost antagonist, the United States, seems likely to pursue a two-level policy in its relations with Russia: on the first level, U.S. attention will focus on how to assist Russia attain domestic stability; on the second level, U.S. policy will center on how to deal with the new Russia as a key power in both Asia and Europe. In economic terms, participation in the modernization process of Russia may present major opportunities for Germany, Japan, and the United States. In political and strategic terms, however, Russia may cause great concern among the other major powers if it embarks upon an expansionist course.

The states that gained independence as a result of the disintegration of great empires in this century have faced difficulties because of the radial nature of imperial relations between the metropolitan countries and their colonies. Although the British Commonwealth was unable to become a multilateral structure satisfying the needs of the former colonies, it was able to maintain certain ties between them. The structure of the Russian empire and of its successor, the Soviet Union, was somewhat different from that of the British Empire. The Soviet empire was a continental empire, with an interconnected infrastructure, a division of labor between countries, and Russia playing a central role in the interdependent environment that emerged. Even after the dissolution of the Soviet empire, and despite the presence of national and ethnic antagonisms among various successor states that may at times overpower economic rationality or obscure mutual economic interests, some form of cooperation among the successor states is likely to endure.

Like Russia and Germany, Japan is also a prominent player in the new multipolar environment, and its bilateral relations will thus be critical to the political and economic future of the world. Problems regarding U.S.-Japanese, Sino-Japanese, and Russian-Japanese relations suggest that a complicated network of relationships will develop in post–Cold War Asia that will have a major impact on global and multilateral relations. Japan is, for example, increasingly pursuing a selective bilateral policy dictated by Japanese strategic interests in Asia.

Aside from the advent of multipolarity, the importance of bilateral relations to the major powers will be ensured by the fact that bilateralism remains the easiest, most direct, and often most efficient means of harmonizing the interests and coordinating the policies and actions of nations. As might be expected, the greater the diversity among countries, the more difficult it is to create such harmony and coordination within a multilateral framework. It is easier in bilateral relations to uniquely define—to customize, so to speak—national policies toward different partners.

Furthermore, bilateralism may also be attractive to some powers because it offers them opportunities to apply direct, though internationally nontransparent, unilateral pressures on weaker bilateral partners. Smaller countries have always been exposed to the geopolitical and geoeconomic consequences of the unilateral actions of larger states. In the past, smaller countries had few options when it came to choosing political partners: generally, either they were subsumed within the sphere of influence of an expanding great power, or they tried—and usually failed—to maintain some freedom of action by acting as buffer states between opposing powers.

The selection of partners in economic relations has been affected by a much broader group of factors than has governed the choice of political partners. In the past, strong bilateral relations were frequently established on the bases of geographical proximity (not least because of problems and costs of transportation) and complementary natural endowments.[11] Common cultural traditions, together with considerations of political and strategic interests, also encouraged the development of bilateral economic relations.

Those factors continue to figure prominently in the choice of bilateral partners. So too does the size of a country. Small countries are rarely able to satisfy each other's economic needs. Possessing often highly specialized economic structures, limited technological potential, relatively narrow internal markets, and small volumes of savings, small countries can help each other overcome their structural problems and meet their capital needs only through the deliberate and intensive division of labor among them and with the aid of institutionalized and liberal trade policies. In the creation of these conditions in today's global economy, transnational corporations can perform a very important role. But transnational corporations cannot substitute for the balancing role played by the major countries within a region. Large countries provide an outlet for the goods of smaller countries, are sources of technology and capital, and produce a broad range of exports that can satisfy the varied needs of smaller countries. A small country's specialization in a particular field that satisfies a larger country's needs may promote an efficient level of production given the economies-of-scale effect. For instance, a small country may be able to produce customized products to meet the needs of particular segments of the market of the larger partner. This practice establishes specific relations of dependence between the small and the large country, which may occasionally lead to some degree of interdependence as well.

Differences in levels of economic development will continue to play a very important role in the shaping of partner relations. For example, exports from a more developed to a less developed country can result in stagnation or decline in the technological performance of the exporter, unless the exporter is obliged to compete with other players in the world market and thus is forced to improve its standards of industrial and market organization. In a less developed country, the higher quality requirements of more developed markets and their demonstration effect on organization, marketing, and consumption patterns can help upgrade the less developed economy. Alternatively, if a less developed country is a dependent supplier of traditional commodities to a more developed partner, the low-tech nature of the less developed economy may be preserved.

In the global economic system, bilateral relations and multi-lateral structures will continue to coexist and influence each other. Indeed, they may do so to a greater degree than before because the number and scope of cooperation regimes and multilateral agreements will increase. The GATT system is itself an interesting example of multilateral commitments realized through bilateral negotiations and agreements. Other patterns of bilateral and multilateral relations may emerge in the future. If, as seems probable, regional trading blocs develop in the future global economy, then in a technical sense their relations with external powers could be considered bilateral; within the blocs themselves, however, multilateral cooperation would obtain. In the single market of the EC, bilateral economic relations between member states will be replaced in many areas by a multilaterally structured, integrated market that, as a cohesive unit, would then establish bilateral or multilateral relations with other countries and regional groupings.

The combination of bilateralism and multilateralism may assume different institutional forms within different cooperation regimes. In the future, some states may prefer to avoid the "excessive institutionalization" of multilateral cooperation regimes by operating within frameworks in which they negotiate identical bilateral agreements with one another, thus providing for reciprocal rights and duties, and by enacting national legislation regarding agreed-upon means to achieve specific ends (as has been the case in the case of the exploitation of seabed resources). Through such frameworks, these states could avoid the establishment of inter-governmental operational organizations and yet achieve limited multilateral results. Daniel Cheever refers to this form of relations among states as "bilateral multilateralism."[12]

The Growth of Regionalism and Its Consequences for Global Cooperation

The pursuit of regional cooperation has a long, varied, and check-ered history.[13] For centuries, attempts have been made in Europe to create regions of peace and cooperation, thereby eliminating the causes of tensions and conflicts between nations. In the 18th century, the establishment of the United States on the American continent inspired political thinkers and statesmen to construct similar federal arrangements in other parts of the world. Some of the Hungarian revolutionaries in the mid-19th century dreamt about a federation of nations in the valley of the Danube that would be established on the ruins of the Austrian empire. Nineteenth-century Latin American revolutionaries like Simón Bolívar sought to create a federal structure to maintain, protect, or increase the autonomy of the new countries of Latin America against external powers. In this century, many African revolutionaries have thought in terms of a united, federal Africa. The vision of a united Arab world has been promoted time and again, with pragmatic, albeit ultimately unsuccessful, steps taken toward its realization by such pan-Arabist politicians as Egyptian president Gamal Abdel Nasser. In the early stages of planning for the post–World War II order, Winston Churchill suggested the establishment of a number of regional councils through which the great powers could exercise leadership in the world.

These are examples of unfulfilled ambitions. In the post–World War II era, however, a large number of regional organizations have been successfully established in a wide range of area. These organizations include military alliances like NATO; essentially political groups like the OAS, the OAU, and the Arab League; and economic bodies like the European Economic Community and about 30 other integration groups and free trade areas, regional development banks, and the regional economic commissions of the United Nations. The EC has been by far the most successful and important regional organization, exercising considerable influence on both its member states and the international system as a whole. Regional organizations have differed in their geographical breadth; in their specific mandates and political, economic, or military responsibilities; and in their relations to global cooperation structures.

Regionalism (or regionalization)—a term that has been used to describe very different institutionalized preferences and trends in international political, military, or economic relations within sets of countries—has been promoted by many of its advocates as an interconnecting, unifying process that is a natural outgrowth of bilateral relations. In the early 1960s, Harlan Cleveland characterized regionalism as "a halfway house at a time when single nations are no longer viable and the world is not ready to become one."[14] According to this definition, regionalism could be seen as a bridge between bilateral and global cooperation.

In the past, regional regimes and agencies have often performed a valuable service by enhancing cooperation. Since the 1980s, however, the strengthening of the process of regionalization has raised concerns about its adverse effects on the future of worldwide cooperation. There is, indeed, a real danger that the emergence of regional "fortresses" and the functioning of regional political and economic structures within the global system may be fragmenting the post–World War II order into competing regional blocs. Fears have been expressed, for example, that the global trading system may disintegrate into a number of trading blocs, regional integration groups, or special cooperation zones, which would usher in new forms of competition and conflict. In addition, the passage of the Maastricht Treaty has prompted concern that it may encourage other regions to form political and economic power centers similar to that emerging in Europe, thereby undermining collective global cooperation and security efforts.

As of the mid-1990s, three main trends are apparent in regionalization: the organization and consolidation of regional integration groups; progress toward the establishment of regional security arrangements and institutions; and the development of "economic spaces" within which countries make preferential agreements for free trade, create customs unions, and harmonize their policies. The European economic space is, in fact, an extension of the EC to countries that may join it later. This extension is based on agreements that focus on liberalizing trade relations with the community. The creation of an American economic space, known in the Western hemisphere as the "American Enterprise," was declared as a continental goal by President George Bush in June 1990, when he spoke of establishing a free trade zone "from Anchorage to Tierra del Fuego."[15] The realization of the North American Free Trade Agreement has been widely regarded as the first major step toward achieving this goal. NAFTA, however, could represent a significant step toward splitting the American continent into blocs, each of which would establish preferential trade and investment conditions for its members.

The idea of a third economic space centered on the Pacific has been raised by a number of Asian countries and pursued by the United States. A concrete step was taken in 1989 with the establishment of the Asia-Pacific Economic Cooperation group (APEC). Proposals made in 1993 to strengthen APEC (an idea that did not receive universal support from within the region) were justified in part by the need to respond to the "escalation of inward-looking regionalism throughout the world"—a thinly veiled reference to the EC.[16]

Post–Cold War regionalism in its different forms has many political and economic sources, the most important of which is probably the failure of global cooperation regimes to create a credible structure of global security and peace and to respond effectively to regional conflicts. In the post–Cold War era, most international political disputes and military conflicts are widely expected to be confined to a given region. At least in principle, the management and resolution of these conflicts should prove easier to accomplish if undertaken by entities with a more limited geographic and political scope than that of the UN Security Council. In practical terms, however, the case of the former Yugoslavia has shown that this principle may not always apply: a regional entity may be hamstrung in its efforts to resolve a conflict because its members have bilateral ties to opposing sides, or because it possesses limited resources to intervene in a large-scale conflict, or because (as in the case of the CSCE) its requirement of consensual decision making prevents a timely response to a fast-moving situation. In recognition of these problems, efforts are under way in Europe to increase the role and enhance the efficacy of regional institutions in security matters. These efforts include proposals for the formation of a European court of conciliation and the establishment of a European security council with a mandate similar to that of the UN Security Council.[17]

Another reason why regionalism will become more important is the emergence of a multipolar world. Russia is certain to be substantially less involved in remote regions of the world than was the Soviet Union. For Russia, the main sphere of interest and influence will be the territory of the former Soviet Union. The United States too seems likely to show less interest in many regions of the world than it did during the Cold War. In the absence of a globally pervasive bipolarity, many regional powers will have the opportunity to strengthen their international positions by forming regional structures within which they can enjoy great influence. Regionalism also offers many less powerful countries—especially those in the developing world—the chance to improve their bargaining positions in the global policymaking arena by combining to form a formidable collective unit.

A growth in regionalism accords with the direction of several ongoing economic trends. Capital flows and technological cooperation have been increasing more rapidly within certain regions—Europe and Asia, most notably—than between regions. In addition, certain currencies are playing a more prominent role within particular regions. In Europe, the leading currency is the German mark, which, together with the ECU, is also the de facto common currency unit within the EC. Likewise in the Far East, economic currents are shaping a yen-based economic bloc.

The progress of regionalization and globalization (and the fragmentation of existing structures) is tied to specific political and economic interests of countries and powerful groups such as the transnational corporations. Regional institutions like the EC are also playing a demonstrative and self-generating role, promoting integration as part of their institutional duty. However, like global or bilateral cooperation, regional cooperation is also facing significant obstacles and uncertainties. In Europe, for example, the question is often asked: Can the momentum that resulted in regionalism be sustained in view of the changing interests of the participating countries? Another fundamental question concerns the extent to which regional cooperation can more efficiently satisfy the political, security, and economic needs of countries than can traditional forms of bilateral cooperation or global multilateralism. A further, more delicate question is whether or not regionalism will be able to provide greater security for smaller nations against the actions of regional hegemons than global institutions have been able to achieve.

Where regional cooperation is most advanced, the impediments to its further progress tend to be more concrete. For example, as discussed in part II of this book, Europe in the 1990s will have to grapple with several major problems. One such problem concerns the widening and deepening of the EC. To date, the EC has been able to maintain a delicate balance of collective and national interests. Any increase in the membership or powers of the community might easily upset that balance, imperiling the interests of member countries and provoking domestic opposition to supranational policies. Ultimately, this may halt or derail the process of integration. Another problem for Europe will be how to respond to threats to the security of the region, especially those arising in the countries of Central and Eastern Europe. The Yugoslavian imbroglio has proved that no European institution by itself is yet sufficiently well organized and powerful to ensure regional security.

The experiences of other regions are even more discouraging. Although such continental organizations as the OAU and the OAS serve as forums for negotiations, they have achieved only limited success in building security structures and promoting qualitative improvements in economic cooperation. In many sub-regions of the developing world, the work of integration groups has hardly progressed beyond the declaration of intentions. Remarks made in 1985 by Maurice Bertrand, a former member of the Joint Inspection Unit of the United Nations, regarding the implications of regional cooperation in some parts of the world may still be valid today:

> They [integration groups] mainly provide the occasion for a large number of meetings, either at an administrative level or at that of officials, but because of the poverty of their means of action, the limitation of the level of their jurisdiction and the failure of the models used to adapt to local problems, they frequently do not do more than increase the complexity of handling national problems without helping either to identify or take over the specific problems of the region.[18]

As Bertrand's observations suggest, regional cooperation institutions are not always more effective than are global organizations and regimes. Indeed, both regional and global bodies suffer from similar problems: the heterogeneity of interests of their member states, an unreliable propensity for cooperation, inadequate financial resources and expertise, bureaucratization, and so forth.

Joseph Nye has enumerated three arguments against the establishment of economic blocs in Europe, the Far East, and North America: one, they run counter to the thrust of global technological trends and the interests of transnational corporations; two, they are counter to interests of smaller states, which need a global system to protect them against domination by their larger neighbors; and three, they cannot diminish the fears of nonnuclear nations regarding their nuclear neighbors in the region.[19] Although these arguments are sound, we cannot afford to disregard the possibility that 21st-century power politics may be characterized by increasing interregional conflicts and regionalism, with competing regions structured as security and economic networks centered around major regional powers.

The regionalization of the global bargaining process and of security issues, the establishment of regional security complexes, and the compartmentalization of global cooperation and institutional structures could, however, very possibly obstruct global cooperation if different regions choose to structure themselves as regional fortresses. In such a situation, interregional relations would become a zero-sum game played by competitive blocs.

Alternatively, however, more intensive regional cooperation could complement and enhance global cooperation and networking. As Harlan Cleveland suggested, regionalism could serve as a bridge between countries and global processes by facilitating internationalization and greater liberalization within regional structures. Compared to their global counterparts, regional structures are more transparent and more familiar to their member states; they enjoy the cohering effects of common cultural and economic ties; and they allow the gains and losses that cooperation produces to be more easily balanced. Furthermore, regional structures could promote different forms of cooperation among countries in a wide variety of areas, ranging from the fight against poverty and the control of migration to the development of physical infrastructure and the establishment of regional information and telecommunications structures. Regionalism could also facilitate the coordination of policies and the elaboration of common attitudes on such issues as environmental protection and demilitarization.

These two scenarios of the character and consequences of future regional cooperation have been the subject of heated debate within industrial countries, especially with regard to the future of the international trading system. Take, for example, the following extract from a summary report of an OECD conference:

> Some observers have expressed deep concern about the increased regionalization of the world economy. They point out in particular, that the preferential trade liberalization features of such agreements

could be a major source of trade diversion which may well offset their trade-creating effects. Moreover, regionalization could have adverse overspill effects since it may induce outsiders who bear the brunt of trade diversion to retaliate by seeking preferential trade agreements among themselves so as to offset their loss of markets and strengthen their bargaining power. This process of competitive regionalization may undermine the multilateral system and, far from contributing to global liberalization, could turn the world into one of hostile economic blocs and discriminatory trade regimes similar to those that prevailed in the 1930s.

Others disagree. They welcome regional and plurilateral strategies as perhaps the best way to foster global liberalization, given the growing obstacles which have brought multilateral negotiations to a virtual halt at present and which are not likely to disappear in the future. . . . [R]egional agreements are attractive, because they make negotiations more manageable: a relatively small number of like-minded countries are involved, which reduces the likelihood that liberalization will be held hostage by a recalcitrant power.[20]

In principle, bilateral or regional and global multilateral cooperation should not necessarily be seen as contradictory forms of relations. They can coexist, and they may even be mutually supportive in open democratic institutional systems. In closed or constrained systems of cooperation, however, they may be conflictual.

The fundamental issue for the political future of regionalism is whether it can outperform globalism in facilitating the maintenance of peace and stability and the protection of human rights. The economic future of regionalism will depend to a large extent on the ability of regional structures to satisfy their members' needs for economic development (higher output and incomes, greater trade and capital flows, increased entrepreneurship, and so forth). In this context, it may be noted that the transnational business sector could better harmonize the processes of globalization and regionalization within its corporate structure than could the small-business sector. Another factor shaping the future of regionalism is the institutional efficiency of regional governance: its cost effectiveness; its timely and flexible response to the needs of member countries; its management of relations within the region and with the rest of the world; and its ability to sustain development and cooperation on a global level, satisfying the new needs of the participants in the global system.

chapter 21

Post-Cold War Politics and Multilateral Institutions

The end of the Cold War and the emergence of a more favorable global political environment have raised expectations that the community of nations will take advantage of the benefits that a system of multilateral institutional cooperation can offer. By themselves, however, the political changes of the late 1980s and early 1990s by no means ensure that global multilateral cooperation will increase. Rather, the future will depend on the attitudes and behavior of states toward such cooperation; as such, those factors that shape attitudes and behavior will ultimately determine the future forms of governance.

These formative factors fall into two interrelated categories. One category includes states' past experiences with international multilateral cooperation; their new needs, preferences, and capabilities in the system; the degree of their shared understanding of mutual problems and sources of risk; and the extent to which their commitments to collective risk management converge. The other category relates to the institutions and regimes of multilateral cooperation themselves, and concerns the extent to which those institutions and regimes can improve their operational efficiency by such measures as bolstering the legal status of resolutions they adopt and enhancing the professional expertise of their staffs. The process of institutional adjustment will have to be related to the changing needs of countries and to the degree that they are prepared to provide the resources necessary to ensure the effective operation of multinational organizations. The adjustment process will be made all the more complex by the increase in the number of states and their differences of opinion regarding the role of the United Nations in such areas as peacekeeping and the revitalization of the development process.

Can the United Nations Respond to the Demands of the Post–Cold War Era?

In discussing the collective response of multilateral cooperation regimes to the future needs of the global community of states, we will focus primarily, though not exclusively, on the United Nations. The UN system is the largest, most comprehensive, and most democratic intergovernmental cooperation system in existence. Were the United Nations and its charter to be eliminated, the international environment would be dominated by unrestrained power politics, chaos, and violence. But will the United Nations be able to respond to the new demands of the post–Cold War era? Will it be able to harmonize the policies of states and take into account the growing role of nonstate actors?

There are three hierarchies in the UN system: organizations and cooperation regimes under the authority of the General Assembly; the specialized agencies with their own governing structures; and the Bretton Woods institutions. The global political changes under way since the late 1980s have increased the demands placed on all of these hierarchies and inspired a wealth of suggestions as to how the United Nations can improve its efficiency and meet the new needs of the international community. Not only have academics, politicians, and IGOs offered an array of new ideas about multilateralism,[21] but also member governments have engaged in a comprehensive review of the subject. At the January 31, 1992, meeting of the Security Council, at which council members were represented for the first time by heads of state and government, recommendations were made that went beyond the usual rhetoric and reflected a new sense of awareness and commitment.

Whether the United Nations is flexible enough to adapt and respond to the evolving agenda of global needs with the necessary speed and efficiency remains to be seen. Certainly, that agenda is broad, broader indeed than at any time in the history of the world body. Issues regarding an increased UN role in maintaining international peace and security are especially numerous and wide-ranging, involving such matters as not only the establishment of international norms of behavior but also the enforcement of those norms. The provision of advanced warning (also known as early warning), mediation, and arbitration services and peacemaking facilities and peacekeeping forces have also become central tasks for institutional development. It is encouraging to note that in June 1992 UN Secretary-General Boutros Boutros-Ghali presented a comprehensive proposal, entitled "An Agenda for Peace," for establishing the peacekeeping and peacemaking activities of the organization on new foundations. The document called for enhancing the role of regional organizations in security matters; improving the speed of response to crises by the creation of a permanent contingent of peacekeeping forces; and providing better training and greater financing, information-gathering, and logistical support.

UN peacekeeping is, above all, a political task, and it must be undertaken in accordance with the UN Charter. This means that each operation must have a clear political goal and a precise mandate. It also underlines the importance of conflict prevention and advanced warning. The improvement of the UN capacity to offer advanced warning of incipient conflicts or crises and thus permit timely preventive action to be taken has actually been on the agenda since the 1980s. Previously, however, the task was confined to the prediction of interstate conflicts. In coming decades, although external threats will still endanger national security in some parts of the world (especially in light of the disintegration of countries like the Soviet Union and Yugoslavia), the sudden and episodic outbreak of domestic ethnic conflict is likely be the main source of violence causing extensive human suffering and mass movements of refugees. The ability to predict and prevent these kinds of conflicts has therefore become an important concern for the United Nations.

In 1991, the General Assembly adopted and the Security Council endorsed Resolution 46-59, which requested that the Secretary-General monitor the state of international peace and security to provide early warning of disputes and other situations that threaten international peace and security. The resolution also recommended that the information-gathering capabilities of the UN secretariat be strengthened. Given the complex nature of the sources of instability, the often intransigent attitudes of countries involved in disputes, and the costs involved, implementing the resolution will be difficult.

Calls for the United Nations to undertake a greater peace enforcement role may have far-reaching implications and have been criticized by a number of states. Peace enforcement goes beyond traditional and impartial forms of peacemaking and peacekeeping to involve coercive military intervention against an aggressor undertaken by the United Nations on the basis of a General Assembly resolution and a mandate given by the Security Council or, in special cases, the UN Charter. To date, only two enforcement actions have been taken by the United Nations: the first in Korea in the early 1950s; the second in the Persian Gulf in the early 1990s. Both of these were prompted by the actions of one state against another. In the future, though, the United Nations may well be expected to legitimize collective intervention in response to internal actions, such as the gross abuse of human rights or the production of weapons of mass destruction.

Speaking to the Security Council in 1992, Boutros-Ghali underlined this new consideration:

> State sovereignty takes a new meaning in this context. Added to its dimension of rights is the dimension of responsibility, both internal and external. Violation of state sovereignty is, and will remain, an offence against the global order. But its misuse also may undermine human rights and jeopardize a peaceful global life. Civil wars are no longer civil and the carnage they inflict will not let the world remain indifferent. The narrow nationalism that would oppose or disregard the norms of a stable international order and the micro-nationalism that resists healthy economic and political integration can disrupt a peaceful global existence.[22]

Intervention for humanitarian reasons, however, is an extremely complex and controversial issue. The UN Charter explicitly upholds the principle of nonintervention, the observance of which has done much to maintain global peace and stability and to safeguard smaller and weaker countries against their more powerful predatory neighbors. The principle of nonintervention has often been justified by the argument that intervention means war, which in itself is an inhumane act, and may cause conflicts to escalate further. If the United Nations is to intervene for humanitarian reasons in a state's affairs despite that state's objections, it seems essential that the criteria for intervention be based on a broad consensus, that decisions to intervene be deliberated and agreed upon in the Security Council, and that intervention be multilateral in nature and combined with political and humanitarian measures.

Except in instances of enforcement, UN peacekeeping operations have traditionally required that the host country consent to the deployment of UN troops. Since their inauguration in 1948, UN peacekeeping operations have involved the participation of more than half a million military and civilian personnel in many different corners of the world. The record of UN peacekeeping forces has been mixed, with operational inefficiencies, uncertain political and financial support from members of the Security Council, and the intractability of some conflicts combining to undermine any hopes for the success of some missions. In the mid-1990s, although significant opportunities exist to strengthen the peacekeeping and peacemaking capacities of the United Nations, spectacular improvements will only be achieved if greater political support and increased financing are forthcoming.

In the past, the United Nations was often unable to deal with ethnic strife and civil wars until they grew to pose a major danger to regional or subregional stability. But new opportunities for early, preventive action are now emerging through a convergence of views within the Security Council. The permanent members seem highly unlikely to exercise their power of veto to the same extent that they did during the Cold War. (Between 1945 and 1990, 279 vetoes were exercised in the Security Council, many of them to prevent action in the more than 100 major conflicts that occurred during the same period at a cost of more than 20 million lives.) The more cooperative relationship that has developed among the members of the Security Council may facilitate improved coordination between UN peacekeeping activities and regional security arrangements. It is, however, far from clear whether the permanent members and other powerful nations will increasingly offer the services of their highly professional and well-equipped military forces to the United Nations or be readier to finance not only specific missions but also improvements in the training of peacekeeping forces and the efficiency of the central command structure. Strong opposition has been voiced in countries like Germany and Japan to the participation of their military forces in peacekeeping operations. Debate on the same subject has also been widespread in the United States.

Security, of course, has nonmilitary as well as military, and domestic as well as international components. Environmental, social, economic, and cultural issues all have the potential to divide the international community along a variety of geographical and political faultlines. For instance, a key element of the domestic component is the security of persons within their own countries, which in practical terms means institutionalized state guarantees of respect for human rights. Although the Universal Declaration of Human Rights adopted by the United Nations in 1948 has helped significantly to internationalize human rights issues, it has served to set international standards rather than to build a global consensus on human rights. Indeed, in practical terms the United Nations has encountered three major problems in its efforts to advance respect for human rights: an essentially sociopolitically motivated disagreement among member states on human right issues; the reluctance of states to accept international scrutiny; and the weakness of the UN institutional capacity to deal with human rights issues. By agreeing in 1993 to the creation of the position of high commissioner for human rights, the United Nations accepted the principle of the internationalization of human rights issues. Achieving recognition of human rights as a component of a comprehensive global security structure is still an unfulfilled goal, however. As people become increasingly aware of their rights as human beings and readier to protest the violation of those rights, and in light of the revival of racist, ethnic, religious, and nationalistic ideologies that tend to disregard human rights, the work of advocating and protecting human rights is unlikely to diminish in its importance to the international community.

Human rights are but one of the very many nonmilitary issues that are intimately related to global security and that will require more effective collective action in the future. Already, very many international organizations devote a great deal of attention to nonmilitary issues. In the early 1990s, for example, more than three-quarters of UN activities (and an even higher proportion of the activities of non-UN multilateral bodies) centered on economic and social affairs. Whether or not these activities have always been efficient and purposive, however, is another matter. Within the United Nations, many organizations, agencies, regimes, groups, and programs not only complement and cooperate but also compete and overlap with one another. The UN agencies have been linked to the New York secretariat and General Assembly only loosely. Institutionally, the UN Administrative Committee on Coordination has been the only forum for the harmonization of policies, programs, and actions, and its record has not been good. The absence of coherent leadership and effective joint planning based on functional rationality and institutional competence has been all too apparent.

The institutional weaknesses and inconsistencies have been especially pronounced in economic and social areas. In the future, the United Nations will have to respond to the rising demands of many countries, especially within the developing world, that it build a new global partnership for development. The repetition of past errors—creating institutions and programs for rhetorical rather than practical purposes—would seriously undermine the credibility of the United Nations in the new era. Consequently, the organization must demonstrate greater selectivity in the issues it addresses and focus on those tasks that are most important and that it can accomplish within its framework and with its limited resources. These tasks include giving early warning of major crises, elaborating recommendations for collective action, and improving coordination among the specialized agencies. It is becoming increasingly evident that a new division of labor must be developed among global, regional, and national organizations, and among governments and nonstate actors, to permit the more effective management of the many sources of economic, social, and environmental risks.

The role of the "G" groups also requires clarification, since those groups significantly influence the process of macroeconomic coordination among the main industrial countries and thus help shape international economic policy issues. In the 1980s, according to many experts, the G-7 countries increasingly bypassed not only the UN system but also the policymaking bodies of all the other international agencies.[23]

The division of labor among different regional and global agencies and cooperation regimes is not merely a legal or institutional question. Suggestions for institutional changes are usually politically motivated and reflect different, and sometimes conflicting, objectives and preferences of groups of countries. For example, some developing countries have complained that many proposals made by industrial powers for institutional restructuring and improving institutional competence are really motivated by a desire to strengthen those powers' control over the most important multilateral institutions and assign only a complementary role to the UN system in the governance of international social and economic policy issues, thereby violating the democratic principles of the UN Charter.

Enhancing global economic security through cooperation based on the democratic principles of the charter is indeed a crucially important task for the United Nations. However, managing cooperation and resolving socioeconomic disputes are often very specific tasks and require various mechanisms to deal with matters such as trade relations and capital flows. The credibility of any system of international cooperation depends not only on the ideas it represents and the importance of the issues it addresses but also on the instruments it has available for achieving its goals. With their long experience in policy analysis, the central organs of the United Nations could play a key role in developing the main principles of cooperation (for instance, that the gains from economic relations should be more equally distributed and that the rich and powerful as well as the small and weak countries should make adjustments to their policies); formulating new global priorities (like the revitalization of growth and the struggle against poverty); and warning of potential sources of crises and conflicts (such as the adverse consequences of protectionism and trade wars). The UN specialized agencies could increase their role in a large number of areas requiring international regulation and control: the global fight against AIDS and the confinement or elimination of other epidemics; the control of drug trafficking;

the formulation of policies to address the consequences of demographic changes; the achievement of global food security; the management of trading regimes and disputes; cooperation on telecommunications and information-flow issues; the protection of intellectual property rights; and the management of environmental cooperation. Increasing the efficiency of the existing institutions that deal with these issues is a more complex task than improving their coordination.

Relatively informal cooperation regimes like the "G" groups also need to be linked more closely to the global multilateral system. For instance, it is vital that the G-7 countries, the domestic policies of which directly influence the rest of the world, should maintain a structured dialogue with the international community as a whole, assess the international or global consequences of their policies, and harmonize their policies and actions with the interests of other countries.

The "G" form of cooperation has been criticized by some countries for eroding the position of the principal multilateral agencies for international cooperation and disregarding the interests of developing and smaller countries.[24] However, while the consortium-like process of the G-7 represents a retreat from global multilateralism, it is a process that is likely to remain in operation. Almost certainly, global and regional multilateral institutions and agencies will coexist in the future with a variety of representative groups or other informal networks of different powers in areas where their cooperation cannot be realized in a global framework. In 1990, the member countries of the G-7 accounted for over 70 percent of world output, more than two-thirds of global merchandise in exports, and more than 90 percent of the new money for global capital markets. Their policies and market performance have had major consequences for the global economy. Were those policies to diverge from the interests of the rest of the world (were they, for example, to shift toward protectionism), the global economy as a whole would suffer.

These smaller, powerful groups may, though, also promote global stability or support the interests of the global economy by enacting policies to stimulate economic growth or liberalize trade and capital flows. Groups such as the G-7 may have compelling reasons (such as the dangers posed by the development of regional trading blocs) to agree on institutional guarantees for cooperation, including a more open and transparent bargaining process between themselves and the rest of the world, and to support a more efficient global cooperation system.

The Difficult Path of Institutional Reforms

Although the post–Cold War world offers many excellent reasons for undertaking major, well-conceived reforms of multilateral cooperation structures, especially the UN system, actually achieving those reforms will not be a straightforward matter. Improving operational efficiency requires not only streamlining existing institutions but also restructuring the organizational network on global and regional levels, which includes merging existing organizations or regimes, establishing new structures, and phasing out those institutions considered superfluous.

The functioning of the global system of IGOs depends on three structures, and on recent changes that have influenced each of them. One is the *national political structure* (the legislative and executive branches of national government), which establishes international organizations, ratifies and codifies their decisions, and either implements or ignores them. A second structure is the *intergovernmental machinery* composed of the governing bodies of multilateral organizations and cooperation regimes, their committees and subcommittees, and also global strategic conferences that have often inspired or catalyzed significant change. The intergovernmental machinery chiefly involves government delegations, politicians, diplomats, and government experts. A third structure is the *secretariat* of any given international organization or cooperation regime; this international civil service enjoys varying degrees of freedom of action and autonomy.

Reform and restructuring are not unfamiliar to international organizations and agencies. For instance, when the OEEC became the OECD, it underwent a major restructuring. Far-reaching changes have also occurred within the structure of the EC. After years of sporadic and sometimes counterproductive attempts to improve the efficient functioning of the community, the conclusion of the Single European Act in 1985 permitted substantial steps to be taken toward achieving consistency and harmony in the operation of the EC's institutions. Even so, the process has not been smooth and has underscored the difficulties involved in reorganizing an entrenched international bureaucracy. No doubt, progress toward monetary union and political integration will encounter similar obstacles.

Efforts to reform or restructure the UN system have been less successful than those made within the EC. As Joachim Muller, the author and editor of a major documentary work on reform of the United Nations, has observed:

> [T]he word "reform" [has] acquired a particular meaning at the U.N. First, it is seen as a response to new challenges or emerging concerns of member states. There are, however, other interpretations. Reform efforts have been viewed as attempts to undermine the interests and concerns of member states which consequently react to preserve the status quo. Others see reform as a process through which economies can be achieved by curtailing or cutting activities, often without concern for substance. Still others view reform as conspiracy: conspiracy on the part of the secretariat to enhance its position or on the part of member states to promote their interests at the expense of others. Quite often, such attempts have resulted in a stalemate and the exchange of accusations, including laments over the absence of vision or the lack of political will.[25]

Between 1960 and 1991, 18 major reform initiatives were undertaken within the United Nations. Only on two occasions were these reforms the outcome of collective efforts based on the analysis of past performance and future obligations. One was the "Capacity Study"–better known as the "Jackson Report," for its main author, Sir Robert Jackson[26]–which analyzed the policies and practices of development cooperation in the UN system and concluded by recommending its fundamental restructuring. The other notable effort at reform grew out of ideas for creating a new international economic order that dominated debates in the United Nations throughout the 1970s and resulted in the restructuring of the economic and social sectors of the UN system, with most reforms affecting the financing, planning, and budgetary activities of the United Nations.

The various reform and restructuring initiatives that have been undertaken within the UN system can be grouped into five categories:

1. Amending the UN Charter.
2. Establishing new agencies, cooperation regimes, and programs.

3. Restructuring existing organizations, including making changes in the intergovernmental governing bodies of different agencies and programs.

4. Reforming the administrative, planning, and budgetary procedures.

5. Restructuring the secretariat.

Since the founding of the United Nations, its charter has been amended only twice. Other attempts at reform have targeted the other categories given above. Until the 1980s, most reforms sought to expand the United Nations; this resulted in extraordinary and unnecessary structural complexity and excessive institutional fragmentation, making coordination practically impossible. In the 1980s, with the United States and the Soviet Union both favoring zero growth in the organization's budget, the United Nations entered a fiscal crisis that spurred attempts to streamline its operations.

The most far-reaching and costly changes to the UN system were suggested in a 1975 report based on an in-depth study of the UN intergovernmental structure and its functions in the economic and social fields. (The report was subsequently endorsed by the Ad Hoc Committee on the Restructuring of the Economic and Social Sectors of the United Nations.) The secretariat structure has also been reviewed, leading to the establishment of the Office for Research and the Collection of Information, which assesses global trends and provides early warning of developing crises that may warrant the attention of the Secretary-General. In addition to such official, government-directed efforts as these, numerous reviews have been undertaken by academic groups, nongovernmental organizations, and private individuals. Some of their resulting reports and proposals for reform have influenced intergovernmental decisions.

A major restructuring of the UN system, including its intergovernmental bodies and the secretariat, could, at least theoretically, be implemented in one of two ways: as a comprehensive package deal or in piecemeal fashion. Given that the first approach would require holding global negotiations and attaining consensus on many major issues, it seems highly unlikely to be taken. The piecemeal approach has a greater chance of producing tangible results, especially in those areas where the main actors are in agreement, where resistance from individual countries is weak, and where the Secretary-General is given sufficient discretion and authority to implement the agreed-upon reforms (this authority, it should be noted, was granted in restructuring the political and the socioeconomic offices of the UN secretariat in 1992 and 1993).

Different UN conferences on organizational reform have adopted a variety of principles, most of which remain relevant to any future reform activity:

- Before deciding *how* to undertake organizational reforms, agreement should first be reached on *what* reforms are necessary, taking into account the original mandate and new needs of an organization.
- All functions that can best be performed by existing organizations should be assigned to those organizations most capable of carrying them out efficiently. No new machinery should be created unnecessarily.
- Efficiency is often best attained not by relying on global "super agencies" but by using a well-coordinated network of national, regional, global, and functional and sectoral organizations that can supplement and complement one another.
- Many global cooperation agencies or regimes will increasingly be required to work on a regional level, but they must only do so if equipped with a well-defined mandate and authority, and only then through relations with regional structures or organizations.
- The highest priority should be given to the coordination and rationalization of existing activities. Scarce financial and human resources should not be wasted on duplication of effort. The intergovernmental policymaking entity that oversees or coordinates the activities of a given agency should not itself initiate new operational functions that compete with the functions performed by other agencies.
- Reform measures should strengthen the democratic and participatory character of the system, in harmony with the UN Charter.

Encouragingly, these principles are gaining greater acceptance among national governments, which are demanding less costly and more efficient services from international agencies.

Some potential institutional reforms are supported by recent political changes in a very direct way. The end of the Cold War opened the way for the reform of the political structure of the United Nations. It has facilitated the simplification and restructuring of the different political committees of the General Assembly; permitted the phasing out or substantial reduction of activities directly related to the Cold War, such as the work of the UN Disarmament Center; and encouraged the restructuring of those arms of the secretariat that deal with peace-making and peacekeeping.

Political changes have also affected socioeconomic areas. Since the dissolution of the Soviet empire, the Bretton Woods institutions have gradually become universal (in principle, all countries can become members). This presents the opportunity to merge several existing UN agencies and cooperation programs and establish a new division of labor among them. After the successful conclusion of the Uruguay Round, for example, it is possible to establish a single global organization to focus on issues of economic development and cooperation. This would not represent an attempt to resurrect the idea behind the ITO; instead, it would involve the establishment of a coordinated and institutionalized network by tying together and gradually merging a wide range of existing agencies like the OECD, the GATT, the United Nations Conference on Trade and Development (UNCTAD), and the United Nations Industrial Development Organization (UNIDO) that deal with resources, energy, new technologies, and transnational corporations.

Two advantages of such an organization would be the greater transparency of the system (achieved through the elimination of parallel activities) and its greater policy relevance for all countries (accomplished by amalgamating the best elements— be they technical expertise, field experience, or whatever— of each agency or country). It could also facilitate the development of a more comprehensive and longer-term approach to global economic security. In the event of any such institutional merger, the character and mandate of the Economic and Social Council would have to be changed. To this end, proposals have already been made for the establishment of either an Economic and Social Security Council with new powers and responsibilities, or a World Economic Council based on a system of regional representation that would assume the responsibilities of the G-7.[27]

Programs for the restructuring of international agencies will have to include closer coordination among regional and global organizations and, in some cases, the merging of parallel regional institutions. Relations among existing subregional structures and regional institutions of the United Nations and its agencies will also have to be more precisely defined.

Today, an unprecedented demand exists for an expansion of the knowledge base of different international agencies and for new solutions to common problems. To meet this demand, international agencies must improve their capacities in a wide range of areas: generating new ideas; developing new practices for global governance; facilitating joint exercises in problem solving; and coordinating the activities of cooperation regimes and member states in areas of research, data collection, information processing, information use and interpretation, and dissemination. The way in which the international system has handled environmental issues (integrating the work of governments and the academic community) demonstrates how the professional competence of international organizations can be enhanced. In this area, the role of nongovernmental organizations has also been very important. Any restructuring effort must recognize the new needs and possibilities engendered by the information revolution. IGOs should utilize electronic networks for the rapid collection and dissemination of information. The information revolution must be exploited to produce a qualitative improvement in, and acceleration of, the learning processes of international organizations.

Ernst Haas has defined the learning process of international organizations in the following way:

> Learning in and by an international organization implies that the organization's members are induced to question earlier beliefs about the appropriateness of ends of action and to think about the selection of new ones, to "revalue" themselves. As this happens, international institutions are being used to cope with problems never before experienced. And as members of the organization go through the learning process, it is likely that they will arrive at a common understanding of what causes the particular problems of concern. A common understanding of the causes is likely

to trigger a shared understanding of solutions, and the new chain implies a set of larger meanings about life and nature not previously held in common by the participating members. . . . "An international organization learns" is a shorthand way to say that the actors representing states and members of the secretariat, working together in the organization in search for solutions to problems on the agenda, have agreed on a new way of conceptualizing the problem.[28]

However, as the 1992 Rio conference on the environment and development illustrated, the learning process is not necessarily symmetrical, and joint understanding of specific problems and their causes does not necessarily create common interests in their management or solution.

Any increase in the number of international multilateral institutions or in their responsibilities and capacities will, of course, require an increase in available financial resources. The end of the Cold War and the consequent reduction of defense expenditures raised expectations that more money would be made available—and on a more reliable basis—for international multilateral programs. These expectations have not been met. Many countries financed a large part of their defense expenditures by borrowing; reducing their defense expenditures simply reduced their deficits. Furthermore, while military expenditures have decreased, many other national demands remain to be satisfied. Even that money allotted to improving international relations may be spent on bilateral assistance to individual countries rather than on multilateral ventures.

Under any circumstances, the amount of financial resources made available for multilateral cooperation depends first and foremost on the attitudes of the larger and wealthier states. As the following chapter reveals, these states are not necessarily willing to allow international agencies to expand their activities into new areas, especially into economic and social fields.

chapter 22

The Changing Attitudes of States toward Multilateral Cooperation

Since the end of World War II, states have generally shown increased interest in participating in IGOs. As of 1990, the average number of different IGOs in which each country was participating was 30. Some nations have been particularly inclined toward IGO membership: 25 nations have participated in more than 140 IGOs, with the United States having belonged to about 200, and France topping the list with membership in about 270. However, while a high participation rate indicates that countries are interested in intergovernmental cooperation, it does not necessarily mean that they are actively involved in the work of IGOs.

The future needs of collective risk management will require not only the formal membership of most states in IGOs, but also a widespread change in the policies and attitudes of states toward international cooperation. Relations between individual member states and the IGOs they establish have been always complex and sometimes conflictual. As was especially evident during the Cold War, bilateral considerations have frequently taken precedence over the responsibilities and duties attached to membership in an IGO (the concept of responsibility is understood here normatively, as essentially a moral commitment). When IGOs acquire new members, other member countries often find themselves uncomfortable with the resulting increase in ideological and intellectual diversity. Even when the composition of an IGO does not change, the interests and attitudes of states may change, undercutting their earlier rationales for membership.

Another fundamental problem has been the selective interest and involvement of states in different cooperation regimes and programs. In IGOs, governments define their attitudes on the basis of national objectives. The general objectives shared by states are security and welfare. States also have prestige- and value-oriented objectives such as the spread of ideas concerning peace, democracy, and human rights or solidarity with the humanitarian goals and actions of a given international agency. The more specific objectives of states are connected with functional issues like health care, food and agriculture, finance, trade, and telecommunications. For many countries of the world, these functional goals play a greater role in forming their attitudes toward IGOs than do the prestige-oriented goals.

One consequence of this diversity of interests and goals is that states demonstrate very different degrees of responsibility and accountability to those IGOs of which they are members. The Charter of Economic Rights and Duties of States, adopted by the General Assembly in 1974 despite criticism of its statist content by some countries, spoke of the responsibility of states in IGOs in terms of organizational policy and efficiency. Accountability would seem to involve somewhat more than this, and would include states accepting that if they act against the principles and charter of an IGO, they could face the suspension of their voting rights or expulsion.

There are three main areas where the responsibilities of member states to international organizations can be identified: the political, the financial, and, in some cases, the managerial aspects of an organization's operation. All three related to collective decisions and actions. In the post–Cold War era it will be necessary and possible to relate the attitudes and responsibilities of countries to their original commitments to a given organization. This was not so during the Cold War, when mutual accusations of nonfulfillment of obligations were a regular rhetorical refrain. The Cold War relations of member states within organizations were governed primarily by the bilateral relations of states. When they disapproved of certain policies or actions, some countries simply withdrew from an organization (as the United States and United Kingdom did from UNESCO), while others simply refused to pay for the program concerned (as the Soviet Union did with most UN peacekeeping operations).

The Orientations of States toward IGOs

The attitude of a country vis-à-vis an international organization or the multilateral system in general can be gauged by at least two indicators: one is the way a country relates to the functioning state system; the other is based on the orientation of a government's policies toward multilateral agencies. Looking back over the past 50 years, it is possible to identify three main policy orientations of individual countries or groups of countries toward IGOs: state-system centered, concerned with maximizing national security; state-system centered, supportive of interdependence and common security; and supranationalist, accepting of the increasing role of international structures.

State-system Centered, Concerned with Maximizing National Security

In countries where politics assumes the primacy of states within the international system and is dominated by attempts to maximize national security, governments have regarded international organizations primarily as tools of their national security policies. This approach has been taken predominantly by the larger powers that have special interests in the global system—powers such as the United States, France, Great Britain, and the Soviet Union. In their policies toward adversaries, these countries have emphasized military deterrence. Within the United Nations, and especially within the Security Council, they have used their special position to establish a framework for shared hegemony, imposing joint decisions on other, weaker states.

Not surprisingly, when politics becomes entirely subordinated to national security interests as determined by military-industrial complexes, the system of internationally organized cooperation is adversely affected. At such times, major powers attempt to force their own security interests onto the international system, often provoking conflict with the interests of other states and paralyzing the functioning of the system. These ill effects were apparent during the Cold War, when because their relative power positions and domestic political systems differed, the U.S.- and Soviet-led blocs were continually at odds.

Unwilling to compromise its position as the leading communist power in the post–World War II world, the Soviet Union rejected any form of supranational decision making.[29] Through its frequent use of its veto power in the UN Security Council, its denial of the principle of international civil service neutrality, its opposition to a broad interpretation of the power and role of the Secretary-General, its politicization of the specialized UN agencies, and its selective participation in peacekeeping operations and cooperation regimes, the Soviet Union did little to further international cooperation. Although Soviet policies toward the United Nations were adjusted several times, and by the late 1980s became more supportive of the work of the organization, some of the Soviet Union's fundamental reservations about IGOs persisted until the country's disintegration. As Robert Gregg has observed of the Soviet Union's earlier (pre-Gorbachev) attitude toward the United Nations:

> To be sure, the Soviet Union played an important role in the design of the United Nations. Distrustful of international organizations, but aware of their value for relationships with non-communist states, the Soviets were tenacious (and on the whole successful) in their efforts to make sure that the U.N. authority would be severely circumscribed. The Soviets were more concerned with hobbling the U.N. than in turning it into an important instrumentality for global problem solving. Preoccupied with security and ideologically convinced that no useful purpose could be served by entrusting a capitalist dominated body with economic and social responsibilities, the USSR was basically disinterested in ECOSOC [the Economic and Social Council] and indeed in all of those Charter provisions concerned with economic and social affairs.[30]

The United States has taken a very different approach. At the earlier stages of the organization's existence, the United States advocated strengthening the operational capabilities of the United Nations, including making institutionalized arrangements for standby peacekeeping forces. After all, the United States was the chief architect of the post–World War II global multilateral cooperation system, and a segment of U.S. public opinion has always supported the ideas of the United Nations' founders. And yet, as World War II has receded and a new power structure has evolved within the United Nations, the United States has exhibited an increasingly selective and ad hoc approach to its relations with intergovernmental agencies.

In principle, the UN Charter and most UN activities have been in harmony with the tenor and substance of much of the U.S. constitution and with U.S. moral and political support for democracy and human rights. In practice, however, the interplay of the U.S. domestic political process and changing global circumstances has altered the original U.S. commitment to the UN system. Within the United States, opinion has been divided on the merits of international cooperation. At one extreme are the isolationists, who have been hostile to all international organizations and have advocated the withdrawal of the United States from the United Nations and the removal of UN headquarters from U.S. territory. At the other extreme are the liberal internationalists, who have supported the United Nations in general but have also sought to reform it in order to promote its credibility at home and efficiency abroad. Between these two extremes lies the mainstream of opinion, which is interested in the United Nations insofar as it can promote, and certainly not compromise, U.S. security. Some sense of the character of mainstream U.S. opinion is indicated by the following statements by three leading U.S. scholars:

> The United Nations is not a world government, and there is no evident desire by its members to have it evolve toward greater supranationality. Most Americans hardly want yet another level of political authority reaching down into their lives.[31]

> American officials have been ambivalent toward the United Nations since its early days, rarely turning to multilateral diplomacy until all else failed. The threat or act of withdrawal has become an accepted American tactic. . . . Too often . . . the United States and other countries have stressed using multilateral forums to persuade other countries to endorse their foreign policy actions and to condemn those of their adversaries.[32]

> Contrary to popular myth, there never was a "golden age" in U.S.-U.N. relations. . . .
> The ideal form of an international civil service was diluted in the United Nations right from the start. The great powers

began immediately to jostle for senior secretariat positions for their nationals. The Soviet Union persistently accused Trygve Lie, the first Secretary General, of pro-Western bias. . . . And McCarthyism in the United States spilled over to impugn the loyalty of U.S. citizens working for the United Nations. . . .

[T]he posture of the U.S. towards the U.N. has oscillated wildly between accommodationism, rejectionism, and pragmatism, but at no time has it been guided by a clear strategic concept of the potential contribution of the United Nations to the kind of world order we desire.[33]

U.S. attitudes toward the international system of cooperation have been clearly reflected in U.S. policy regarding the financing of IGOs. In the 1980s, the Reagan administration's review of U.S. policies toward the United Nations coincided with rapid growth in the domestic budgetary deficit of the United States. The U.S. Congress grouped international organizations into four financing categories. The first category represented institutions of extreme strategic importance that would receive full funding at all times, like NATO and the International Telecommunications Union. In the second category were organizations such as the OECD, the GATT, the International Atomic Energy Agency, and the World Health Organization that were judged to be of importance to the United States and to have demonstrated a readiness to change their policies as required by the United States; these also received full funding. The third category, which received 85 percent of the assessed U.S. contribution, included organizations like the International Labor Organization and UNIDO that were considered less important and also less willing to implement reforms at the behest of the United States. The fourth category, which received only 75 percent of the scheduled U.S. contribution, included the United Nations itself and the Food and Agricultural Organization. No explanation was offered for this treatment of the United Nations.[34]

Although the United States has generally regarded the World Bank, the IMF, and the GATT more favorably than the United Nations, the 1980s saw a marked shift in the U.S. attitude toward the former. This shift, characterized by a move away from multilateral economic decision making and toward unilateral measures or preferential regional agreements, was remarked on in 1986: "As America's preponderance declined, so did the

American sense of responsibility for the health of the international economic system. The result has been drift, uncertainty, and deterioration."[35]

The Soviet and U.S. examples are two of the many variants of an orientation toward international cooperation that is distinguished by a focus on maximizing national security within a state-centered international system. Another variant is displayed by many developing countries, which see international agencies merely as instruments for obtaining development assistance.

State-system Centered, Supportive of Interdependence and Common Security

The politics of the state–system centered and interdependence-oriented countries is typified by their acceptance of the notion that states may no longer be able to accomplish their goals through their efforts alone and that a greater degree of international policy coordination is to the benefit of the entire international community. On this basis, they accept a system of multilateral cooperation that has required significant compromises for the sake of harmonizing interests and policies. They want, however, to maintain the sovereignty of states in the making and execution of decisions within the system of international cooperation, with a view to protecting their national interests and values against far-reaching international measures.

Most countries today, especially the small and medium-sized states, belong to this group. Many of them were born after World War II and have been helped by the United Nations to establish themselves within the international community. Typical of their outlook is the comment from a Singapore delegate to the UN General Assembly: "The small states, which make up the vast majority of membership, have never lost faith. They know that global adherence to the principles of the United Nations Charter is crucial for their survival."[36] The attitudes of interdependence-oriented countries are not only supported by government policies but also, in some cases, by their constitutions. Article XI of the Italian constitution, for example, states: "Italy repudiates war as an instrument of offensive action against the liberty of other peoples and as a means for the resolution of international disputes; it consents, on conditions of parity with other states, to limitations of sovereignty necessary to an order for assuring peace and justice among the nations; it favors and promotes international organizations directed toward that end." A constitutional declaration of the limitation of national sovereignty for the same purposes has also been codified in Germany.

Supranationalist, Accepting of the Increasing Role of International Structures as Institutions for Collective Sovereignty

Those countries that favor a supranationalist approach to IGOs pursue a deliberate integration strategy by building international structures to manage collective institutions. These countries have not relinquished the ideas and practices of the state system. Rather, they have accepted that supranational structures with well-defined and limited responsibilities in an increasing number of economic activities have a special role to fulfill. The supranational approach has become characteristic of the practices of the EC. Supranational bodies, however, are not distinct from their member states, being themselves international institutions created and controlled by states through various channels.[37] The central, supranational institutions are accountable and responsible to their member states' governments and to a parliament directly elected by the citizens of the member states. Decisions taken by supranational bodies in the areas of their mandates automatically become structural components of national law and government policies. Originally, different governments often had different reasons for transferring power to supranational authorities. Some countries, like France, sought to maintain influence through the machinery of collective decision making; other states simply wanted to impose constraints on others. All European states wished to take advantage of the opportunities presented by large markets increasingly unrestricted by national regulatory power. In the increasingly competitive global market, the supranational structures have become instruments as much of collective protectionism as of collective liberalization. Their role in strengthening the international competitiveness of the member states has become indispensable.

The attitudes of states to international cooperation are changing. Several trends can be observed in the mid-1990s. The Maastricht Treaty represents a trend toward supranationality, albeit with increasing checks and balances. The difficulties of the GATT negotiations reflects, by contrast, the strength of the state-centered system, although the successful conclusion of the Uruguay Round indicates a widespread recognition of the influence of interdependence. The increasing number of peacekeeping operations has been a sign of a growing readiness to take collective security measures, although the failures of peacekeeping in Bosnia shows the limits of that readiness.

While the world is still a long way from accepting a "global policy" approach to multilateral cooperation on the state level (such an approach would focus on general global security interests and the maximization of welfare at the global level), in specific areas some movement has been made in this direction. Most countries of the world, for example, were ready in the 1980s to accept binding norms in order to protect the ozone layer. As yet, however, it is still too early to judge the extent to which the post–Cold War era will see states demonstrate a shared collective responsibility, even for the well-being of the environment, and an increased readiness to engage in multilateral cooperation on a global level.

Changing Interests, Shifting Attitudes, New Dilemmas

Despite an abundance of rhetoric suggesting an international consensus on the need to revitalize multilateral cooperation, the political changes that have occurred since the end of the Cold War have not yet inspired most national policymakers to lend greater moral, political, and financial support to global multilateral cooperation. There seems to be a strengthening correlation between the level of domestic socioeconomic and political turbulence and the willingness of countries to support a higher level of international multilateral cooperation. Still, although it is now generally recognized that no country can disregard the problems posed by the new global environment or deal with the main global issues through unilateral action, few if any national leaders appear prepared to accept the *full* impact of the new realities of the world and to act accordingly. The costs of doing so—in financial, political, and ideological terms—seem perhaps too high. Instead, despite the growing sense of global interconnectedness, politicians and publics alike, especially within the major powers, seem to be focusing increasingly on national problems.

Part II of this book has discussed many of the changes currently under way in the international outlook of the leading actors in the community of states. Here, we will briefly assess the likely future attitudes of Russia and Central and Eastern Europe, the United States, Europe, Japan, China, India, and the developing world toward multilateral cooperation.

Russia and Central and Eastern Europe

The systemic transformation under way in the former Soviet Union and Central and Eastern Europe varies from country to country and is at an early stage. Consequently, it is as yet difficult to evaluate the impact of that transformation process on the future of multilateral cooperation.

In principle, a strong and effective international system of multilateral cooperation would be greatly in the interests of the states in the region. Those states need long-term and effective international support in solving or moderating their economic problems. Strong and credible international guarantees in the field of human rights, especially minority rights, are particularly important to a region that lacks democratic traditions. Multilateral cooperation can also serve to "communicate" the democratic principles laid down in the UN Charter. An efficient global collective security structure supported by regional arrangements offers probably the only hope of resolving existing conflicts and avoiding the outbreak of new violence. The region also needs safeguards against the rebuilding of the traditional client-state system and the playing of dangerous power games.

Some political forces in the region well understand the importance of multilateral cooperation and security guarantees. In areas like peacekeeping, countries like Russia, Ukraine, Poland, and Hungary have already been actively involved. However, there is no uniformity of thinking in the former Soviet bloc on the course of internal transitions, let alone on the subject of a new world order or new multilateralism. The key issue is the future attitude of Russia, which is highly uncertain.

Although Russia has inherited the Soviet Union's seat on the UN Security Council and all other multilateral bodies, there is little immediate continuity between the global interests and international priorities of the two states. Unlike the Soviet Union, Russia is not a military-ideological power and does not claim any leadership role over any group of countries, at least so far. While it has inherited much of the Soviet Union's nuclear arsenal and military capacity, Russia is highly unlikely to employ its forces in a worldwide or regionwide conflict; rather, it must attend to the dangers of becoming embroiled in smaller-scale conflicts with other former Soviet republics or in ethnic disputes within its own territory. The urgent task of economic consolidation requires Russia to pursue international cooperation and political stability.

Russia will most probably remain strongly state-system oriented but less preoccupied with global military-security considerations than was the Soviet Union. More interested in the comprehensive character of its security, Russia is likely to develop a stronger orientation toward international cooperation in its different forms, including active participation in multilateral organizations and programs that involve a broad area of activities, from environmental protection to peacekeeping. Russia will probably be readier to participate in collective international actions together with other major powers. Although it is unlikely to develop any specific grand design for world peace, Russia seems certain to support comprehensive reforms that aim to strengthen global security.

Moreover, Russia will be greatly interested in future arrangements with European and Asian-Pacific regional cooperation structures. For the other successor states of the Soviet Union, their participation in international organizations will help to defend and assert their sovereignty and independence. Like Russia, they will also be preoccupied with their domestic or regional security problems, which in some cases may require the involvement of the United Nations or regional groups.

The United States

With the disintegration of the Soviet Union, the United States is now the only global power, and its interests would seem to be best served by its assuming many global and regional responsibilities. But to what extent will the United States be ready and able to do so? Will it be readier than it has been in the past to work through the United Nations, cooperating with other nations, especially with the permanent members of the Security Council, to preserve global security at a time when long-standing military alliances are disappearing or undergoing radical changes?

Toward the end of the Bush administration, a number of policy statements were issued that indicated new U.S. preferences in security matters. As regards the future U.S. position on multilateral security structures, one Pentagon document declared:

> While the United States cannot become the world's policeman . . . neither can we allow our critical interests to depend solely on international mechanisms that can be blocked by countries whose interests may be very different from our own. Where allies' interests are directly affected, we must expect them to take an appropriate share of the responsibility and in some cases play the leading role; but we must maintain the capabilities for addressing selectively those security problems that threaten our own interests.[38]

This statement suggested that the United States would take a selective and more positive approach to multilateralism in such areas as peacemaking and peacekeeping.

President Bill Clinton and leading members of his administration have publicly remarked on the need to strengthen the United Nations and other multilateral cooperation structures in the post–Cold War era. Warren Christopher, in Senate hearings to confirm his nomination as U.S. secretary of state, commented on the future policy of the Clinton administration:

> It will be this administration's policy to encourage other nations and the institutions of collective security, especially the United Nations, to do more of the world's work to deter aggression, relieve suffering and keep peace. In that regard, we will work with Secretary-General Boutros Boutros-Ghali and the members of the Security Council to ensure that the United Nations has the means to carry out such tasks.

But, Christopher added: "Ultimately, when our vital interests are at stake, we will always reserve our option to act alone. As the President-elect has said, our motto in this era should be: Together where we can; on our own where we must."[39] Anthony Lake, Clinton's national security adviser, offered more specific indications of the direction of future policies: "Certainly, we face new threats, from weapons proliferation to violent ethnic conflict. But we also have the opportunity to pursue new forms of global problem-solving—through reinvigorated multilateral institutions, and through new partnerships that the Cold War had made impossible."[40] The multilateral inclinations of the Clinton administration may also be gauged from such measures as the resumption of U.S. assistance to the UN Fund for Population Activities and the creation of a new position within the State Department of assistant secretary of state for global affairs.[41]

In 1993, Madeleine Albright, the U.S. ambassador to the United Nations, suggested the following as foundations on which to build a new consensus in the United States regarding the world organization:

- The United States should be actively engaged in furthering free markets, democratic values, and adherence to international law.
- Multilateral peacekeeping should be seen as a "potentially valuable foreign policy tool" and not as a "guarantor" of U.S. vital interests.
- UN capacities and decision-making procedures must be strengthened and budget processes reformed. Sources of civilian and military personnel must be more dependable. Training, intelligence, equipment, command and control, and availability of resources must be improved.
- The United States should provide personnel and technical equipment "credited against our assessment" to improve the management and effectiveness of UN peacekeeping capabilities.
- The U.S. share of UN peacekeeping must be reduced from its present level of just over 30 percent.
- The United States should participate in some peacekeeping operations when it is in the national interest to do so. Most often, U.S. support should be in the areas of logistics, intelligence, public affairs, and communications rather than in combat capacity.[42]

Notwithstanding the positive signals, the fact remains that U.S. policy toward multilateral cooperation will always depend fundamentally on national security considerations. In addition, the different forces shaping U.S. interests in multilateralism are unpredictable in their course and consequences. The international regionalization process and the sharpening of global economic competition, for example, may have an increasingly adverse impact on U.S. public opinion and place new limits on the level of U.S. commitment to multilateral agencies. This, in turn, would decrease U.S. interest and activity in the expansion of multilateral cooperation structures and increase U.S. demands for greater sharing of the existing burdens of multilateral programs.

Europe

Of all the continents, Europe has the largest number of regional multilateral cooperation organizations. As far as global institutions are concerned, the future policies of the European states (especially Germany, France, and Great Britain) are likely to depend primarily on progress toward political union within the EC. In security matters, it is probable that Europe will increasingly rely on regional structures, but will also be interested in global multilateral peacekeeping and peacemaking operations. Most European countries, particularly the larger powers, already have a powerful voice in a number of UN structures, especially those that deal with human rights, development cooperation, and humanitarian assistance. If the EC were to speak with one voice, it would become a major power in all the UN agencies. In those agencies, the policies of all European countries, but especially of the smaller West European countries and the Nordic countries, will probably remain interdependence-oriented, with an active interest taken in global economic security and the problems of the developing world. European states are also involved in the reform of the governance of the United Nations, with the aim of making it more democratic, transparent, and efficient.

Japan

Until the 1990s, the strengthening of multilateral cooperation was never high on Japan's international agenda. Today, however, Japan is searching for new opportunities to foster international cooperation. As a likely future permanent member of the UN Security Council and as an economic superpower, Japan is well equipped to strengthen economic and environmental security and play a key role in enhancing a global multilateral strategy that is based on active engagement to promote world peace and military restraint. Japan's search in the 1990s for a new identity in the United Nations and other multilateral organizations has already resulted in a change in Japanese policy toward peace-keeping operations. In terms of practical involvement, Japan played a key part in promoting the peaceful settlement reached in Cambodia. And in terms of organizational reform of peace-keeping, Japan has suggested new consultative mechanisms to ensure the participation of all interested parties on an equal footing. In addition, Japan urged the strengthening of UN capabilities to deal with nonmilitary threats to security and to prevent the proliferation of nuclear and other weapons of mass destruction.

Its position as the leading donor country in the mid-1990s has given Japan a prominent role in shaping development cooperation regimes. With economic power coming to rival military and political strength within the international arena, Japan seems likely to continue to advance an agenda in the United Nations and other multilateral agencies that is based on peace, global interdependence, and economic statecraft.

China, India, and the Developing World

With the disappearance of the Soviet Union, China and India will probably play leading roles in the United Nations and other multilateral bodies, advocating the interests of the developing world and emphasizing such principles as the sovereign equality of member states and the strict observance of noninterference in internal affairs. During a visit to India in 1991, Chinese prime minister Li Peng warned of the "emerging international oligarchy," and both Chinese and Indian officials spoke out against hegemonism.[43] Speaking at the United Nations in January 1992, Li Peng offered a broad interpretation of human rights, which he said "included not only civil and political rights but also economic, social, and cultural rights." At the same time, he indicated that China gives less prominence to human rights than does the West, noting that "as far as the large number of developing countries were concerned, the rights to independence, subsistence and development were of paramount importance."[44]

China, India, and the vast majority of the developing countries have a strong economic interest in enhancing and strengthening multilateral cooperation, but there is an important difference between them and the majority of the developed industrial countries concerning the role of multilateral agencies in the global economy. This difference is rooted in the old East-West conflict between those (like many developing countries) that favor international agencies acting as regulatory institutions—believing that only regulation can overcome disturbances and inequalities in the contemporary system of international economic relations—and those (like the majority of the developed nations) that support the more liberal expression of global free market values and norms—believing that the greater the degree of economic liberalization, the greater the level of economic rationality, competition, and, ultimately, prosperity. This debate will remain a prominent feature of North-South dialogue.

A number of proposals and steps initiated by developed countries for reform of the United Nations have already received sharp criticism from prominent figures and institutions within the developing countries. For instance, the South Centre (a research body sponsored by a number of developing countries and private organizations) issued a document in October 1992 that suggested that a number of proposed reforms were inspired by a desire to maintain the status quo in international relations, eliminate pluralism from the existing world order and silence dissent, and extend the present undemocratic decision-making process in some UN organizations.[45] These views were not officially sanctioned by any government, but they clearly reflect the concerns of many governments in the developing world that in the post–Cold War era the industrial countries will bargain on a take-it-or-leave-it basis.[46]

The Role of National Legislatures and Bureaucracies

The political relations between states and international organizations are shaped to a large extent by national political processes. In democratic states, legislators (and the voters who elect them) have a major impact on intergovernmental cooperation through their role in policy formation; the ratification of internationally agreed policies, resolutions, and legal obligations; and the authorization of funds for international organizations. In many countries of the world, especially in the larger and more powerful states, legislators have tended to favor bilateral over multilateral relations, particularly when multilateralism has involved trade policy concessions, financial sacrifices, or a perceived limitation of national legislative power. In this respect, the U.S. Congress has proved to be a perennial source of difficulty for the executive in the latter's conduct of day-to-day negotiations and the process of bargaining within multilateral policy forums. Within the EC, the legislatures of member states have been highly ambivalent about transferring some of their authority to supranational bodies. Should progress toward economic and political union be made according to the provisions of the Maastricht Treaty, the power of national legislatures will be substantially reduced while that of the directly elected European Parliament will grow accordingly.

Seeking to overcome domestic legislative suspicion of IGOs, many governments have invited members of their legislative bodies to participate in, or consult with, national delegations to multilateral agencies. This tactic has been notably successful in cases of humanitarian assistance programs, not least because legislators have been able to boost their domestic political support by associating themselves with such humanitarian endeavors. Nongovernmental organizations (NGOs) have also helped to expose legislators directly to international multilateral cooperation. For example, the Interparliamentary Union, one of the oldest and most prestigious of international NGOs, has served as an important bridge between national parliaments and the system of IGOs.

As of the mid-1990s, it is still too early to judge whether national parliaments will be more or less supportive of international cooperation than they were during the Cold War. Given the growing scale of domestic social and economic problems, international issues may well attract diminishing attention from legislators, who may be not only discouraged from supporting new commitments but also reluctant to fulfill old ones. Such uninterest or disinclination is likely to influence the attitudes of governments in countries where legislatures play a significant role in determining the formation of international policy.

National bureaucracies influence the relationship between governments and IGOs in a number of ways: by the bureaucracies' responsibility for the technical implementation of international agreements, and by the direct participation of bureaucrats from various national agencies in the work of IGOs and in the policymaking bodies of their own nations. The importance that governments attach to intergovernmental cooperation is usually reflected in the way in which matters concerning IGOs are perceived and ranked by bureaucracies against other policy priorities. Revealingly, UN activities have not been highly ranked in the past, nor do they seem to be receiving much greater consideration today, despite the numerous global summits organized within the framework of the United Nations in the 1990s.

Just as IGO activities have not been a priority for national bureaucracies in the past, neither do recent global political changes appear to have prompted fresh efforts to improve future coordination among the various governmental agencies involved in intergovernmental cooperation. This lack of attention on a national level hinders the process of improving coordination among different multilateral organizations. In the past, the unplanned growth of international organizations and cooperation regimes, mostly along various functional lines that had not been coordinated within state bureaucracies, created unnecessary duplication of effort, competition within and between IGOs, and inefficiency. It even produced situations in which officials were unaware of the mandate or services of IGOs that they had, sometimes unwittingly, helped to establish. For example, government officials concerned with the Food and Agricultural Organization probably were unaware that various programs approved by that organization might very well have been realized earlier in UNIDO.

Since the end of World War II, some interplay has developed between national bureaucracies and the international bureaucracy based not only on their mutual interests in strengthening each other, but also on the influence of internationally agreed-upon norms and technical procedures in functional areas such as health, transportation, and telecommunications. Tens of thousands of government experts have participated in IGO workshops and committees that have permitted the exchange of expertise on a wide variety of technical matters. This interplay has benefited both sides. It has broadened the support within individual nations for IGOs, increased the expertise available to them, and in some instances inspired the creation of valuable new programs. In some cases, however, it has also led to IGOs undertaking parallel projects or assuming marginal and incremental tasks that are ill suited for international action and that only increase the operational costs of IGOs. IGOs need to improve the level of coordination among themselves and among their component parts (for example, among the various agencies of the United Nations). But better coordination is also required among the specialized national bureaucracies, which tend to compartmentalize their relationships with international agencies and not share relevant information with one another. Governance in international organizations cannot be made more efficient unless national institutions are also reformed and more coherent national policies are developed for multilateral cooperation.

chapter 23

The Governance of International Intergovernmental Organizations

The key issues of governance in all IGOs are the quality and relevance of the outcome of their work for the member states individually and for the international community as a whole. Outcomes are judged not only by the passage of resolutions but also by their effective implementation. A "good" outcome depends on good governance, which in turn depends largely on five factors: the quality of leadership shown by member states; the effectiveness of the intergovernmental decision-making machinery; the appropriate selection of programs for action; the level of financing an IGO enjoys; and the ability of an IGO's secretariat. This chapter addresses each of these areas, paying particular attention to the kinds of improvements needed to make each adequate to the demands of the post–Cold War era.

Leadership in an Era Free of Bloc Politics

Leadership is a complex phenomenon within a multilateral organization, where the presence of equal voting rights does not reflect differences among the military and economic capacities of states, and where there is a greater equality between member states

315

than in the "real" political and economic system. Among the
many conditions for achieving a leadership role are moral stature—the advocacy of widely accepted values and norms, and a
credible record of having honored them—and political commitment—an abiding interest in multilateral cooperation or at least
in a particular institution and regime. A country must possess a
respectable degree of intellectual capacity and an efficient organizational culture within its national bureaucracy; these are seen
to be attributes that can benefit the international community.
Leaders must also demonstrate the ability to form coalitions by
forceful persuasion, diplomacy, or the imaginative formulation
of widely acceptable policies.

However, while leadership can sometimes entail a collective
effort among powers if their interests and values converge sufficiently, multilateral organizations always require strong and
committed leading powers. The value of political, military, and
economic strength may be reduced within international organizations, but it is by no means eliminated. Major powers within
the international political and economic systems also tend to be
major players within IGOs, which need the financial resources,
political influence, and sometimes military capabilities that only
the larger countries can provide. It is interesting to note that
the first draft of the UN Charter sought to institute a weighted
voting system that would distribute electoral power in proportion to the contribution of each member to the UN budget. This
idea was abandoned, however, partly as a political gesture to
smaller states, and partly because it was correctly assumed that
the larger contributors would have greater influence over the
organization anyway.[47]

The question of which country or countries will play leading
roles in IGOs in the post–Cold War period, and what forms
those roles will have to take, is a complex one. Leadership in
the UN system during the Cold War years was, for practical
purposes, a matter of bloc leadership and politics. The global
political, military, and economic power realities were omnipresent in the bargaining process at the United Nations—the principles of sovereign equality, equal voting rights, and the special
responsibilities of the great powers notwithstanding. Now, in
the absence of two confrontational global powers and military
blocs, the situation is destined to change. Leadership no longer

implies the struggle for control over an organization to legitimize the policies of one adversary against another. Although their veto power in the UN Security Council will continue to endow the permanent members with substantial power, mid-level powers will find that they have more room to influence the organization in many issue areas.

The role of member states in financing IGOs is not identical with their role in forming and implementing the policies of those organizations, but neither are the two roles unrelated. For the rest of the 20th century and into the 21st century, significant shifts will occur in the funding—and thus also in the policies—of IGOs as countries like Japan and Germany increase their financial share in relation to that of the United States, traditionally the largest contributor. Since the mid-1980s, "burden sharing" has become a catchphrase much used by both the United States and IGOs. In response, many of the United States' partners have commented that burden sharing must inevitably be reflected in power sharing. Whether either side fully appreciates the complexities of power sharing—which can involve changes in voting rights, policymaking processes, leadership personnel, and so forth—is questionable. One hopes that future discussion of shifts in the distribution of power within IGOs will heed the following cautionary note sounded in the mid-1980s:

> [E]ven if the United States tried, it could not, by itself, alone bring about the changes that are called for. Whether one calls it collective leadership, burden sharing, or simply more cooperation, what is needed cannot be supplied unless a number of countries—most importantly Japan and the countries of Western Europe as well as the United States—accept the idea that they have a stake in the health of the system as such, not just a concern in the way the system affects their own particular interests.[48]

Intergovernmental Decision-making Machinery

The new needs and political circumstances of the post–Cold War world require changes in the functioning of the intergovernmental decision-making machinery of multilateral organizations. Reform in this area involves questions of professional competency, the level of government representation and commitment, and the nature of the voting system.

The need for such changes has already been articulated in the EC, where the transition from a structure of nation-states to a political and economic union is on the agenda. The way in which the EC's legislative institutions—the European Council and the European Parliament—will function in the future will determine the character of the transition process and its outcome. It is not just a question of whether member states will accept these legislative bodies as common democratic instruments, but also of whether these bodies will be able to acquire new competencies in the process.

The same question of competency applies equally to the United Nations. The intergovernmental political bodies of the United Nations (the two most important structures are the General Assembly and the Security Council) fulfill various important functions. They are forums for discussion, policy formation, bargaining, and the introduction of new actions and program initiatives. They elect or appoint the leading officers of the different UN secretariats and evaluate their work. In the case of various intergovernmental conferences on strategic global issues organized under the auspices of the UN system, political bodies very often initiate new programs, cooperation regimes, and standing committees.

Work in multilateral intergovernmental structures requires knowledge not only of substantive but also of procedural matters. Negotiation itself may not be considered a distinct function separate from more substantive activities, but the ability to understand, articulate, and accommodate interests is certainly necessary to effective participation in intergovernmental bodies. In light of the fact that multilateral negotiation generally requires greater political sophistication and professional expertise than does bilateral negotiation, it is vital that delegates to the intergovernmental political bodies be people of the highest competence. In most cases, delegates to political bodies are drawn from national diplomatic missions to the United Nations. Prior to the 1980s, the United States, the Soviet Union, and most other powers did indeed staff their UN missions with highly skilled and experienced diplomats, who were supported by an array of technical experts in such fields as legal affairs, economics, social policy, and finance. This practice unfortunately declined during the 1980s, although the situation appears to be improving again in the 1990s.[49]

Equally as important as professional competency to the efficient functioning of the UN system is the level of government representation within, and commitment to, governing or policymaking institutions. Heads of states or governments, foreign ministers, or heads of other ministries and government agencies are often present at intergovernmental meetings and conferences.

Since the late 1980s, governments that wish to give prominence to particular issues have often initiated "summits" in the United Nations. For example, three UN summits held in the early 1990s sought to generate greater international attention to the problems of children worldwide, the deteriorating state of the global ecosystem, and the need to strengthen global cooperation on security issues, especially peacemaking and peacekeeping. International cooperation requires such demonstrative events as these summits, but by themselves they can only voice concern and approve resolutions; they cannot guarantee that any resolution is implemented. To ensure that action is taken, intergovernmental structures must generate sustained political support from both the legislative and the executive branches of national governments.

Like the level of government representation and professional competence, the nature of the voting system has always been crucial to the governance of IGOs. Reform of the character of the voting system and of mechanisms for adopting resolutions is vital if IGOs are to remain relevant and responsive in the future. Within the United Nations, debate on this topic has centered on two questions: One, can the level of international cooperation be raised to meet the needs of the post–Cold War world under the present voting system, or is that system essentially dysfunctional? And two, in light of the increasing number and diversity of member states, and given the changing global power structure, should the power of veto be taken from some countries and given to others, should it remain as it is, or should it be abolished outright as a superfluous safety valve in a more harmonious world?

In the past, the major powers were reluctant to enter into serious discussions over how reflective the UN voting system actually was of global changes in the relative power capacities of states. There were probably good reasons for this reluctance. To begin with, the major powers did not want to relinquish their voting power by making the system more acceptable to other member states. In some cases, the major powers were able to mobilize a sufficient number of votes to maintain the status quo; and even when they could not, the "Big Five" still retained their veto power. Consequently, the permanent members could disregard any UN resolution that failed to serve their interests. The major powers were probably also unwilling to initiate changes in the voting system because they did not relish the prospect of being accused by other countries of promulgating antidemocratic measures.

However, some changes have been made to the voting system. The one-country, one-vote system was established in the United Nations on the basis of the principle of the sovereign equality of states. This system was somewhat modified in the 1980s with regard to budgetary issues, where committee consensus is now required to approve the budget, thereby giving an effective power of veto to any country represented in committee. A variety of groups have recommended that the voting on certain issues should be restructured along the lines of the system used in the Bretton Woods institutions. In those institutions, decisions are made by boards of executive directors. Each of these boards has more than 20 members, each representing a constituency—a constituency is usually a group of countries but can also be a single country, such as the United States, which by virtue of its financial contribution enjoys a veto power over many issues. Voting power is weighted according to predetermined quotas based on financial contributions; changes in quotas thus bring changes in voting power (Japan, for example, has acquired increased power since the mid-1980s). The decisions of the executive directors are formally binding, whereas UN resolutions, except for those approved by the Security Council, are basically recommendations.

In practical terms, the decision-making process in the UN system has been strongly influenced, and often dominated, by blocs and groups. Blocs have been formed by member states that share common economic and political interests, political and ideological affinities, and security alliances. Groups have been formed on the basis of geography, with various subregional or regional groups displaying varying degrees of homogeneity. Some groups have become very large and are highly divided, like the group of nonaligned nations.[50]

The UN voting system made the passage of resolutions dependent on the formation of voting coalitions that sometimes crossed group boundaries. The blocs in the United Nations, however, usually voted unanimously, partly on the basis of common interests, although very often because of bloc discipline and/or satellite relations that linked smaller countries to the leading power of the bloc. In many cases, countries did not officially declare their membership in a given bloc or group yet voted with it when their votes were needed.

Member states, NGOs, and academics have offered many and varied proposals for changing the UN voting system. Almost 30 different formulas have been debated over the past 50 years. One proposal sought a return to the 1944 suggestion that voting weights be established in proportion to budgetary contributions. Another reform scheme proposed to weight voting power according to a combination of such indicators as the territorial size of a country, its population, GNP, and UN assessment. None of these proposals has received broad support from member governments, however.

The introduction in the 1980s of "consensus voting" (where decisions are made on the basis of formally required or informally achieved unanimity) represented a compromise between those who wished to maintain the simple majority system based on the one-country, one-vote principle and those who wanted a qualified voting system based on each country's budgetary contribution or another form of weighting. Consensus voting was supported for two reasons. One reason, which arose in the 1970s during a period of détente, was the desire to demonstrate unity on issues of great importance to world peace. A second reason was the desire to protect minority rights against the "dictatorship of the majority," a concern prompted by the admittance of a great number of ministates and microstates to the world organization. During the Cold War, the developing countries (which have long constituted the majority of member states) and the socialist countries could easily form a two-thirds majority against the Western powers. Despite the introduction of consensus voting, the long-running debate on voting continues.[51]

Another issue of governance related to the voting system is the system of representation by which not all countries vote directly in all UN committees; instead, in some cases, groups of countries select or elect a representative who advances and defends their joint interests in a particular committee. One proposal for reform of the voting system has suggested that only the large countries and voting federations of groups of small countries should have equal voting rights. Representation, it may be noted, has been a regular practice in the World Bank and the IMF. In the United Nations, however, representation has been more informal and arranged through a process by which groups of countries bargain for certain committee memberships or offices. A more sophisticated system than the present system of representation would retain the one-country, one-vote formula insofar as each country within a representative group would have one vote on decisions taken within that group. A drawback to this proposed system is that the bargaining process would become more protracted, with each federation or group obliged to refer back to its members on changing positions. The possibility of representation emerged also in debates over the veto power. According to one proposal, veto power should be extended to all the main regions of the world, each of which would be represented in the Security Council by one country elected by all the members of that region.

Given the sensitivity of countries to the issue of sovereign quality, changing the voting system will probably be the most protracted and strongly contested of all UN reforms. Rather than seeking a single comprehensive solution, it may be easier to introduce a greater variety of decision-making processes, each determined according to the nature of the issue at question and the mandate of the UN institution involved.

Programming and Financing

The operational direction and activities of IGOs are defined by their choice of programs. Which programs are adopted, and in what manner they are implemented, depends heavily on the level of financing that an IGO's member states are willing to provide. The level of funding made available is, in turn, a reflection of the priorities of the member states.

All IGOs, whether regional or global in nature, have experienced grave difficulties in prioritizing their programs. The United Nations has suffered particularly in this regard because member states and powerful groups within the organization disagree almost constantly on the selection of programs. Frustrated with this state of affairs and conscious of the growing demands placed on the United Nations in the post–Cold War era, some countries have urged that the Secretary-General, rather than the member states, draw up a list of program priorities, albeit after consultation with the member states, which would be free to influence, criticize, or disregard the Secretary-General's selection.

Since the 1970s, the United Nations has developed an elaborate four-phase program cycle: medium-term planning, program budgeting, monitoring of program implementation, and evaluation. The last two phases of the cycle, however, have been more or less completely ignored. Programs that have achieved their objectives or lost their relevance seldom have been eliminated. As a result, the agenda of the United Nations has lengthened unnecessarily and its intergovernmental machinery and bureaucracy have expanded significantly. With programs becoming increasingly fragmented among different subsidiary bodies and agencies, it has become almost impossible to monitor many activities, let alone to coordinate them. This situation worsened significantly in the 1980s. At one point in the second half of the 1980s, more than 150 committees, commissions, subcommissions, and working groups were operating in the economic and social fields on more than 1,000 issue areas.

In 1986, the programming activities of the United Nations were examined by a group of high-level international experts, known as the Group of 18. Their highly critical report stated that the medium-term plan—a regularly used instrument for managing UN programs—did not serve the supposed goal of the organization and was frequently ignored. Inputs by member states to the preparation of plans and programs usually came late in the process, thereby influencing the outcome marginally, if at all. Priorities within programs were established only infrequently, and then in a perfunctory fashion.[52]

Some analysts have recommended replacing the process of prioritization with a system of consultation among member states for building consensus on which programs to undertake and a system for managing the activities on which consensus is achieved.[53] Even if this suggestion is adopted, setting priorities will remain a necessary, albeit difficult and contentious business. In the absence of major reforms, the present divisions among nations and regions, and between the North and the South, are unlikely to produce an environment conducive to greater rationality.

More encouragingly, initiatives by Secretary-General Boutros-Ghali have helped to create a comprehensive basis on which the UN agenda for the 1990s can be elaborated. The "Agenda for Peace" published in 1992 and the "Agenda for Development" published two years later serve as frameworks for UN programs and define priorities for UN action—this marks a welcome departure from the chaotic and piecemeal process of UN agenda setting that has obtained previously. It is also heartening to note that the intellectual and informational resources of member states and the global academic community have been better utilized than they were in the past. Even so, the further development and implementation of those programs will require significantly greater interaction among government representatives, secretariats, and scholarly communities. For example, the United Nations University, which acts as a global community of scholars, is ideally placed to assist in the preparation of medium-term plans and program priorities, harmonizing the approaches of different governments and translating the resolutions of different governing bodies into long-term programs. A much more efficient interchange of ideas between the UN specialized agencies and other IGOs is also needed.

The implementation of programs depends largely on the financial resources available to IGOs. Financing has a technical-managerial and a political dimension, both of which overlap in several issue areas. As is the case in most IGOs, the budget of the United Nations comes from two major sources: assessed contributions and voluntary contributions. Assessments are a form of international tax levied on the basis of the volume and per capita level of national income. There is a fixed per capita ceiling, and all states that fall below this ceiling pay proportionally less. Although the payment of assessed contributions is a legal obligation imposed on all member states under the UN Charter, many members have not fulfilled their obligations. The only sanction that can be applied for nonpayment, however, is the suspension of voting rights in the General Assembly should a member's arrears exceed two full years of its assessed contribution. Voluntary contributions, which are the only sources of funding for organizations like UNDP and UNICEF, are made on the basis of a particular country's commitment to multilateral assistance in specific issue areas or projects.

Technical deficiencies in the UN system of financing have led to the passage of several resolutions on the processes of budgetary authorization and program budgeting. The problems of funding, however, are fundamentally political. Nations are conspicuously reluctant to devote more of their financial resources to IGOs than they deem absolutely necessary. At the end of the 1980s, the amount spent on international multilateral cooperation, including all existing regional and global organizations and integration groups, corresponded to less than 5 percent of global defense expenditures.

The history of the financial crisis of the United Nations illustrates the political roots of the financial problems that beset almost all IGOs. During the 1970s, especially the latter half of that decade, the developing countries mustered their collective voting power to initiate a number of resolutions and programs in the United Nations designed to reshape the international economic order. Debates, even on technical matters, became increasingly politicized, and the developed industrial countries and the Soviet bloc sought to curb the huge bureaucratic growth that the new programs threatened. The ideology with which these countries justified their actions, wrote Maurice Bertrand in 1989:

> was initially based on a criticism of "management." By concentrating on waste, inefficiency, excessive staff salaries, duplication of work and the like, the foundation was laid for demanding economies. This type of criticism had in fact been traditional since the creation of the Organization, but a truly systematic campaign along these lines began in the early 1980s. It culminated in the slogan of "zero growth" for the budget of all the organizations in the United Nations system and it actually succeeded in stopping any increase in these budgets after 1982–83.[54]

Bertrand also observed that the chief critics of mismanagement were, in fact, the major contributors, which thus had the most direct influence on the selection of UN top management, including the choice of Secretary-General. This fact had apparently eluded the critics.

Though there was a great deal of truth in the criticisms, especially concerning waste and mismanagement, Bertrand was right to point out the political character of the complaints. Furthermore, the politics of the issue extended beyond the question of the operational efficiency of the United Nations. For all member states, domestic political considerations were, and remain, very influential. For instance, in some countries, notably the United States, popular and political opposition has been mounting since the early 1980s to any increase in public expenditure, especially on international problems and institutions. Unfortunately, in the virtual absence of cost-benefit analyses of the IGOs, it has been difficult to counter the growth of this sentiment with statistical evidence that international cooperation can fulfill certain tasks more cheaply and efficiently than could a national government acting alone. The benefits of international cooperation are, of course, exceedingly difficult to quantify. Even so, it seems evident that multilateral development cooperation programs and projects do make a qualitative contribution to the easing of international tensions and the creation of new opportunities for mutually beneficial coordination of policies and actions.

Indeed, the more efficient use of scarce resources, reduction of bureaucracy, elimination of waste and duplication, and improvements in operational efficiency and the quality of services rendered, taken together, would be convincing proof of the greater value of the multilateral system of cooperation. Steps taken since the early 1990s in the UN system represent real progress in most of these areas.

The financial crisis besetting the United Nations cannot be overcome without a new and more realistic approach by the member states to the political, as well as technical and managerial, dimensions of the problem. The demands and expectations placed on the United Nations by its member states must be balanced by their readiness to provide the resources necessary for the organization to realize those expectations. The current failure of member states to do this not only throws into doubt the sincerity of the rhetorical commitments made by some countries to the United Nations in the post–Cold War era, but also presents the danger that the UN financial crisis may develop into a credibility crisis.

It may be necessary to heed the suggestion made by a number of countries that international organizations cut their programs and seek funding only for those on which there is general agreement. This approach may be appropriate in certain cases, but if it is adopted without a thorough evaluation of the risks involved, it may substantially reduce the collective capabilities of countries to deal with many key global issues at a stage when they are still manageable.

Many technical suggestions have been offered for overcoming the financial problems of IGOs in general and the United Nations in particular. During the 1991 session of the General Assembly, a variety of technical recommendations were put forward, including charging interest on assessed contributions not paid on time, increasing the Working Capital Fund (which covers day-to-day operations), establishing reserve funds for peacekeeping and humanitarian assistance, and, as a longer-term measure, founding a UN peace endowment fund from assessed and voluntary contributions. Outside of the United Nations, a much-debated proposal has been the introduction of a global tax levied on international travel and communication, financial transactions, and transborder data flows. Its advocates (most of whom are within the NGOs) have suggested that the tax might also be paid by corporations and governments that exploit or pollute parts of the global commons, such as the seabed or atmosphere. Clearly, however, none of these technical proposals can be implemented without the political commitment of member states.

From International Bureaucrats to Global System-Engineers

Three generations of international civil servants have already staffed the UN secretariat, and the end of the 20th century will witness the entrance of a fourth. Although these generations have inevitably overlapped, it is possible to distinguish the distinct character and qualities that each brought to its work.

The first generation was drawn chiefly from national or colonial civil services and diplomatic corps, although a number of academics were also recruited. They soon came to recognize a fundamental difference between the international civil service and its national counterpart. In the latter, officers shared a common cultural background and a natural allegiance to the institutions in which they worked. By contrast, the international civil service brought together men and women from many cultures and with diverse professional and diplomatic experiences. This variation was to some degree masked during the first years of the UN secretariat by the dominant influence exercised by the organizational cultures of the U.S., French, and British national bureaucracies.

The second generation was a strange mixture of academics, government bureaucrats, and diplomats. They began working in the early 1950s, during the most hostile years of the Cold War. The rivalries and suspicions of that conflict colored the selection of personnel and promoted narrow national political considerations above the claims of professional competence and the best interests of the United Nations. Whereas the UN Charter stipulated that UN staff should be appointed according to the highest standards of efficiency, competence, and integrity, the superpowers required above all the political loyalty of their citizens who worked as international civil servants. McCarthyism spread to affect U.S. citizens working at the United Nations, with their loyalties being examined in hearings held at UN headquarters in New York.[55] For its part, the Soviet Union considered its officials working at the UN secretariat to be an extended part of the Soviet national bureaucracy. Other countries too made appointments that reflected political allegiances rather than personal abilities or professional qualifications. Most secretariat officials from the newly independent developing nations, for instance, were closely associated with the anticolonial movements and the ruling elites in their countries.

The disease of politically inspired appointments left its mark on the secretariat. According to a report published in 1985:

> The average level of qualification of the staff in the professional grades (staff engaged in program design, management, research, and drafting) bears no relation to their responsibilities. In the United Nations, for example, 25 percent of these professionals have had no university training and 10 percent have had less than three years of university studies. The situation is comparable in most other agencies. . . . It is probably in the higher posts that this situation of unsuitability for the duties actually performed is the most serious.[56]

Member states were not only charged with exerting political pressure and interfering at all levels of the secretariat in the areas of recruitment and promotion,[57] but also, and particularly in the case of the Soviet Union and some of the East European countries, with using many of their nationals in the United Nations for intelligence gathering.[58] The situation within the United Nations was made worse by the fact that most of its various secretariats were overstaffed and the workload was usually poorly distributed.

Yet, despite these and other problems, the various secretariats became ever more cohesive bodies and increasingly efficient in areas such as statistics, analysis, and management of cooperation regimes.

The third generation of international civil servants entered the organization in the 1960s and 1970s, a time of new needs and receding political tensions. Those who occupied the high- to mid-level positions were more likely to be technocrats who understood the nature of the problems confronting them, were familiar with the procedures and internal politics of the United Nations, and were firmly committed to the goals of the organization. This group of international civil servants raised the level of technical expertise within the UN system, particularly as regards the standard of fieldwork performed by the various UN agencies.

The fourth generation of personnel, who will enter international organizations during the 1990s, are increasingly products of a global educational system influenced by the information revolution and the spread of modern methods of data processing, analysis, and management. Compared to their forebears, this group will find their work more difficult because of the emergence of new, post–Cold War challenges, norms, and requirements that call for managing, or engineering, international cooperation systems on different levels. They will enter the United Nations through a process of international competition and entrance examinations with universal standards. In the absence of the Cold War, the fourth generation will inevitably be less ideologically driven and politically divided. They will find it easier, and more helpful, to identify themselves with the ideology of a world organization guided by general global and human interests.

The fourth generation will face many new challenges and responsibilities. In an increasingly diverse world, the United Nations will need excellent negotiators who are well versed in history, politics, and law and able to mediate between adversaries divided by racism, religious bigotry, and ethnic hatred. One new area into which the international civil service must venture is that of "international system-engineering"—that is, not merely fulfilling the traditional job of running an international organization but also being actively involved in building global cooperation at different levels and in a greater variety of functional areas. International system-engineering also calls for much closer relations between the United Nations and national institutions. Future international officers will have to be proficient in engineering the microsystems of the global community and able to understand the complex functioning of urban and rural communities within given societies. Given the complex international web of states, IGOs, and transnational corporations, the fourth generation will have to possess exceptional professional abilities and personal qualities to accomplish the many operative, practical, and managerial functions assigned them, while also running ad hoc or long-term operations in areas of development and peacekeeping.

To provide a staff able to undertake such a workload, the personnel policies and management of the entire UN system will have to be radically altered. Reform in these areas should seek to promote greater flexibility in deciding the distribution of posts according to the national origins of UN staff and to achieve an optimal combination of temporary employment and long-term career development. Employees should be chosen according to their abilities to perform the specific tasks assigned them, not according to petrified principles and practices. Policies regarding the professional development of UN staff likewise require radical reform. In most UN agencies, the personnel receives virtually no advanced training. According to a 1991 study, UN staff members receive on average only 2 or 3 days of training per year; by contrast, private-sector personnel at all levels, including that of senior management, receive an average of 15 to 20 days annually. The UN system is far away from achieving its modest target of having 1 percent of the salary base of each organization devoted to personnel development and training. Advanced training is vital to the efficient functioning of an international staff.[59]

The many different groups that have urged a comprehensive review of UN personnel policies in light of the new demands placed on the organization have almost unanimously called for improvements in the living conditions and remuneration of UN staff. They have also pointed out the adverse impact of the "competitive conditions" that exist among different UN agencies—the international financial institutions and regional development banks, for example, offer much higher salaries than do other UN organs.

Improving the functioning of the UN secretariat requires not only a thorough review of personnel policies and practices but also the introduction of yet more far-reaching changes. One major impediment to the efficient operation of the secretariat is the limited autonomy given to administrative organs in implementing the decisions of the intergovernmental structures and initiating new actions. Although some observers have compared the situation within the United Nations to that which typically exists between national legislative and executive bodies, in practice the UN secretariat faces greater financial and operative constraints than do national executives, not least because of the sheer number of member governments with often competing interests and goals, all of which must be taken into account by the UN agencies. Whether the secretariat will enjoy greater autonomy in the post–Cold War world is unclear.

The quality of leadership is another key issue for the UN secretariat in New York, as it is for the secretariats of other agencies as well. The chief administrative officer of any agency, but especially the Secretary-General, possesses considerable power and influence, even in those cases where member states limit or meticulously control his or her role. Depending on his or her skills and qualifications, an executive director can influence the policies of member states and exploit their conflicting interests to neutralize pressures from national governments.

A very interesting study by Brian Urquhart and Erskine Childers undertaken in the late 1980s and published in 1990 as *A World in Need of Leadership: Tomorrow's United Nations* provides an excellent summary of leadership problems in the UN system from both an historical and a forward-looking perspective.[60] The study draws attention to several important facts:

- The UN Charter is ambiguous concerning the qualities of the Secretary-General. It recognizes the political importance of the post and its need for autonomy and integrity, yet makes no provisions regarding a Secretary-General's qualifications. The Secretary-General is not elected but is appointed by the General Assembly, a procedure that underscores the administrative character of the duties involved. The political and coordinating functions of the Secretary-General have not been sketched out.

• Different member states have looked for different qualities and attitudes in a Secretary-General. The five permanent members of the Security Council have been reluctant to accept an independent-minded Secretary-General; instead, they have given their support to persons whose opinions on a number of key issues have been similar to those of the permanent members themselves. Many industrial powers have preferred that the Secretary-General be a guardian of the status quo, whereas most of the developing countries have wanted a person who would stimulate change. Some countries have looked for a person who is primarily a mediator; others have wanted a manager and coordinator. Many countries have regarded the ability and readiness of the Secretary-General to present new ideas as of paramount importance; others, however, have held to the belief that the Secretary-General should simply communicate to the wider public the ideas generated by the intergovernmental structures.

• Among the personal qualities required in a Secretary-General are moral stature and integrity; diplomatic skill; fair-mindedness; analytical capability; administrative, managerial, and executive skills; the ability to communicate; creativity in developing original ideas; physical stamina; and a sense of proportion and humor. Because Secretaries-General naturally have had different personalities, not all of the above requirements have been fulfilled equally. Some Secretaries-General have been better diplomats than managers; others have been analytically creative but administratively weak.

• Although leadership functions and the procedures for selecting and appointing the executive heads of specialized agencies and programs have been well defined and documented, many problems have nonetheless occurred in these areas. Political pressures, for example, have sometimes elevated unqualified persons to positions of responsibility. The leadership posts in the specialized agencies and in the UN funds and programs have become regional or even national monopolies; ending these monopolies may be impossible. In certain agencies, the nature of leadership has become too strongly identified with particular ideologies and policies, resulting in major conflicts within those agencies.

- To improve the quality of leadership within the United Nations, the governments of member states must reconsider their policies and procedures for appointing key executives. "Parochial, national, geographical, or political considerations should cease to dominate the process," argue Urquhart and Childers. "Far more imaginative and wider search procedures are required. . . . The best procedures will, however, be useless without the will and the sustained interest of governments in making them work."[61]

With long experience of the UN system and national politics, Urquhart and Childers have understood that leadership in any large and complex organization is difficult to achieve, and even more so in the United Nations where the constraints on the Secretary-General imposed by member states are considerable. Recognition of this fact has not, however, been able to overcome the obstacles to the Secretary-General's effective coordination of operations posed by the autonomy of the executive heads of agencies (they are not formally subordinated to the Secretary-General) and the diverging interests of governments. If efforts to improve coordination are to achieve more success in the future, one requirement is that the primus inter pares position of the Secretary-General be changed to allow the Secretary-General to exercise greater direct authority.

Many governments have emphasized the need to extend the powers of initiative and inquiry of both the Secretary-General and the Security Council. Under Article 99 of the charter, the Secretary-General is authorized "to bring to the attention of the Security Council any matter which in his opinion may threaten the maintenance of international peace and security." This article has been seldom used, partly because during the Cold War the Secretary-General was trapped between bloc politics and allowed little room for independent action. Such constraints, however, no longer apply, thereby providing the opportunity for the Secretary-General to assume new functions.

In the post–Cold War era, the tasks of the Secretary-General will be even more complex and demanding than they were before. In the absence of bloc politics, the Secretary-General will be exposed to pressure from a greater number of countries on a greater variety of issues. The process of obtaining consent and securing compromises between rival member states will be harder to accomplish than it was when bipolarity ensured a high degree of stability and predictability. The Secretary-General's greater freedom of action will also bring with it greater personal responsibility and accountability, especially in the case of failures. In the new era, the Secretary-General will need the services of high-level personal advisers and assistants, who are independent of, but have access to, governments, NGOs, and the academic world. And with growing demands for the Secretary-General's involvement in mediation and negotiation, he or she will require highly experienced and respected personal representatives.

Encouragingly, many UN observers have applauded the choice of the first post–Cold War Secretary-General. With his long diplomatic and academic experience, excellent intellectual capacity, and vitality, Boutros-Ghali has been seen as ideally suited to the job of managing transition within the United Nations and moderating the problems that confront the international system.[62]

Of course, the success or failure of leadership depends not just on the personal attributes of the Secretary-General and the executive heads of the various UN agencies. Ultimately, the quality of leadership reflects the degree of political commitment by member governments to multilateral cooperation and their ability and readiness to work together in problem solving and risk management.

Reference was made earlier in part IV to the current "crisis of multilateralism." As the above chapters have shown, though the multilateral system is as yet free from a *general* crisis, several of its ingredients are present. We are faced with the enduring consequences of past mismanagement. We are witnessing the disappointment of expectations—expectations that have been raised by rhetorical assertions of the crucial role of multilateral institutions in building a new world order but left unfulfilled by the lack of the required financial and political support. And we are seeing the very visible failures of multilateral cooperation—failures that have been most apparent in peacekeeping operations, which have suffered from ill-defined mandates and the indecision and inadequate level of commitment of member states. The very real danger exists that "reforms" prompted by resource constraints but designed without recognition of new needs and opportunities may paralyze or destroy a large part of the structure of international cooperation. With the United Nations being so often used as a scapegoat for the failures experienced in the transition to a new world order, even the remaining faith in, and credibility of, multilateral cooperation regimes may be undermined.

Part V

Holding the World Together

chapter 24

Adjusting to the New Challenges and Opportunities of the System

Throughout almost all of the 20th century, the national security interests, policies, and conflicts of a few dominant powers have shaped world events. Individually or collectively, these powers precipitated two world wars that brought unprecedented destruction, human suffering, and environmental devastation. Although no global conflagration enveloped the world during the Cold War, numerous small proxy wars were waged that cost millions of lives and turned many more millions into refugees; all corners of the globe became scenes of intense political and ideological confrontations; meanwhile, the superpowers conducted the most extensive and terrifying arms race ever known.

Not surprisingly, the wars and the ideological, political, and economic divisions of this turbulent century have molded the character of multilateral cooperation. The world, however, has now changed. And that change has presented both the need and the opportunity to modify the concept and practice of multilateral cooperation.

But how should they be modified? At this transitional, post–Cold War stage—which we can only name by reference to what came before, not to what we hope or believe may come to be—it is too early to draw a comprehensive and credible picture of recent and ongoing changes and their impact on the regulating forces and processes in the global system. Compared to the circumstances in which the Cold War was waged, the new realities in many ways comprise a more complex and less predictable environment for analysis or policy formulations. History, anyway, has generally shown itself unwilling to comply with prognoses, especially the more colorful and confident of them. At this particular juncture between centuries, it is especially hazardous to presume too much, for recent years have witnessed a rare coincidence of historical turning points with long-term consequences.

Nonetheless, we must not let analytical caution blind us to the need to make some assessment of the likely character of the world order that is currently evolving. Indeed, because of the uncertain implications of the different changes, the international community will have to be highly sensitive to shifting realities, anticipating and managing risks where it is able to do so, and maximizing the opportunities for sustaining a peaceful order that present themselves. Here, in the final part of this book, while a definitive prognosis is studiously avoided, some tentative conclusions are drawn about how the changes have affected the world, what their likely implications might be, and how the disparate worldviews of the major actors in the international system might be reconciled.

A More Complex Global Security Environment

A new and more complex global security environment is evolving that has major implications for all countries. The ending of the Cold War has made the world a safer place in which to live. The dangers of a global nuclear holocaust, which had overshadowed human life for almost half a century, have disappeared. To say that this has been an important global change is an understatement; it has been an unqualified victory of the human instinct for survival and of reason over the dangers of mutual annihilation. Whether this will be only a temporary respite or a definitive turn in human history, however, will be determined by the capabilities of present and future generations to resolve their disputes and conflicts in a peaceful fashion.

The words of Raymond Aron are no less relevant today than they were when penned in the mid-1960s:

> Mankind has always lived dangerously. The dangers are no longer the same, but they have not disappeared. One mankind, united under a sole rational administration . . . would correspond to one possible end of human adventure. The adventure is still far from its final state, conforming not to the logic of history but to a partial logic that fascinates because it at once attracts and repels.[1]

Aron also wrote: "History has more imagination than wise men do. It has thus far refused to choose between collective suicide and the abdication of states. It has gradually brought a certain order out of the anarchy common to all international systems, an order favoring the limitation of armed conflicts."[2]

The end of the Cold War and the diminishing dangers of nuclear holocaust support Aron's analysis. Those same developments, together with the disintegration of the Soviet empire and the collapse of communism as a major political force, also present new opportunities for all nations to improve their relations and cooperate at all levels. Whether countries are willing and prepared to take those opportunities and collaborate to achieve effective global governance is unclear, however.

The international agenda brims with old and new problems, each complex and interrelated with many others. Some problems are rooted in the uncertainties of the transition process and the largely unpredictable consequences of the evolving new global power structure. Other problems are connected with the globalization of particular issues. Population growth, for example, is an acute problem that endangers the ecological, political, and economic systems of the entire world. Similarly, increasing social tensions, unemployment, and poverty are not merely domestic problems, but reach across borders in myriad different ways, affecting in the process the global system as a whole. Ethnic tensions and human rights violations can provoke wars that not only engulf nations but also disrupt the political and economic stability of entire regions. The global economy is becoming more competitive, and in different segments of the world market new challengers are contending with old powers for dominance. Trade wars may split the world into hostile regional blocs. Such problems remain manageable in the 1990s. However, if they are not treated promptly, appropriately, and jointly by the members of the international community, they are sure to threaten the future of humankind in short order.

More States, New Interests, and Power

The increasing number of states and the changing character of their relations are a major source of uncertainties for the 1990s and beyond. The present stage of the transition to a new era has often been characterized simply as the end of bipolarity and the beginnings of multipolarity. It is, in reality, much more complex than that. As the number of states grows, so do differences among them in terms of their interests, values, intentions, and political, military, and economic potentials. Multipolarity as a category of global power relations does not sufficiently reflect the complexity of the relations among the global and economic superpowers, middle powers, and small—even tiny—states that coexist on the planet.

If present trends persist, the vast majority of new nation-states will be created from the fragmentation of larger states. The political consequences of this are impossible to predict with confidence, but one recalls the remark attributed to the French statesman Georges Clemenceau that small states are quite as bad as large ones, only they cannot afford to be bad on so grand a scale. Indeed, the history of many small states in different parts of the world is rich in examples of the abuse of power. In the second half of the 20th century, when the majority of states are small, several have become sources of global risk through their own domestic instability or by initiating major regional hostilities. Some small states have insufficient political capacity to manage their domestic problems; Somalia has already provided an example of a state existing within the international system without a government.

The economic problems of small states are even more acute than their political woes. Underdeveloped national markets in small developing countries hamper or make impossible the process of economic modernization based on manufacturing industries and the development of a modern service sector. This problem can only be overcome through effective regional cooperation undertaken with the support of the wider international system.

The main powers in the international political system of the late 20th and early 21st centuries will be the United States, Japan, Russia, and Germany. China and India, as the two most populous countries of the world (they are projected to have about 21 and 17 percent, respectively, of the world population by the year 2000), may also become major regional and global actors if they can demonstrate an ability to manage their domestic problems and maintain political stability. Other important regional powers will be Brazil or Argentina in Latin America, Nigeria in Africa, and Indonesia, Pakistan, and (if it is united) Korea in Asia. Although the interests of the main powers are converging in some areas— most notably, in their shared concern to achieve global peace and stability—their search for solutions to their domestic difficulties is leading them into conflict over other issues.

The evolving global power structure may be further complicated by relations and potential conflicts among the emerging regional blocs. The outcome of the integration process that may result in a United States of Europe is still highly uncertain, but the process itself will have a major impact on European and global politics and economics, especially in the next century. Achieving cooperative relations among smaller and larger powers through an international framework created to solve the many specific economic and political problems of the smaller countries will be a vital task in the coming decades. Only multilateral cooperation and a relatively open economic system can provide reliable guarantees against the creation of new client-state networks around regional and global powers.

The New East and the Changing South

The development of North-South relations and the way in which the successor states of the Soviet Union and the countries of Central and Eastern Europe are integrated into the global political and economic systems will be extremely important in the coming decades. As these processes evolve, the new linkages formed between states will demonstrate the potential for both cooperation and conflict, for convergence and divergence.

By contrast to the two post–world war eras, the post–Cold War world is not divided into political winners on one side and losers on the other. After all, the collapse of totalitarian regimes was not a loss for those who had lived for decades under oppressive communist rule. In strict economic terms, however, there are winners and losers. Inequalities in wealth and poverty among countries and regions are growing, encouraging the richer areas to erect formidable barriers of one kind or another along their frontiers. The influence of economic inequalities is especially significant in North-South relations. In the coming decades, most of the socioeconomic problems of the world—poverty, hunger, unemployment, and so forth—will be concentrated in countries belonging to the South. The South, and especially Asia, will also encounter rapid and widespread economic development, structural transformation, and increasing international economic competitiveness. In the mid-1990s, one can confidently assert that a North-South political conflict will not, as some observers have predicted, replace the previous East-West conflict, simply because the issues that divide North from South are more socioeconomic than political or ideological in nature. Furthermore, states in both the North and the South are, and will remain, divided among themselves on many issues.

North-South relations are nonetheless bound to change now that the Cold War is over. Although some parts of the South may no longer be host to proxy wars, other areas may become increasingly unstable and violent as traditional rivalries reassert themselves in the absence of the constraints imposed by one or both of the Cold War blocs. Early indications suggest that the post–Cold War era in the South may also witness an extensive proliferation of sophisticated arms and weapons of mass destruction. Many countries in the South have been, or still are, ruled by authoritarian, often repressive, regimes. The experience of such governments has inspired profound popular disillusionment with state structures. Even in those areas where democratization trends have been strongest, as in Latin America, a similar disenchantment has grown as democratically elected governments have, in many cases, failed to meet public expectations. This sentiment, fueled by deteriorating living conditions and mass unemployment, will continue to engender substantial social discontent and political unrest. It may also encourage mass migration from the South to the North. For this and for many other reasons, the states of the North have a vested interest in forming a new partnership with the South (and the East) that will contain the extent of political and social dislocation within the framework of a new, more secure global order.

Faced with a range of potentially explosive issues, the countries of the North and the South must devote much greater attention to understanding, exploring, and more effectively managing the problems that divide them. Most of the mechanisms invented to manage North-South relations have been shaped by Cold War rivalries. But bipolarity is gone, and the most dangerous of today's problems between the North and South are socioeconomic and environmental in nature. Although they may not necessarily have any less devastating an effect, socioeconomic and environmental risks certainly do have a different character than the risks associated with military buildups and confrontations. As the North and the South seek to manage these new risks and forge a new relationship based on the principles of common and comprehensive security, they will have to construct more efficient international mechanisms, accords, and compromises than those developed over the past 40 years. Arrangements will have to be made on all levels, global as well as regional, multilateral as well as bilateral.

A World without Blocs and Discipline?

The bipolar power structure was a primary source of international risk and instability during the Cold War. The dangers of a global conflagration were real, and the effects of such a war would have been devastating in the extreme. Many regional wars were stimulated by the contest between the superpowers for political and ideological dominance. Yet, the Cold War was also to some degree a restraining influence. Both sides appreciated the scale of destruction that a war between them would unleash, and thus they strove to avoid it. Furthermore, both superpowers exerted pressures on their clients or partners to avoid pursuing policies that threatened to destabilize countries within their spheres of influence. To varying degrees, the major actors in the international system subordinated their own agendas to bloc agendas. Ideological and political discipline preserved the division of much of the world into two hostile camps, but it also made international relations more predictable, encouraged the articulation of mutual interests, imposed constraints on regional powers, and moderated the scale and intensity of many conflicts.

Bloc discipline no longer exists. Indeed, other than the fear of reciprocity and various legal and moral accords that are difficult to enforce, today's international system possesses no means of disciplining its members. Some degree of discipline is often imposed on the behavior of Western-style democratic states by various domestic forces, which can incline their states to act on the basis of the UN Charter and the principles of international law, but which can also interpret those same principles solely on the basis of perceived national interests.

A more peaceful and democratic world may have no need for discipline of a Cold War nature, but it certainly does require mechanisms of some sort that are able to prevent the emergence of new and unconstrained risk factors. In a future multipolar system, one with a larger number of global and regional actors having competing interests, the sources of potential conflicts will be qualitatively different than those within a bipolar system, and their management will require different structural forms and machinery and new institutional safeguards. The increasing technological sophistication of the arsenals of smaller countries; the rising tide of ethnic conflict; the continuing activities of international terrorist groups: these and many other dangers to international peace demand that the international community develop new, more democratic mechanisms to substitute for those stabilizing forces born of common strategic interests in the Cold War.

Macropolitics and the Grass Roots of Democracy

These early years of the post–Cold War era are characterized by an unprecedented spread of universal suffrage and by greater pluralism and a greater number of both democratically elected governments and global democratic institutions than the world has ever seen. Massive violations of human rights are less tolerated within the international system than they have been before. Although greater democracy brings with it risks—it permits, for example, the more forceful articulation of conflicting interests and the stronger assertion of minority demands for autonomy or secession—on the whole, democratic governments better serve general human interests by safeguarding peace than do dictatorial regimes. In the absence of their common enemy, however, it remains to be seen whether the main pillars of global democracy will be able to continue to harmonize their interests and sustain the momentum of the global crusade for democracy.

Despite the remarkable gains achieved in recent years by democratic forces, democracy in many parts of the world remains a fragile construct, with weak socioeconomic foundations. Advocates of totalitarianism are busily exploiting the freedom of expression that democracy allows to press for a return to dictatorial political structures. The economic hardships that are plaguing many newly democratic nations are further undermining popular support for open societies and free markets.

In this context, it has become a serious responsibility of the international community to provide further support and international guarantees to the democratization process and to make democracy sustainable in Central and Eastern Europe, the successor states of the former Soviet Union, and other parts of the world by promoting sound and broadly based socioeconomic progress. These tasks are all the more demanding because they require simultaneous changes in the domestic management of the democratizing countries and the system of international cooperation. Democracy must also be sustained and strengthened in interstate relations.

The strengthening of civil society both at national and international levels and the increasing role of nonstate actors like NGOs will be important safeguards of the democratization process in the interstate system. The world of the NGOs has always been a complex structure that has functioned according to the changing level of contemporary concern regarding major social, economic, ecological, and, most importantly, political issues. Indeed, during the Cold War, very many NGOs were instruments of global political and ideological confrontation. Since the end of the Cold War, however, most NGOs have expressed a growing awareness among citizens of international problems, especially problems related to poverty, human rights, gender issues, and the environment. NGOs—the number of which now exceeds 3,000—have introduced a new dimension into the functioning of the international cooperation system. In some cases, especially in the environmental and human rights fields, NGO initiatives have grown into world movements of decisive significance. NGOs are increasingly needed as forces of independent and innovative political thinking and as champions of pluralism and democracy. The future vitality of international multilateralism depends on NGOs continuing to place critical issues on the global agenda and mobilizing national publics to ensure that collective action is taken and programs are implemented.

Collective Security Needs and Domestic Policies

National governance and international cooperation must rise to meet the new security challenges of the post–Cold War era. In this regard, it is encouraging to see that the global community as a whole and individual states have come to accept a broad concept of security, one that encompasses not only military and political but also economic, social, and environmental components. Awareness is growing that geographic distance from the epicenter of a crisis or conflict is no guarantee of safety; national or subregional instability—whether military, political, economic, social, or environmental in origin—creates shock waves that can easily spread throughout the international system. However, although the concept of common and comprehensive security has been accepted, it has yet to lead to the necessary transformation in the values and processes of national and international political structures. Countries have still to fully understand the positive implications of their interconnectedness and interdependence and the need to incorporate into their policies such ethical norms as predictability, responsibility, and solidarity.

A new relationship is developing between domestic and international issues that is influencing a great number of processes. The development models that have characterized the main countries and regions during past decades are being increasingly challenged by evolving domestic and international problems. At the risk of oversimplification, the Cold War years could be characterized as a period in which international problems dominated domestic issues. Even the strongest countries significantly subordinated their domestic policies to foreign policies that would guarantee their power positions in the Cold War conflict. Attempts to destabilize the sociopolitical life and economies of opponents were common tactics of Cold War games.

In the post–Cold War period, the pendulum has started swinging toward the other extreme. Domestic stability, internal security, and the attainment of political and economic consensus have always been important to nations, but they are substantially more so today. Domestic economic competitiveness and power are especially highly prized; thus the foundations of national economic power have acquired increased significance.

As all nations compete to maximize their economic gains and bolster their power, progress toward more effective international cooperation is likely to be obstructed. Indeed, national policies aimed at maximizing gains and that assume international conflicts to be zero-sum games are much more dangerous and counterproductive in the new era than they were during the Cold War, when bloc discipline moderated their consequences. Therefore, the global community must devote more attention to sustaining and strengthening the multilateral trading system and give greater support to mutual adjustment measures.

Making Multilateralism Work

The necessity of multilateral cooperation, global governance, and collective risk management has been emphasized by practically all states. However, in an era when so many old and new unresolved problems occupy the international agenda—when such forces as unilateralism, neoisolationism, neonationalism, bilateralism, and regionalism are simultaneously influencing the dynamics of international relations—major disagreements exist about which direction future institutional changes should take. The turbulent undercurrents of global change have thus far resulted in much journalistic and academic debate about a new order, yet few concrete policy measures have been taken. The post–Cold War world still possesses no grand design for institutional reform that could bring about a qualitatively new era of intergovernmental cooperation. Nor is there any overall scheme for facilitating efficient collective risk management procedures and responsible global governance. Expectations stimulated by earlier rhetoric about a new global order are now fading, with complex domestic socioeconomic problems and devastating civil wars having taken center stage. The initial steps taken by some countries in the early 1990s toward reformulating national strategic interests and goals are limited and uncertain. Many countries have adopted a wait-and-see attitude.

Changing the objectives and instruments of foreign policy is always difficult. Transforming international organizations and cooperation regimes requires lengthy negotiations and much bargaining. In the present transitional phase, the process is especially complex and demanding. Both positive and negative factors influence the main trends in international relations and the readiness of countries to implement radical reforms intended to improve cooperation regimes and promote a more peaceful and democratic order. Negative factors such as civil wars, ethnic conflicts, and poverty not only create instability and risks by themselves but also may produce new sources of risks through their combined effects.

The very rapidity with which change is occurring, the emergence of new forces and factors in the global system, and the increasing number of states and the widening divergences among their interests: these factors, either individually or collectively, do not permit fast and radical improvements to be made in multilateral programs and structures, not even in those areas—such as the promotion of environmentally sustainable development and conflict prevention—where general agreement exists on the need for action.

However, the risks posed by the expanding number of states may be balanced, to some extent, by a positive development in the international system, namely, growing international pressure to hold states more accountable for their actions. This pressure is exerted not only in cases of international violence but also when human rights have been violated and, albeit to a lesser extent, when major environmental damage has been wrought. Adherence to international normative standards, and accountability for their transgression, will enable states to pursue their interests peacefully and honorably.

Another trend that includes conflicting elements is associated with collective security. Although conflict prevention, peacemaking, and peacekeeping enjoy widespread support, and despite the fact that the end of the Cold War would seem to have improved the conditions for the enforcement of peace, the major powers have actually displayed a diminishing readiness to run or support collective military peacemaking in a conflict where their immediate security interests are not threatened. As the U.S. experience in Somalia in 1993 has shown, there is considerable domestic resistance to the involvement of national armies in dangerous peacemaking operations. Given such resistance and the increasing costs of peacemaking operations, the threshold of readiness for collective peacemaking will become higher still. Unable to depend on collective security structures, many countries may be forced to strengthen their own military capabilities.

National governments seem much readier to participate in cooperative action that responds to environmental dangers. In the environmental field, the complex nature of many of the tasks facing the international community are now well understood and interests, values, and goals have been clearly articulated. In the economic and social fields, however, the collective institutional capacity of countries to manage factors of risk (including poverty, migration, and unemployment) is outdated and needs to be adjusted to respond to new global realities. Yet, though updating and improving institutional mechanisms would be in the interests of all countries, the developed industrial countries seem to focus on the their own economic and social problems and priorities and pay much less attention to those of the developing countries and the new market economies of the East. Some industrial countries prefer unilateral to multilateral measures and appear unconcerned about the international consequences of their actions. This approach may prove counterproductive. If national decision makers do not take into account the implications of their country's policies for the rest of the world, then other countries may find their economies ruined or may respond with reciprocal measures that will undermine constructive efforts at international cooperation.

In the final analysis, however, the character of future multilateral cooperation will be influenced by the peculiarities of the political system. That system is an hierarchical one in which the United States is, and will remain, the strongest military and economic power. Yet, even the United States, the only state with multidimensional sources of power in the evolving international power structure, cannot act unilaterally or construct a political and institutional structure that meets the criteria formulated by U.S. leaders for the post–Cold War era. The burden of sustaining a new order based on the rule of law and intent on eradicating the worst forms of poverty, conserving the environment, and accomplishing a broad range of security tasks is far too heavy for any one country to bear. The United States' partners in the UN Security Council—Russia, China, France, and Great Britain—are recognized as great powers in the global hierarchy. Even these four countries, however, lack the economic power necessary to create and maintain the new order. In today's world, where economic power is considerably more important than military strength for the governance of the global system, the establishment of a new world order depends on Japan and Germany joining with the Security Council members in a common endeavor. Sharing economic burdens and political power in the key institutions of collective security will thus occupy a prominent place on the future reform agenda.

Only a determined and collective effort to secure the qualitative improvement of international cooperation can guarantee a politically, socially, economically, and ecologically sustainable common future. Individually, even the strongest nations must give much higher priority to multilateral relations and regimes; collectively, they must undertake institutional, structural, and managerial reform of the entire system of multilateral cooperation, and ensure that the members of that system display greater predictability, reliability, and accountability.

20th-century Reforms and 21st-century Dynamics

The reforms of the UN system that began to be implemented in 1992 may reshape, at least to some extent, the organization's hierarchies, functions, structures, and programs. This process of reform is unlikely to represent a fundamental restructuring, but one hopes that it will be sufficiently far-reaching to bring the organization closer in line with the realities of the post–Cold War world and thus strengthen the foundations of the United Nations and enhance its ability to tackle the major issues of the 21st century.

The community of nations that the United Nations will serve in the next century will be quite unlike that group of countries that formed and shaped the organization after World War II. The dominant powers of the Cold War years sought above all to maintain and expand their spheres of influence; their desire to win the Cold War was much weaker than their fear of losing it, so they tended to prize stability and stifle change. The hallmarks of the 21st century will not be bipolar stability and Cold War continuity but rather uncertainty and dynamic, multifaceted change. The fundamental task for the global community will be to manage this change in a relatively peaceful manner, defusing potentially explosive situations and averting major crises. Accomplishing this task will require a system of international cooperation that is more democratic, complex, and flexible than the existing one. In some areas, the system will have to be more decentralized, though its components will also have to be better harmonized. In all areas, the system will have to be supported by adequate human and financial resources and effective institutional structures.

Prophesying doomsday has been a popular occupation in the second half of the 20th century. Upbeat forecasts based on technological optimism or exaggerated expectations of the potential for the United Nations to act as some sort of world government have also been numerous. Despite enjoying public appeal, however, all such predictions have proved inaccurate and have had little influence on the policies of nations and international organizations. Here, we will not contribute to the list of gloomy forecasts, nor will we join the ranks of the unjustifiably optimistic. We must, though, recognize the existence of real and new dangers, and of real alternatives to deal with them. Indeed, in this transitional era, the alternatives, like the uncertainties, are many. The longer action is delayed, however, the greater is the decline in the number and quality of those alternatives.

Even so, in most areas there are still options—still opportunities to prevent the worst from happening. By taking advantage of the opportunities to improve the efficiency and quality of the multilateral cooperation system, the global community could facilitate the solution of many of its problems, create greater harmony between general global interests and specific national needs, better accommodate an increasingly diverse cast of non-state actors, and protect the interests of future generations. The world must be held together for the achievement of those goals.

Various forms of risk, uncertainty, and instability will always be present in the global system. Humankind, as Aron stated, will probably continue to live dangerously. Many of the sources of dangers and risks that are expected to arise in the coming decades are already visible, and many more will emerge in the complex and probably increasingly chaotic global system. How the dangers and risks evolve, and what consequences they will bring, will almost certainly change. The capabilities of countries to deal with them will have to improve.

The future tasks of global governance, however, cannot be confined to the anticipation and management of risks. In this era of interdependence and interactivity, with information highways crisscrossing the globe, qualitatively new solutions must be found to problems in an increasing number of areas. States, which are likely to remain the key members of the global society, will have to harmonize their actions in a broad range of areas and extend their cooperation if they are to enjoy the beneficial consequences of their interactions. They will also have to manage international changes and disputes peacefully. Whereas the Cold War system was based on costly and dangerous deterrence, the new era will have to be based on peaceful cooperation. Just as deterrence required very substantial investments of financial, material, and human resources (in military research, production, infrastructure, and the formation of public opinion), so too will cooperation. The investments in cooperation, however, will have to be made in other areas: research on major problem areas of the future such as energy, health care, and food supplies; information acquisition and dissemination to improve cooperation among international organizations and programs; peacekeeping operations; humanitarian assistance; development cooperation—the list is long. Building an efficient and enduring system of international cooperation will be expensive, but it will be less expensive than creating and maintaining a system of nuclear deterrence was. If properly conceived, cooperation will also yield far greater benefits.

Harmonizing diverse interests, perceptions, policies, and actions in a dynamic world will never be easy. But it can best be achieved, and achieved democratically, within a constructive multilateral framework of shared responsibility and mutual accountability.

Notes

Introduction

1. There are many different understandings of the "global," "world," or "international" system. For instance, Wallerstein has posited its foundation in the capitalist world economy, whereas Ougaard has emphasized the system's connection to social formations. See Georg Sorensen, "A Revised Paradigm for International Relations: The 'Old' Images and the Postmodernist Challenge," *Cooperation and Conflict* 26 (1991): 85–116.

A more recent and comprehensive definition is offered by Stanley Hoffman:

> The world system today is . . . a complex game played at three levels: a world economy that creates its own rewards and punishments and provides both opportunities and constraints for the players (not all of whom are states); the states themselves; and increasingly, the peoples who intervene insofar as they are unhappy with the effects, inequalities and inefficiencies of the world market, or with the inadequacy of established borders or with the nature of their governments.

See Stanley Hoffman, "Balance, Concert, Anarchy, or None of the Above," in Gregory F. Treverton, ed., *The Shape of the New Europe* (New York: Council on Foreign Relations, 1991), 196.

2. John Spanier, *Games Nations Play: Analyzing International Politics* (New York: Holt, Rinehart and Winston, 1984), 91.

3. A paper presented at the World Bank's 1991 conference on development economics emphasized that governance:

is not a word that has been used extensively in the past by political scientists and its recent appearance in popular usage has not been very rigorous. It has become in many ways both all-embracing and vague. According to the Oxford Dictionary, governance means "the act or manner of governing, of exercising control or authority over actions of subjects; a system of regulations." In essence, therefore, governance may be taken as denoting how people are ruled, and how the affairs of a state are administered or regulated. It refers to a nation's system of politics and how it functions in relation to public administration and law.

Pierre Landell-Mills and Ismail Serageldin, "Governance and the External Factor" (Staff Papers, The International Bank for Reconstruction and Development [The World Bank], 1992), 304.

Part I: Global Orders

1. See Ralph Buultjens, "The Destiny of Freedom: Political Cycles in the Twentieth Century," *Ethics and International Affairs* 6 (1992): 58.

2. Ted Galen Carpenter, "The New World Disorder," *Foreign Policy* no. 84 (Fall 1991): 27.

3. W. W. Rostow, *Theorists of Economic Growth from David Hume to the Present, with a Perspective on the Next Century* (New York and Oxford: Oxford University Press, 1990), 448.

4. Robert W. Cox, "Structural Issues of Global Governance: Implications for Europe" (Paper prepared for the United Nations University, Tokyo, September 1991), 9–10.

5. Ibid., 11.

6. My definition is not dissimilar to the formulations offered by a relatively large number of scholars, the most oft-cited of whom is Hedley Bull, who defined international order as "a pattern of activity that sustains the elementary or primary goals of the society of states or international society." See Hedley Bull, *The Anarchical Society: A Study of Order in World Politics* (New York: Columbia University Press, 1977), 8.

7. Robert Gilpin, *War and Change in World Politics* (Cambridge: Cambridge University Press, 1981), 7.

8. See James Rosenau, *Turbulence in World Politics: A Theory of Change and Continuity* (Princeton: Princeton University Press, 1990).

9. See R. J. Stoll, "System and State in International Politics: A Computer Simulation of Balancing in an Anarchic World," *International Studies Quarterly* 31, no. 4 (1987).

10. A profound analysis of the views expressed by the different schools of thought on issues of order and anarchy is offered by Helen Milner in her article, "The Assumption of Anarchy in International Relations Theory: A Critique," *Review of International Studies* 17, no. 1 (1991): 67–86.

11. Aurelio Peccei, *One Hundred Pages for the Future* (London: Futura, 1982), 158–159.

12. Emeric Cruce, *The New Cyneas,* trans. and ed. Thomas W. Balch (Philadelphia: Garland Publishers, 1909), 104, 120–122.

13. William Penn, "Essay Toward the Present and Future Peace of Europe," in *The Fruits of Solitude and Other Writings* (New York: Dutton, 1915).

14. Castel de Saint-Pierre, *Le Project de Paix Perpetuelle* (1713).

15. Immanuel Kant, *Perpetual Peace, and Other Essays on Politics, History, and Morals,* ed. Ted Humphrey (Indianapolis: Hackett Publishing Co., 1983).

16. See, for example, Harry G. Johnson, "International Economic Questions" (British-North American Research Association, June 1970, Mimeograph), 24.

17. See F. L. Schuman, *International Politics,* 6th ed. (New York: McGraw-Hill, 1958), 207.

18. The concept of collective security had much earlier been raised, albeit in different rudimentary forms. One interesting example of this is seen in William Penn's 1693 essay, "Essay Toward the Present and Future Peace of Europe," in which he called for the establishment of a parliament of princes mandated to uphold the rule of law and adjudicate territorial controversies.

19. United Nations Declaration of January 1, 1942, reiterating the terms of the Atlantic Charter, signed by Roosevelt and Churchill on August 14, 1941.

20. See, for example, J. Shiskow's summary of a debate on the unity of the world economy in *Mirovaia Ekonomika i Mezhdunarodnoe Otnoshenia* (Moscow), no. 4 (1984).

Part II: The International Political System

1. Robert Jervis, "The Future of World Politics: Will It Resemble the Past?" *International Security* 16, no. 3 (Winter 1991–92): 67–86.

2. John Paul II, "On the Hundredth Anniversary of *Rerum Novarum*: *Centesimus Annus,*" *Encyclical Letter,* May 1, 1991 (Publication 436-8, Office for Publishing and Promotion Services, United States Catholic Conference, Washington, D.C.), 82.

3. Of the definitions of economic power, one that is widely used in international literature is that of the American economist F. D. Holzman. According to Holzman, two things are to be understood by economic power. One is the operation of monopolistic market forces in the classical sense, by means of which the seller or the buyer exercises sufficient control over supply or demand to influence the conditions and outcome of transactions. The other is that a few actors are in a position to control the flow of an immense volume of resources. F. D. Holzman, *International Trade under Communism, Politics and Economics* (London: Macmillan, 1976), 54.

4. The most conspicuous manifestation of the use of economic power in the international system is the functioning of the so-called hegemonic economies. According to French economist François Perroux, a hegemonic economy exercises a particularly great influence on other economies (occasionally independently of its manifest intentions) simply by virtue of its large dimensions and technological development and as a consequence of the scope of its international economic operations. A change in the internal relations of such an economy—economic growth, level of employment, rate of interest, or production and consumption patterns, for instance—makes its effects felt throughout the system of international relations, with significant repercussions in particular countries. Perroux considers the United States a typical example of a hegemonic economy. François Perroux, *L'économie du XX-eme siecle* (Paris: Presses Universitaires de France, 1961), 27–56.

5. Robert Art, "A Defensible Defense: American Grand Strategy after the Cold War," *International Security* 16, no. 1 (Spring 1991): 5–53.

6. Samuel P. Huntington, "America's Changing Strategic Interests," *Survival* (January–February 1991): 3–17.

7. Draft of the "1992 Defense Guidance," published in *The New York Times*, March 8, 1992, 14.

8. In this regard, many analysts have drawn attention to the problems of inflexibility and coalition building within the U.S. Congress on foreign policy issues. As Peter Trubowitz has observed, "American leaders' autonomy in making foreign policy is contingent upon domestic politics." Peter Trubowitz, "Sectionalism and American Foreign Policy: The Political Geography of Consensus and Conflict," *International Studies Quarterly* 35, no. 2 (June 1992): 173–190.

9. Carpenter, "The New World Disorder," 33–34.

10. W. W. Rostow, "The New World Order and the United States" (Highland International Issues Forum, June 28, 1991, Mimeograph).

11. Ibid., 6.

12. Henry Kissinger, "What Kind of New World Order?" *The Washington Post*, December 3, 1991, A21.

13. President George Bush, "Toward a New World Order," *U.S. Department of State Dispatch* 1, no. 3 (September 17, 1990).

14. John J. Mearsheimer, "Back to the Future: Instability in Europe after the Cold War," *International Security* 15, no. 1 (Summer 1990): 5–56.

15. Here, the concept of nationalism is broadly defined as not just an effort to pursue national interests and subordinate everything else to them, but as an ideology that is exclusionary and presumes superiority over other nations. Nationalism may become the motive force behind policies to justify subordination, domination, and violence.

16. The nature and implications of Europe's environmental problems are discussed in part III of this book.

17. *The European* (London), September 13–15, 1991, 8.

18. *The Economist*, July 4–10, 1992, 15.

19. See Rodolfo Stavenhagen, *Problems and Prospects of Multi-Ethnic States* (Tokyo: The United Nations University, 1986).

20. "France is finding it especially painful to accept Germany's new profile," said *The New York Times*. "For 35 years France enjoyed political leadership of the [European] community, thanks to its alliance with Germany's economic power." The newspaper quoted a German official, who said, "The myth of French grandeur is disintegrating and this is creating a deep crisis of confidence in France." See "After the Cold War: At the East-West Crossroads," *The New York Times*, March 25, 1992, A10.

21. See Dominique Moisi, "The Place for France Is in NATO," *International Herald Tribune*, November 7, 1991.

22. See *National Security: Papers Prepared for GAO Conference on Worldwide Threats*, Supplement to a Report to the Chairmen, the Senate and House Committees on Armed Services (Washington, D.C.: General Accounting Office, April 1992), 34–35.

23. Quoted in Stephen Blank and Thomas Durell Young, "Challenges to Eastern European Security in the Nineties" (Strategic Studies Institute, U.S. Army War College, April 1992, Mimeograph), 30.

24. In April 1992, the first meeting of the defense ministers of NATO and the former Warsaw Pact countries took place. They agreed to establish a joint working group to organize panel discussions on practical defense planning, restructuring of armed forces, conversion of the arms industry to peaceful programs, and so on. It was also agreed that NATO would send military and civilian experts to East European countries if asked. The defense ministers will meet at least twice a year.

25. See François Heisbourg, "From a Common European Home to a European Security System," in Treverton, ed., *The Shape of the New Europe*, 55–56.

26. See "West European Force to Be Formed," *The Washington Post*, June 20, 1992, A18.

27. See "After the Cold War: At the East-West Crossroads," *The New York Times*, March 25, 1992, A10.

28. In June 1992, the nine member states of the WEU, in response to the crises in Yugoslavia and Nagorno-Karabakh, decided to organize a small military force to play a role in military situations in which NATO would be unwilling or unable to act. These forces could be used at the request of the UN Security Council or the CSCE. The duties of this WEU force may include participation in humanitarian assistance and peacekeeping missions and the deployment of combat forces for crisis management.

29. Pacific-Asia is used here to mean simply those Asian states open to the Pacific.

30. Yoshikazu Sakamoto, "Conditions of Peace in the Asia-Pacific Region," in *Asia: Militarization and Regional Conflicts* (Tokyo: The United Nations University, 1988), 223.

31. This factor had been a conerstone of the 1951 U.S.-Japanese peace treaty and the security agreement of 1960.

32. See Tommy T. B. Koh, "Asia Needs U.S.-Japanese Cooperation," *International Herald Tribune*, December 17, 1991, 4.

33. See Iriye Akira, ed., *The Chinese and the Japanese: Essays in Political and Cultural Interactions* (Princeton: Princeton University Press, 1980).

34. An interesting reference to this problem is made by Jim Hoagland in "An Arms Race in East Asia," *The Washington Post*, July 14, 1992, A14.

35. Such an argument has been mentioned, for example, by Masaru Tamamoto in "Japan: Uncertain Role," *World Policy Journal* (Fall 1991): 591.

36. See Michael J. Green, "Japan in Asia: The American Connection," *Global Affairs* (Summer 1991): 59.

37. See, for example, Chen Xiaogong, "Anxieties Mount over Japan," *Liberation Army Daily*, September 7, 1990, 2.

38. See, for example, Murray Weidenbaum, "Greater China: A New Economic Colossus?" *The Washington Quarterly* 16, no. 4 (Autumn 1993): 71–83.

39. See Hassan Mahamadi Nejad, "The Middle East: Building a Community of Nations," *Bulletin of Peace Proposals* 23, no. 2 (1992): 159–167.

40. A detailed and interesting analysis of this process is given by Lisa Anderson, "Remaking the Middle East: The Prospects for Democracy and Stability," *Ethics and International Affairs* 6 (1992): 163–178.

41. See United Nations Development Programme, *Human Development Report, 1992* (Oxford and New York: Oxford University Press for UNDP, 1992).

42. United Nations, *World Economic Survey, 1991* (New York: United Nations, 1991), 181–182.

43. See Kenneth W. Stein, Samuel W. Lewis, and Sheryl J. Brown, eds., *Making Peace among Arabs and Israelis: Lessons from Fifty Years of Negotiating Experience* (Washington, D.C.: United States Institute of Peace, October 1991).

44. Ten million Kurds live in Turkey, five million in Iran, four million in Iraq, one million in Syria and some 4,500,000 in other regions. See Nejad, "The Middle East: Building a Community of Nations."

45. A fascinating analysis of the problems and perspectives of the region is offered by Helio Jaguaribe, "Latin America and the Challenge of the 1990s," in L. Emmerij, ed., *One World or Several?* (Paris: OECD Development Center, 1989), 67–75.

46. Based on statistical data in United Nations, *World Economic Survey, 1991.*

47. Ibid., 178.

48. See, for example, Robin Wright and Doyle McManus, "History Tomorrow: Four Choices between Reason and Chaos," *The Washington Post*, December 29, 1991, C3.

49. See, for example, references in Owen Harries, "Lower Case: The Third World R.I.P.," *The National Interest*, no. 26 (Winter 1991): 109–112.

50. This attitude is reflected in the document adopted in 1991 at the Caracas conference of the Group of 15, a body formed in 1990 to represent the major regions and countries of the South. "The Doctrine for a Truly New World Order" considers the eradication of poverty, the rejection of closed economic blocs, and the solution of external debt problems as essential prerequisites for a new world order. See *Interpress News Service*, no. 20, 1991.

Part III: The Global Economic System

1. Data calculated by the author on the basis of *SIPRI Yearbook, 1990: World Armaments and Disarmament* (Oxford: Oxford University Press for SIPRI, 1990); Congress of the United States, Office of Technology Assessment, *Global Arms Trade: Commerce in Advanced Military Technology and Weapons* (Washington, D.C.: Government Printing Office, 1991); and different publications of the United Nations Department of Disarmament Affairs based in New York.

2. See Simon Kuznets, *Modern Economic Growth: Rate, Structure, and Spread* (New Haven: Yale University Press, 1966), 1–8.

3. See N. D. Kondratieff, *Die langen Wellen der Konjunktur* 56 (Tubingen: Archiv für Sozialwissenschaft und Sozialpolitik, 1929); D. Landes, *The*

*Unbound Prometheus: Technological Change and Industrial Development in West-
ern Europe from 1750 to the Present* (London: Cambridge University Press,
1969); Rostow, *Theorists of Economic Growth from David Hume to the Present*,
486–508; and Joseph A. Schumpeter, *Business Cycles: A Theoretical, Historical, and Statistical Analysis of the Capitalist Process* (New York: McGraw-
Hill, 1939).

4. See J. Attali, *Millennium* (London: Times Books/Random House,
1991), 10.

5. See Angus Maddison, *The World Economy of the 20th Century* (Paris:
OECD the Development Centre, 1989).

6. The elaboration of long cycles theory is credited to the Russian
scholar Nicolai Kondratieff, who concluded that the development of the
capitalist system is not linear, but cyclical. Short waves of development of 1.5
to 3 years are matched by economic cycles of 7 to 11 years and social
and economic cycles of about 50 years. Kondratieff believed that recoveries
occur more often in the upward trend of long cycles than in the downward
trend, which corresponds to much suffering, particularly in the agricultural
sector. The phase of decline is noted for its many innovations, technical
and otherwise, that are employed on a mass scale at the beginning of the
subsequent phase. The upward trends represent phases of growth that
strain economic resources. In these phases wars and revolutions break
out, which in turn influence development.

Long cycles have been examined by several other experts, including
Joseph A. Schumpeter, P. G. Mensch, and W. W. Rostow. Christopher
Freeman and Carlota Perez have also sought to explain the causes of
long cycles; their technological, economic, and social peculiarities; their
political-economic consequences; the corporate organizational forms
within them; power relations; and international organizational structures and institutions. According to these authors, the first cycle began
in the 1770s to 1780s (the beginning of manufacturing industry) and
lasted until the 1840s, with rudimentary mechanization as its technological basis. The second cycle lasted until the 1880s to 1890s, and had
as its base the development of steam engines and railways. The third
cycle lasted until the 1930s to 1940s, its base being the electrical and
heavy machine industries. The fourth cycle came to a close in the 1980s,
and had the characteristics of mass production, the development and
distribution of road and air transportion networks, and the synthetic
chemical and nuclear industries. The fifth cycle began in the 1980s,
and is being fed by information and communications engineering, the
microelectronics industry, the biological revolution, and space technology. See Christopher Freeman, ed., *Long Waves in the World Economy*
(London: Frances Pinter, 1984).

7. Ibid.

8. I consider these regulating forces to be combinations of conscious actions of the main actors in the international system and the operations of quasi-automatic mechanisms that stimulate or constrain the actors. In this context, while my ideas are close to those of Kenneth N. Waltz, who employs the concept of controlling factors and forces, I use the concept of "regulating forces" in a broader framework. See K. N. Waltz, *Theory of International Politics* (Reading, Mass.: Addison-Wesley, 1979) 80, 88, 94, 95.

9. Per capita output in the developed countries was $19,800; in the developing world, the figure was $1,311. See United Nations Conference on Trade and Development, *Handbook of International Trade and Development Statistics, 1992* (New York: United Nations, 1993), table 6a.

10. See United Nations, *Global Outlook 2000: An Economic, Social and Environmental Perspective* (New York: United Nations, 1990); and United Nations, *World Economic Survey, 1991*, part III.

11. See Emmerji, ed., *One World or Several?* 17.

12. The functioning of these models is important from the point of view of long-term resource allocation, the qualitative and quantitative aspects of the growth process, and the distribution of the costs and benefits of development.

13. See Mihaly Simai, *The Process of Privatization in East and Central Europe: Problems and Perspectives* (Seoul: Seoul National University, 1991).

14. As might be expected, the interplay among the three models gives rise to systemic friction. See S. Ostry, "Beyond the Border: The New International Policy Arena," in Organization for Economic Co-operation and Development, *Strategic Industries in a Global Economy* (Paris: OECD International Futures Programme, 1991), 81–92.

15. This increased role was connected with policy commitments to avoiding another major depression. The Full Employment Act of 1946 made economic growth an objective of national economic policy and a responsibility of the federal government in a free, private, and competitive economy.

16. U.S. Department of Commerce, Bureau of the Census, *Statistical Abstract of the United States, 1991* (Washington, D.C.: Government Printing Office, 1992).

17. Ibid.

18. United Nations, *World Economic Survey, 1991*, 52.

19. *Economic Report of the President* (Washington, D.C.: Government Printing Office, 1992), 275.

20. See, for example, Laura D'Andrea Tyson, *Who's Bashing Whom? Trade Conflicts in High-Technology Industries* (Washington, D.C.: Institute for

International Economics, 1992); and Ernest H. Preep, "Who's Benefiting Whom? A Trade Agenda for High Technology Industries," *The Washington Quarterly* 16, no. 4 (Autumn 1993): 17–33.

21. See K. Bradsher, "As U.S. Urges Free Markets Its Trade Barriers Are Many," *The New York Times*, February 7, 1992, D4.

22. The majority of EFTA members seem likely to become members of the EC during the coming years. Sweden, Norway, Finland, and Austria are all engaged in ongoing negotiations with the EC.

23. See World Bank, *World Development Report, 1991* (Washington, D.C.: World Bank, 1991); and United Nations, *World Economic Survey, 1991*, 60–61.

24. See United Nations Development Programme, *Human Development Report 1991* (New York: Oxford University Press for UNDP, 1991), 119.

25. See D. Okimoto, "Between MITI and the Market," in *Japanese Industrial Policy for High Technology* (Stanford: Stanford University Press, 1989).

26. A large proportion of Japanese bank assets consists of direct capital market investments and property; companies and banks are permitted to count up to 45 percent of their unrealized capital gains on such assets as capital.

27. See United Nations, *World Economic Survey, 1992* (New York: United Nations, 1992), 52, 226; and United Nations Conference on International Trade and Development, *Handbook of International Trade and Development Statistics, 1992* (New York: United Nations, 1992).

28. Experts on international trade have debated why the United States, which insisted on liberalization and openness in Europe after World War II, did not pursue a parallel policy with regard to Japan, a country where it had a much greater opportunity to influence economic policies. I suggest that this seeming oversight was in all probability tied directly to U.S. strategic security interests. The United States sought the fastest possible recovery in Japan to create a strong Asian force to countervail the Soviet Union and China. Opening and liberalizing Japan would have been an economically and politically dangerous shock for the leading economic actors in Japan, and it would have run counter to the traditions and the character of the Japanese market. In addition, the United States was preoccupied with the grand design of a liberal global trading system, a system that the United States probably hoped would eventually influence the economic behavior of Japan.

29. World Bank, *World Development Report, 1993* (Oxford: Oxford University Press for the World Bank, 1993); Economic Planning Agency, *Japan in the Year 2010* (Tokyo: Government Printing Office, 1992).

30. D. E. Sanger, "The Power of Yen Winning Asia," *The New York Times*, December 5, 1991, D22.

31. See *The Asian-Pacific Community in the Year 2000: Prospects and Challenges* (Seoul: Sejong Institute, 1991).

32. The chief characteristics of the model of central planning and of its various versions have been summarized and analyzed in an excellent book by the Hungarian economist Jånos Kornai, *The Socialist System: The Political Economy of Communism* (Princeton: Princeton University Press, 1993).

33. See, for example, the report by Michael Camdessus, managing director of the International Monetary Fund, *Economic Transformation in the Fifteen Republics of the Former U.S.S.R.: A Challenge or an Opportunity for the World?* (Washington, D.C.: International Monetary Fund, April 1992), 10.

34. See, for example, William H. Overholt, *The Next Economic Superpower* (London: Weidenfeld & Nicolson, 1993).

35. See United Nations, *World Economic Survey, 1993* (New York: United Nations, 1993), 185–203.

36. Witness, for example, the following UN statement on economic conditions in Africa:

> Thus, following the decade-long decline and woeful economic performance in Africa, the enabling environment is being further eroded. The slowdown in output growth was sufficient enough to arrest the incipient recovery on the continent, and to ensure that per capita income growth remained negative as population pressure continued unabated. In addition to the external debt trap, capital flight and the brain drain phenomena, both of which were significant elements in the reverse flow of resources from Africa in the 1980s, persisted. In short, all the underlying vulnerability, fragility, and the deep structural weaknesses and limitations of the African economies remained manifest on the threshold of the new decade.

United Nations Economic Commission for Africa, *Economic Report on Africa* (New York: United Nations, 1991), v.

37. United Nations Development Programme, *Human Development Report, 1992*.

38. See Mihaly Simai, *Interdependence and Conflicts in the World Economy* (Rockville, Md.: Sijthoff & Noordhoff, 1981), 120–121.

39. See, for example, the statement of the finance ministers of the G-7 published in *International Monetary Fund Survey* 22, no. 10 (May 17, 1993): 148–150.

40. A study directed by Lance Taylor at the World Institute for Development Economics Research of the United Nations University addressed the concept of socially necessary growth rates. This concept incorporates the need to reduce unemployment to manageable levels within a 10-year time horizon; specific minimum standards of human development or basic needs goals in health and education; poverty alleviation; and improvements in income distribution. According to this study, the developing world as a whole would have to grow about 5.5 percent per year in terms of GDP to achieve these goals. Earlier calculations had considered 4 percent annual growth necessary for social sustainability. This definition of socially necessary growth, however, makes no allowance for resources required to support environmental sustainability. See L. Taylor, *Foreign Resource Flows and Developing Country Growth* (Helsinki: WIDER Research for Action, 1991).

41. The idea behind locomotive theory is that expansionary actions in large economies provide positive impulses in other countries, the cumulative effect of which adds steam to the locomotive and to the world economy as a whole. A detailed analysis of the theory is provided by Martin Bronfenbrenner, "On the Locomotive Theory in International Macroeconomics," *Weltwirtschaftliches Archiv* 115, no. 1 (1979): 38–50.

42. The debate about the role of the economic model should take heed of this warning from Attali:

> Outside the emerging Pacific and European spheres, 4 billion people will take faltering steps toward a market society and democracy. But the market alone cannot develop industry or build the basic infrastructure of a health and education system. The market alone cannot make raw materials profitable. Nor can it protect the environment. Nor can it close the immense and growing gap between the privileged regions and the paralyzed periphery. If the market alone is relied upon to build whole societies, it will end up producing the principal revolutionaries of tomorrow who will rise in resentment against the wealthy inhabitants of the privileged centers of the world.

Attali, *Millennium*, 71.

43. See United Nations, *World Economic Survey, 1991*; and S. Cunningham and K. G. Ruffing, "Some Macroeconomic Aspects of Reductions in Military Expenditures" (United Nations, New York, November 1992, Mimeograph).

44. See *Economic Report of the President* (Washington, D.C.: Government Printing Office, 1992), 301.

45. The United Nations has defined globally sustainable development as follows:

> Sustainable development is development that meets the needs of the present, without compromising the ability of future generations to meet their own needs, and does not imply in any way encroachment upon national

sovereignty. . . . It implies, further, the existence of a supportive international economic environment that would result in sustained economic growth
and development in all countries, particularly in the developing countries,
which is of major importance for sound management of the environment.
It also implies the maintenance, rational use and enhancement of the natural
resource base that underpins ecological resilience and economic growth.
Sustainable development further implies incorporation of environmental
concerns and consideration in development planning and policies. . . .

Official Records of the General Assembly, Forty-Fourth Session, Supplement no. 25; A/44/25, Decision 15/2, Annex II.

46. See, for instance, "An Invitation to Dialogue," published in the
newsletter of the Geneva-based South Centre, *South Letter*, no. 17 (Spring-
Summer 1993): 2–5.

47. By 1993, practically all intergovernmental organizations and more
than 1,300 international nongovernmental organizations were dealing with
the management of the ecosystem and environmental cooperation. The UN
General Assembly has adopted a number of detailed resolutions and programs.
Several dozen multilateral intergovernmental declarations, 168 multilateral
conventions, agreements, and protocols, and dozens of bilateral agreements
cover a wide variety of areas for environmental cooperation and joint action.

48. See H. Wiedner, "The Capability of the Capitalist State to 'Solve'
Environmental Problems" (Paper presented at the 15th World Congress
of the International Political Science Association, Buenos Aires, 1991).

49. See J. C. Glenn, *Future Mind: Artificial Intelligence* (Washington, D.C.:
Acropolis Books, 1989), 11–35.

50. Here I use John Burton's definition concerning the needs of human
beings as social units. He characterizes these needs as "conditions and
opportunities that are essential to the individual if he is to be a functioning and cooperative member of society, conditions that are essential
to his development and which through him, are essential to the organization and survival of society." See J. W. Burton, "Human Needs vs.
Societal Needs," in R. A. Coate and J. A. Rosati, eds., *The Power of Human
Needs in World Society* (Boulder and London: Lynne Rienner Publishers,
1988), 38.

51. United Nations Development Programme, *Human Development
Report, 1991*, 160–161. UN population projections are based on the
assumption that fertility will eventually reach replacement levels, in which
each couple replaces itself by having on average 2.1 children. Depending
on how fast the replacement level is reached, global population has been
projected to stabilize at between 9 and 14 billion. Most developed countries
today are 10 to 20 percent below replacement fertility and most of the
developing countries are above it. However, it is almost impossible to

predict changes in behavior according to the projections. If fertility rates are only 5 percent higher than the projected replacement rate, the global population in the mid-21st century will reach 20.8 billion.

52. See United Nations Department of International Economic and Social Affairs, *World Population Prospects, 1988* (New York: United Nations, 1989); and United Nations Development Programme, *Human Development Report, 1991.*

53. The United Nations Department of International Economic and Social Affairs projects that in the coming decades there will be a rapid increase in the fossil fuel consumption of the developing countries, including China, due to population growth and the replacement of noncommercial sources of energy. See United Nations, *Global Outlook 2000,* 115–116.

54. See N. Sadik, "Global Development Challenges: The Population Dimension," in U. Kirdar, ed., *Change: Threat or Opportunity for Human Progress?* (New York: United Nations, 1992), vol. 4, *Social Change,* 25.

55. The United Nations' full-employment pledge is credited to the initiatives of President Franklin Roosevelt and Sir William Beveridge. As World War II ended, many people feared that victory would be followed by a new Great Depression. President Roosevelt proposed a postwar economic bill of rights based on what he believed was a fundamental right to a job with fair wages. Beveridge proposed full employment as a postwar goal for Britain. In both countries, business groups firmly opposed the idea and a fierce debate began. In 1945, when the debate was still going on, the UN Charter was adopted; Article 55 committed the members of the organization to promoting full employment. In 1948, the UN Universal Declaration of Human Rights strengthened this commitment. In 1946, a Full Employment Act was passed in the United States, committing the federal government not to full employment, but rather to preventing a mass depression. Over subsequent decades, however, the idea of full employment has been gradually abandoned in practical policies.

56. Attali, *Millennium,* 76.

57. World Resources Institute, *World Resources Report, 1990-91* (Washington, D.C.: World Resources Institute, 1990), 272–273.

In the early 1980s, the foreign-born percentage of the population in Canada was 16 percent, 6.2 percent in the United States, 20.6 percent in Australia, 16.7 percent in Switzerland, 11 percent in France, more than 7 percent in Germany, 6.3 percent in the United Kingdom, 64 percent in the United Arab Emirates, 42 percent in Israel and Kuwait, and 22 percent in Côte d'Ivoire. See Lin Lean Lim, "Growing Economic Interdependence and Its Implications for International Migration" (Paper prepared for the UN Export Group Meeting on Migration, Santa Cruz, January 1993), 6.

58. See P. B. Levine and O. S. Mitchell, "Expected Changes in the Work Force and Implications for Labor Markets" (NBER Working Paper, no. 3743, National Bureau of Economic Research, Cambridge, Mass., 1991).

59. See United Nations Development Programme, *Human Development Report, 1993* (Oxford: Oxford University Press for UNDP, 1993), 194; and *Human Development Report, 1991*, 51.

60. See United Nations, *Global Outlook 2000*; and UNESCO, *Statistical Yearbook, 1988* (Paris: UNESCO, 1989).

61. The technology life cycle can be divided into four stages: the innovation stage, in which a new product or process is born from R&D; the commercialization stage of demonstration, industrialization, and marketing; the diffusion stage, when markets are penetrated; and the substitution stage, when a technology declines and is substituted by a new technology.

62. See, for example, M. Abramovitz, "Catching Up, Forging Ahead, and Falling Behind," *Journal of Economic History* 4, no. 2 (June 1986): 385–406; and C. Freeman, "Technical Change and Long-Term Economic Growth" (World Bank Seminar Paper, 1988).

63. By "technological culture" is meant a nation's accumulated knowledge and the attitude of its population, including its ruling elite, entrepreneurs, and labor force, toward "new" science and technology. The level of technological culture depends on the level of education in a society and its degree of openness to new ideas.

64. See United Nations Development Programme, *Human Development Report, 1993*, table 39.

65. See S. Deger and S. Sen, "Reorientation and Conversion of Military R&D towards Environmental R&D and Protection," in N. P. Gledtisch, ed., *Conversions and the Environment* (Oslo: PRIO Reports, 1992).

66. See U.S. Office of Technology Assessment, *Redesigning Defense: Planning the Transition to the Future U.S. Defense Industrial Base* (Washington, D.C.: Government Printing Office, 1991); and C. W. Taylor, *A World of 2010* (Carlisle, Penn.: Strategic Studies Institute, U.S. Army War College, 1992), 49–74.

67. See *Business Week*, November 23, 1992, 45.

68. See National Science Foundation, *Science Indicators, 1989* (Washington, D.C.: N.S.C.F., 1989), 371, 375, 377; Jeffrey E. Garten, *A Cold Peace: America, Japan, Germany and the Struggle for Supremacy* (New York: The Twentieth Century Fund, 1992); and Tyson, *Who's Bashing Whom?* table 2.8.

69. See Organization for Economic Co-operation and Development, Directorate for Scientific Affairs, *Gaps in Technology: Comparisons between Member Countries in Education, Research and Development, Technological Innovation, International Economic Exchanges* (Paris: OECD, 1970); Organization for Economic Co-operation and Development, *Selected Science & Technology Indicators: Recent Results* (Paris: OECD, 1986); and United Nations Development Programme, *Human Development Report, 1992.*

70. The direct costs of technology imports are direct payments for the purchases. The indirect costs are the restrictions imposed on the importing countries.

71. See, for example, M. A. Khaminawa, "Science and Technology: Africa's Dilemma," *African Technology Forum* 5, no. 3 (August–September 1992): 4–5.

72. In economic terms, "conjunctural components" tend to be shorter-term factors of supply and demand that influence general economic trends, producing a crisis or temporary upswing.

73. See United Nations Conference on Trade and Development, *Handbook of International Trade and Development Statistics, 1992.*

74. The world consumption of raw materials calculated in metric tons per billion dollars of world output declined between the mid-1960s and the late 1980s in the following fashion: iron ore fell from 51.5 to 30.0; other metals and minerals from 4.0 to 2.8; and oil from 287.0 to 236.0. See S. Fardoust and A. Dhareshwar, "Long-term Outlook for the World Economy" (World Bank Working Papers, W.P.S. 372, Washington, D.C., 1990), 7.

75. The Uruguay Round was the eighth round of negotiations in the GATT since 1947. Each round tends to be named after the country or city where the talks began or after a person who played a prominent part in the negotiations.

76. See the *1989 Annual Report of the Bank for International Settlements* (Basle: Bank for International Settlements, 1990).

77. The size of a capital market is usually characterized by the average market capitalization as a percentage of the GNP in a given country. At the end of the 1980s, the capital market was 92 percent in Japan, 80 percent in the United Kingdom, 58 percent in the United States, 21 percent in Germany, and 18 percent in France. See World Bank, *World Development Report, 1989* (Washington, D.C.: World Bank, 1989).

78. See Federal Reserve Bank of New York, "Summary of Results of U.S. Foreign Exchange Market Survey Conducted in April 1989" (Report released September 13, 1989).

79. The United States became the world's main debtor due to the enduring deficit in its balance of trade and budget, which it could finance only by borrowing from external sources. The Federal Republic of Germany and Japan, which financed the greater part of the United States' international borrowings, became the chief creditors in the world economy. Since its reunification, Germany has significantly reduced its role as a creditor.

80. See United Nations Conference on Trade and Development, *Trade and Development Report, 1991* (New York: United Nations, 1991), 88–89.

81. See P. S. Armington, "Global Demand for Capital, the Rate of Interest and World Models" (Unpublished report, World Bank International Economics Department, 1991).

82. Globalization could be defined as the entirety of such universal processes as technological transformation; increasing interdependence caused by mass communications, trade, and capital flows; and the homogenization and standardization of production and consumption patterns. Internationalization could be characterized as the predominance of a world market orientation in trade, investments, or other transactions. Another approach to the definition of globalization could be institutional, and it could be taken to mean the identity or similarity of economic regulations, institutions, and policies across national boundaries.

83. See two reports prepared for the 19th session of the Commission on Transnational Corporations of the United Nations Economic and Social Council: *The Universe of Transnational Corporations* (New York: United Nations, April 1993), 5–6; and *The Growth of Foreign Direct Investments in the 1980s* (New York: United Nations, March 1993), 24.

84. See "An Exchange on Multinationals," *The National Interest*, no. 27 (Spring 1992): 104.

Part IV: Multilateralism of the 21st Century in the Making

1. See Rosenau, *Turbulence in World Politics*; and Ken Booth, "Security and Emancipation," *Review of International Studies* 17, no. 4 (1991): 314–315.

2. The system was based on the Bretton Woods Agreement of 1944, named after the New Hampshire resort where representatives of 28 nations met to organize a system of international monetary cooperation.

3. As of the mid-1990s, the World Bank is cooperating with a number of regional banks established to assist development not only in Latin America, Asia, and Africa but also in Eastern Europe.

4. See the "Special Survey" in *The Economist*, October 12, 1991, 6.

5. See for details, Eric Helleiner, "States and the Future of Global Finance," *Review of International Studies* 18, no. 1 (1992): 31–49.

6. These include the United Nations Conference on Trade and Development, which was established in 1964, and the United Nations Industrial Development Organization. In the late 1970s, the influential position of director for development and international cooperation was created in the UN secretariat.

7. See F. T. Haner, with J. S. Ewing, *Country Risk Assessment, Theory and Worldwide Practice* (New York: Praeger Special Studies, 1985); and, from the point of view of international banking, Georg Junge, "Country Risk Assessment, Swiss Bank Corporation Approach," in Swiss Bank Corporation, *Economic and Financial Prospects Supplement* (Basle-Zurich: Swiss Bank Corporation, February–March 1988).

8. John Maynard Keynes, "Part 2: Defense and Development," in *The Collected Writings of John Maynard Keynes: The General Theory and After*, ed. Donald Moggridge (Cambridge: Cambridge University Press, 1973), vol. 14, 112–113.

9. Richard J. Herring, ed., *Managing International Risk* (Cambridge: Cambridge University Press, 1983), 3, 23.

10. Here, multilateralism is understood in its broader definition to mean an organizational design for the collective management of international agencies and cooperation regimes for the elaboration of common norms defining the rights and obligations of countries and the implementation of policies of collective sanctions when necessary. To date, some multilateral organizations have been of a multipurpose nature, whereas others have fulfilled more limited functions. The "functional" approach to the international cooperation system can be used in different senses: functionalism may relate to such problem areas as politics or economics, or more specifically to legal problems, trade, human rights issues, or capital flows. It does not precisely define the structural nature of organizations.

11. See Simai, *Interdependence and Conflicts in the World Economy.*

12. Daniel S. Cheever, "The U.N. Convention on the Law of the Sea: Regime Change and Regime Maintenance?" (Paper presented at the Annual Convention of the British International Science Association, London, 1989), 17.

13. A region can be defined in many ways. The geographical concept of a region is usually based on the physical characteristics of a given area. From an economic point of view, a region is a zone within which countries cooperate more intensively among themselves than with the rest of the world. Geostrategically, a region is a specific area of cooperative and/or conflictual political relationships. The cultural definition of a region may emphasize similarities in historical development in regard to such factors as ethnicity, religion, life-style, or language. Regions can, of course, be identified within countries or within a larger, international framework. In this book, "region" is used in the international sense.

14. Harlan Cleveland, "Reflections on the Pacific Community," *Department of State Bulletin* 48, no. 1243 (April 22, 1963): 614.

15. See R. E. Feinberg and Dalia M. Boylan, "Modular Multilateralism," *The Washington Quarterly* 15, no. 1 (Winter 1991): 195–196.

16. Quoted from an edited excerpt of a confidential report to the Asia-Pacific summit meeting. See "Now Let's Build an Asia-Pacific Economic Community," *International Herald Tribune*, November 4, 1993, 8.

17. See The British American Security Information Council, *Basis Report*, no. 21 (April 10, 1992): 2.

18. Maurice Bertrand, *Some Reflections on Reform of the United Nations* (Geneva: United Nations Joint Inspection Unit, 1985), 56.

19. Joseph S. Nye, Jr., "What New World Order?" *Foreign Affairs* 71, no. 2 (Spring 1992): 87.

20. OECD Forum for the Future, *Long-Term Prospects for the World Economy: Outlook, Main Issues and Summary of Discussions* (Paris: OECD, 1992), 17–18.

21. See, for example, Peter J. Fromuth, ed., *A Successor Vision: The United Nations of Tomorrow* (New York: United Nations Association of the United States of America, 1988); Maurice Bertrand, *The Third Generation World Organization* (Dordrecht: Martinus Nijhoff Publishers, 1989); Nordic UN Project, *The United Nations in Development: Reform Issues in the Economic and Social Fields—A Nordic Perspective* (Stockholm: Nordic UN Project, 1991); and William J. Durch and Barry M. Blechman, *Keeping the Peace: The United Nations in the Emerging World Order* (Washington, D.C.: Stimson Center, 1992).

22. *The Statement of the Secretary-General of the United Nations at the Security Council Summit Meeting* (New York: United Nations Department of Public Information, January 31, 1992).

23. See, for example, J. Kaufman and Nico Schrijver, *Changing Global Needs: Expanding Roles for the United Nations System* (Hanover, N.H.: The Academic Council for the United Nations System, Reports and Papers 1990–1995), 43–44.

24. For further details, see *World Economic Summits: The Role of Representative Groups in the Governance of the World Economy*, WIDER Study Group Series, no. 4 (Helsinki: World Institute for Development Economics Research of the United Nations University, 1989).

25. Joachim W. Muller, *The Reform of the United Nations* (New York: Oceana Publications, Inc., 1992), vol. I, 1.

26. Sir Robert Jackson, *A Study of the Capacity of the United Nations Development System* (Geneva: United Nations, 1969).

27. See, for example, *World Economic Summits*, 79–83.

28. Ernst B. Haas, *When Knowledge is Power: Three Models of Change in International Organizations* (Berkeley: University of California Press, 1990), 24–26.

29. When the UN Charter was debated in 1945, the Soviet Union wanted to limit the role of the organization to security functions exercised in matters determined by the Security Council, within which the Soviet Union expected to have the power of veto. The deadlock over this issue was broken only at the last moment in the San Francisco negotiations. See Ruth Russel, *A History of the United Nations Charter: The Role of the United States, 1940–45* (Washington, D.C.: Brookings Institution, 1958), 761–764.

30. Robert W. Gregg, "International Economic Cooperation and Development: The United Nations in Search for a Role" (Paper presented at the 1984 International Studies Association Conference in Atlanta), 12.

31. Donald J. Puchala, "American Interests and the United Nations," *Political Science Quarterly* 97, no. 4 (Winter 1982–83): 573.

32. Edward C. Luck, "The U.N. at 40: A Supporter's Lament," *Foreign Policy*, no. 57 (Winter 1984–85): 155–156.

33. John Gerard Ruggie, "The United States and the United Nations," *International Organizations* (Spring 1985): 344, 351, 355.

34. See the statement of Richard S. Williamson, assistant secretary for International Organization Affairs, before the House Foreign Affairs Committee, in *U.S. Contributions to International Organizations: Hearing before the Subcommittees on Human Rights and International Organizations and on International Operations of the Committee on Foreign Affairs, House of Representatives, February 23, 1988* (Washington, D.C.: Government Printing Office, 1988), Appendix 2.

35. Miriam Camps and William Diebold, Jr., *The New Multilateralism* (New York: Council on Foreign Relations, 1986), 33.

36. Dhanabalan, the delegate of Singapore, Official Records of the General Assembly, Forty-first Session, Supplement no. 1, 67–72.

37. See Peter Ludlow, "Europe's Institutions: Europe's Politics," in Treverton, ed., *The Shape of the New Europe*, 62–64.

38. An excerpt from the "Defense Planning Guidance for Fiscal Years 1994–99," printed in *The Washington Post*, May 24, 1992, A23.

39. See *U.S. Department of State Dispatch* 4, no. 4 (January 25, 1993).

40. Remarks of Anthony Lake as prepared for delivery at the Brookings Institution Africa Forum Luncheon, Washington, D.C., May 3, 1993.

41. Reported in *The Washington Post*, May 12, 1993, A25.

42. Cited in the weekly newsletter of the United Nations, *International Documents Review* 4, no. 37 (October 18–22, 1993).

43. See "New Delhi et Pékin critiquent la domination des Etats Unis dans les affaires mondiale," *Le Monde* (Paris), December 15–16, 1991.

44. See the press release issued by United Nations Department of Public Information in New York regarding the 3,046th meeting of the Security Council, January 31, 1992.

45. South Centre, *Enhancing the Economic Role of the United Nations. The South and the Reform of the U.N.O.* (Geneva: South Centre, October 1992), 4–5.

46. See Shahram Chubin, "The South and the New World Order," *The Washington Quarterly* 16, no. 4 (Autumn 1993): 91–93.

47. See Russel, *A History of the United Nations Charter*.

48. Camps and Diebold, *The New Multilateralism*, 33.

49. Commenting on the early 1980s, one U.S. expert noted that the lack of experienced professionals in key roles severely handicapped the United States in the United Nations. See Seymour Maxwell Finger, "Jeane Kirkpatrick at the United Nations," *Foreign Affairs* 62, no. 2 (1983): 445–447. It should be emphasized that the United States was not the only country thus afflicted.

50. Many scholars have analyzed the voting practices, bargaining processes, and roles of the groups in the United Nations. See, for example, on two separate issues, Jeane J. Kirkpatrick, "The U.N. and the U.S.," in *The U.N. Under Scrutiny* (Washington, D.C.: The Heritage Foundation, 1982), 26; and Robert Rothstein, *Global Bargaining: UNCTAD and the Quest for a New International Economic Order* (Princeton: Princeton University Press, 1979), 197.

51. A good historical summary of how these issues have been dealt with in different international organizations is offered in a comparative perspective by Werner J. Feld and Robert S. Jordan (with Leon Hurwitz) in *International Organizations: A Comparative Approach* (New York: Praeger, 1988), 121–243.

52. *Report of the Group of High-Level Intergovernmental Experts to Review the Efficiency of the Administrative and Financial Functioning of the United Nations* (New York: United Nations, August 15, 1986).

53. See Maurice Bertrand, "Planning, Programming, Budgeting, and Evaluation in the U.N.," in Fromuth, ed., *A Successor Vision*, 264.

54. Bertrand, *The Third Generation World Organization*, 103.

55. In 1953, a concession was made to the U.S. government in relation to its UN staff members, who were obliged to attend clearance hearings on the premises of the United Nations. U.S. citizens on the UN staff who refused to testify before a United States Federal Grand Jury were dismissed. Pressure on the U.S. government led to the later abandonment of this practice.

56. Bertrand, *Some Reflections on Reform of the United Nations*, 12–13.

57. See Seymour Maxwell Finger and Nina Hanan, "The United Nations Secretariat Revisited," *Orbis* 25, no. 1 (Spring 1981): 198.

58. See, for example, *The United States and the United Nations: A Balance Sheet*, Backgrounder Report (Washington, D.C.: The Heritage Foundation, January 21, 1982), 5–6.

59. See United Nations Institute for Training and Research, *The Proposed Changes* (New York: United Nations General Assembly, September 30, 1991), 23.

60. Brian Urquhart and Erskine Childers, *A World in Need of Leadership: Tomorrow's United Nations* (New York: Dag Hammarskjöld Foundation, 1990).

61. Ibid., 40.

62. For example, according to an editorial in one Japanese newspaper, Boutros-Ghali is "a formidable defender [of the United Nations] with abundant faith" in the importance of its mission. See "Questions of Leadership," *Yomiuri Shimbun* (Tokyo), November 12, 1993, A13.

Part V: Holding the World Together

1. Raymond Aron, "The Anarchical Order of Power," *Daedelus* (Spring 1966): 502.

2. Ibid., 485–486.

Index

The designation *t* following a page number indicates that the reference is to a table.

United States Institute of Peace

The United States Institute of Peace is an independent, nonpartisan federal institution created and funded by Congress to strengthen the nation's capacity to promote the peaceful resolution of international conflict. Established in 1984, the Institute meets its congressional mandate through an array of programs, including grants, fellowships, conferences and workshops, library services, publications, and other educational activities. The Institute's Board of Directors is appointed by the President of the United States and confirmed by the Senate.

Board of Directors

Chester A. Crocker (Chairman), Distinguished Research Professor of Diplomacy, School of Foreign Service, Georgetown University

Max M. Kampelman, Esq. (Vice Chairman), Fried, Frank, Harris, Shriver and Jacobson, Washington, D.C.

Dennis L. Bark, Senior Fellow, Hoover Institution on War, Revolution and Peace, Stanford University

Thomas E. Harvey, Senior Vice President and General Counsel, Corporation for Public Broadcasting

Theodore M. Hesburgh, President Emeritus, University of Notre Dame

William R. Kintner, Professor Emeritus of Political Science, University of Pennsylvania

Christopher H. Phillips, former U.S. ambassador to Brunei

Elspeth Davies Rostow, Stiles Professor of American Studies Emerita, Lyndon B. Johnson School of Public Affairs, University of Texas

Mary Louise Smith, civic activist; former chairman, Republican National Committee

W. Scott Thompson, Professor of International Politics, Fletcher School of Law and Diplomacy, Tufts University

Allen Weinstein, President, Center for Democracy, Washington, D.C.

Members ex officio

Paul G. Cerjan, Lieutenant General, U.S. Army; President, National Defense University

Toby Trister Gati, Assistant Secretary of State for Intelligence and Research

John D. Holum, Director, U.S. Arms Control and Disarmament Agency

Walter B. Slocombe, Principal Deputy Under Secretary of Defense for Policy

Richard H. Solomon, President, United States Institute of Peace (nonvoting)

Jennings Randolph Program for International Peace

As part of the statute establishing the United States Institute of Peace, Congress envisioned a fellowship program that would appoint "scholars and leaders of peace from the United States and abroad to pursue scholarly inquiry and other appropriate forms of communication on international peace and conflict resolution." The program was named after Senator Jennings Randolph of West Virginia, whose efforts over four decades helped to establish the Institute.

Since it began in 1987, the Jennings Randolph Program has played a key role in the Institute's efforts to build a national center of research, dialogue, and education on critical problems of conflict and peace. Through a rigorous annual competition, outstanding men and women from diverse nations and fields are selected to carry out projects designed to expand and disseminate knowledge on violent international conflict and the wide range of ways it can be peacefully managed or resolved.

The Institute's Distinguished Fellows and Peace Fellows are individuals from a wide variety of academic and other professional backgrounds who work at the Institute on research and education projects they have proposed and participate in the Institute's collegial and public outreach activities. The Institute's Peace Scholars are doctoral candidates at American universities who are working on their dissertations.

Institute fellows and scholars have worked on such varied subjects as international negotiation, regional security arrangements, conflict resolution techniques, international legal systems, ethnic and religious conflict, arms control, and the protection of human rights, and these issues have been examined in settings throughout the world.

As part of its effort to disseminate original and useful analyses of peace and conflict to policymakers and the public, the Institute publishes book manuscripts and other written products that result from the fellowship work and meet the Institute's high standards of quality.

Joseph Klaits
Acting Director

THE FUTURE OF GLOBAL GOVERNANCE

The text of this book is set in Perpetua; the display types are Futura and Industria Solid. Cover design by Rick Heffner; interior design by Joan Engelhardt and Day W. Dosch; page makeup by Helene Y. Redmond of HYR Graphics. Editorial work by Nigel Quinney, Tim McInnis, and Deirdre Macdonald Green.